FLAT
OUT
Flat Broke

THIRD EDITION

D1419888

FLAT OUT
Flat Broke

PERRY McCARTHY

Haynes Publishing

First published in hardback in July 2002
Reprinted twice in 2002
First published in paperback in September 2003
Reprinted in 2004 (twice) and 2006
Re-issued with revised cover in June 2008
This updated edition published in March 2013

A catalogue record for this book is available from the
British Library

ISBN 978 0 85733 382 7

Library of Congress control no. 2012953865

Haynes North America Inc., 861 Lawrence Drive,
Newbury Park, California 91320, USA

Published by Haynes Publishing,
Sparkford, Yeovil, Somerset BA22 7JJ, UK
Tel: 01963 442030 Fax: 01963 440001
Int. tel: +44 1963 442030 Int. fax: +44 1963 440001
E-mail: sales@haynes.co.uk
Website: www.haynes.co.uk

Printed in the USA by Odcombe Press LP,
1299 Bridgestone Parkway, La Vergne, TN 37086

CONTENTS

DEDICATION

To Karen
There is no cure for birth and death
save to enjoy the interval.
Soliloquies in England (1922) 'War Shrines'

PS I love you. Here's to the next 25 years.

To Julian Bailey, Mark Blundell and Bob Tappin
Well boys... after some of the stuff we've
been involved with
I find it difficult to believe we're all still alive.
My life would have been much different and nowhere
near as much fun without you all.

To Richard Lloyd
Like so many others, I miss you so very much.
Rest in peace my friend.

ACKNOWLEDGEMENTS

There have been so many people who have helped me, directly or indirectly, during my life that I can't thank them all by name, but you know who you are, and how grateful I am. Here are some who deserve special mention:

Alan Howell, remember the dashboard spear? The one you was gonna aim at my throat so I wouldn't brake!

Alex Hawkridge, perhaps one of the brightest people on the planet who has always been there for me. Thanks mate.

Amanda Cross, love ya. Thanks darling for your support and friendship.

Andy Wallace, you've been a great friend for many years and thanks for looking after me AWOL.

Antony Rogers, you know, as kids, some of those Mutt missions were pretty dangerous! Cheers Mutt.

Bernard Ecclestone... thank you very much sir.

Bill Blandford, a great guy who helped me and others.

Bill Schut, loved your company, thanks for looking after me in the States. Lots and lots of good times!

Bob Hawker, a lovely fella who gave me a shot at the big time.

Bobby Rouse, tell me, how much fun have we had? I'm laughing now thinking of it! You must've really hated that Mouse!

Brian Jones, 'there he goes – high, wide and handsome!' Great fun Brian. Thanks.

Chris Hilton, thank you mate. Rest in peace buddy.

Chris Witty, hope you're well. Thanks for everything.

Dad for taking a chance (Rest in Peace Pop, I'm pleased you're out of pain) and mum for cooking all the bacon and eggs for me and Bobby at one o'clock in the morning!

Damon Hill, hey World Champ... thanks for the foreword... cheque's in the post. Some good times huh!

David Berger, thanks for your help and the laughs DB.

David Brabham, Gary Brabham, Geoff Brabham. To a man... open, honest, and fun. Cheers boys.

David Coulthard, don't worry bud, I didn't want to drive for Williams anyway – laughing.

David Ingram, thank you so much for your enthusiasm and support. It's always fun. Cheers DI.

David Price, oy Pricey! I know you never thought I was as good as Senna but we 'ad a laugh eh!

David Tremayne, hey Reptile! Your support and friendship has always meant a lot to me.

Dennis Rushen, hey cool cat! Thanks for your confidence in me.

Derek Blackwell, scaffolding and motor racing: sure, it's a great marketing fit! Thanks as always mate.

Don Hume, I only meant the bit about Tracey in a sisterly kinda way. OK love you too!

Duffy Sheardown... oh boy! Thanks so much for trying mate.

Frank Biela, get that xxxx out of the shower! Great times mate.

Frank Williams, cheers Frank. All the best.

Fred Rodgers, thank you so much for your faith and hard work Fred.

Gary Denham, Gal... I'm by the flyover, it's not too bad, just a few panels maybe! Thanks Gal.

Gary Howell, look, I haven't got a bad temper! Ooops, remember Le Mans? Well, he started it! Thanks Gal.

Gary Savage, just a small detour to get Karen to Sebring. Cheers mate.

Gary Waller... oi, big bruv. Cheers Gal.

Gordon Message, thanks Gordy... it was great to get in a proper one!

Graeme Sutton, you made a big difference, especially when we went out to play! Thanks Graeme.

Grahame Taylor, I've got a plan. Let's stay up really late, have another drink, and put the world to rights!

Guy Edwards, thanks for spending some time trying to point me in the right direction.

Haynes Publishing, thanks so much Mark, Flora, Jeremy and Rebecca.

Ian Shepherd, 'this time next year... ' Thanks for everything me 'ol mate.

Ivan Mant, hey Ivano... luv to the family. Thanks mate.

James Weaver, you are one seriously funny guy. Love your company Jamsie-boy!

Jay Cochran, crazy times baby... I'll never forget my Yank mate!

Jim and Val Waddilove, always good to see you.

Joachim Hausner, my great engineer and friend. Now, can you get me out of the sand!

John Daniels, thanks for looking after me in the case of McCarthy v the world. Always lovely to see ya!

John Hall, from one demolition expert to another! Cheers John.

John MacDonald, not many people know what it's like, do they? I know you do! Thanks Johnny.

John Robinson, yes my boy... there can be only one! Top bloke Johnny.

John Wickham, the target of my telephone terrorism! Thanks for the breaks and the laughs JW.

John Zammit, cheers Zammo!

Johnny Dumfries, you do make me laugh John and I love some of your suits. Only some.

Johnny Herbert, thanks a lot for beating me as much as you did you little sod. Great times Little 'un. Luv Pel.

Julian Randles, oh boy... we gave 'em a run for their money, huh Jules! Cheers mate.

Keith Phillips, hey big boy! Now, tell me just once more... I adjust the computer by... oh, please come over!

Kevin Rose, thanks so much for all your faith and support. Here's to the future.

Les Ager, my dear old friend, you put me on the road and started the adventure. May you rest in peace.

Mark Gallaher, how near were we to the Leyton House drive? Cheers Mark.

Mark Stevens, I need a hundred quid fast! Remember? You always helped out! Cheers mate.

Martin Brundle, cheers mate – thanks for helping with Bennies.

Martin Donnelly, crazier than a March hare. 'Whad a boucha'... me 'ol mate Marty. Great times eh!

Michele Alboreto, great company, great driver, and true gentleman. Rest in peace my friend.

Mike Collier, lots of fun... ok. a bit of damage but thanks for the chance.

Mike Francis, I'll always remember your help. Cheers.

Mike Hughes, a charming and talented fellow who always helped. Rest in peace my friend.

Mike Innes. Thanks for being a good mate.

Mike Theobald, thanks for keeping me fire-resistant.

Mike Whittingham, keep phoning me from your boat... I just love to hear what a great time you're having.

Murray Walker, so enthusiastic. Thanks for helping me. Good Luck.

Nick Wirth... thanks Nick.

Paul Broom, thanks for sticking with me mate. Rest in peace my friend.

Paul Carnill, a great big thanks from me and Julian.

Paul Haigh, hi Petal! You gave me the confidence to succeed. Thanks for the laughs mate.

Paul Whight, one day you will look your age and it will happen overnight when you're asleep! Thanks PW.

Piero's, my second home!

Peter Rogers, a lovely fellow and talented driver. Rest in peace my friend.

Peter Smith, thanks mate. Remember the guy in your office looking at the photos?

Peter Todd, thanks for going into battle for me!

Peter Townsend, it's been a while since our last car chase through Southend. We must get out more!!

Philip Lamb, Jesus... with a mind like yours I'm pleased you're on my side! Thanks Philip.

Poppy, Frederica and Finella, my darling girls... well, sometimes! I love you.

Richard Farleigh, my great buddy – always so much fun. The Dragon and The Stig!

Richard Lloyd, look, the red boots will be fine. Oh Richard, even when you told me off I laughed.

Rod Vickery, thanks mate for your support and enthusiasm on a whole range of McCarthy projects!

Roger Cowman, a true racer and a great mate. How much fun have we had huh? Lots and lots!

Sears, good boy.

Simon Arron, thanks for all your support Simon.

Simon Crompton, hey champ. Remember you, me, KJ, and Lou in the hotel in Belgium? Wow, scary stuff! Thanks mate.

Simon Cummins, for paving the way with *Grand Prix International!*

Simon Kidd, oh God I'm so pleased we're mates. I've seen what your karate blows can do to bricks... wood... etc!

Steve and Debbie Osman, lots of love guys, sorry about the motor Steve!

Steve Rees, talented bright bloke. Thanks for all your help mate.

Steve Sydenham, thanks for all your work with RfB.

Sutton Images, to Keith and the boys. Thanks as always.

Terry Back... TB you nutcase. Thanks so much for everything mate.

The Gang: Gel and Ali, David and Karen, Mike and Jill, Christian and Kirsty. Good times.

Tim Clowes, thank you my 'ol mate for all the help.

Tim Jones, stop worrying, we'll be all right... unlike your overalls.

Tim Spouge, what can I say? Thanks mate. Here's to the future.

Tony Ash, you know, one day I'd like to actually do something back for you! Thanks Tony.

Tony O'Connell: thanks for my prancing Horse Buddy.

Tracey Hume, love ya!

Wolfgang Ullrich (Dr.), it was a pleasure driving for you sir. Good luck to you and all my friends at Audi Sport.

FOREWORD

by 1996 World Champion Damon Hill

There are legions of ex-racing drivers with a tale to tell – of how they could have made it but never had the money, or were cheated out of a drive they believed should have been theirs, or had to admit to themselves the painful truth... that they lacked the total commitment needed to succeed. Of these, most will have come to terms with living without the ever present gut-churning anxiety and heart-palpitating stabs of fear that haunt a racing driver's life. But for those who enjoy that sort of thing, there is no hope of escape. They have to have it in whatever form it takes. These people are known as 'Perry McCarthy'.

If you are ever blessed enough to meet Perry, he will first ask you how much money you have on you, then how much you can get, and finally if you could be so kind as to give it all to him so he can go racing. It's impossible not to like him, despite this. 'No' is a word that Perry has heard more times than the word 'Yes' by a factor of infinity. Yet he still does not give up hope. This is known as 'madness'. So why do we like him? Because no matter how many times he gets knocked down he just gets back up again and has another go. Persistence has not exactly paid off for Perry in the same way it smiled on me, but he will never have to lie in bed staring at the ceiling thinking, 'I wonder if I could have tried harder?'

The real reward for Perry is that, along the way, he has had a hell of a lot of fun times to counter the desperate times. They are all accurately embellished in this book, together with a few things he should have left out, notably the stories with me in them, but I refused to concede to his demands for money yet again.

Life is what happens when you are busy trying to win races, and in this regard Perry is a winner of life itself.

OK. That's enough grovelling. Can I have my money now?

Damon Hill
April 2002

INTRODUCTION

By the middle of 1992 I had to keep reminding myself that I was a grand prix driver. Formula One, pick of the bunch, top of the international motor racing ladder. Well, it didn't seem like it. My life was hell. 'Mirror mirror on the wall, who's the fastest of them all?' I'd ask. The reply: 'Not you sunshine... although you might be the craziest!'

An extract from Christopher Hilton's book *Inside The Mind of the Grand Prix Driver: The psychology of the fastest men on earth* (Haynes, 2001) supported this view:

The next race was at Hockenheim [Germany]. Six cars were to be involved in pre-qualifying on the Friday morning and [Formula One drivers] Julian Bailey, Mark Blundell and JJ Lehto were out on the circuit at a corner, watching as the session began. McCarthy, who certainly did not know Hockenheim in a Formula One car, approached.

McCarthy: 'Where are they braking for this corner?'

Bailey ruminated, because he was thinking about where the good cars braked.

'Just after the 100-metre board.'

McCarthy: 'Right.' He continued his recce.

Bailey to Blundell: 'I don't believe he is going to do this!'

They stood waiting and after a while they heard the

distinctive high-pitched wail of a Formula One engine on its way toward them. It burst into view – what Bailey describes as 'that black Andrea Moda thing [McCarthy's car] going whaaaang'.

Bailey shouted 'No, don't do it!' Bailey was deeply, deeply sure McCarthy couldn't make it.

Lehto put a finger to his forehead, the international sign for madness.

McCarthy was absolutely determined to brake after the 100-metre board.

'How he made that corner that day I don't know,' Bailey says. 'We were actually scared and we told him that... I honestly thought he was going to kill himself there.'

Like my magic mirror, they had a point. I knew it was madness to try that manoeuvre in that car, but I'd come to learn that madness is relative. I was broke, my career was hanging by a thread and I was spiralling into more and more trouble, both on and off the track, just to keep going.

How the hell had I got into the situation? For God's sake, all I wanted was to be Formula One World Champion. That wasn't too much to ask, was it?

PREFACE

In the summer of 1941, the whistle of a Luftwaffe bomb stopped when its fall was skilfully cushioned by a small house in St. Paul's Way, East London. One year later an even smaller place, less than a mile away in Wages Street, saved a different bomb from hitting the ground and was similarly vaporised.

My grandparents, Edward and Marie, along with my dad Dennis, who was just three years old, survived both hits, and although they were homeless, that's about as lucky as the McCarthy family was ever going to get. A year later grandad died from TB and the rest of them were now in serious trouble, even by their standards. Nan, dad and his younger brother Teddy evacuated to Somerset but after six months they missed the sound of exploding streets and, incredibly, moved back. Like many others in the East End, they sang 'Maybe it's because I'm a Londoner' and did whatever it took to stay alive. They must have really hated Somerset.

My old man has, at a conservative estimate, told me this part of the McCarthy history 14 million times, and each time he does, the explosions are bigger and there's even less money. In fact, dad tells everyone; he'll tell his friends, anyone else who's listening, and then anyone who can be *made* to listen. On our family holidays, dad's main pastime was to find a German, buy him a pint, and tell *him* the story as well.

From a young age, this and other do-it-yourself survival lessons must have nailed themselves into my subconscious. In my efforts to become a World Champion racing driver, this 'pick yourself up, dust yourself down' determination has sometimes felt like a curse. It would have been a lot easier to quit, instead of trudging forward like one of those 1960 sci-fi robots who keep repeating the words 'Crush, Kill, Destroy' and asking if anyone's seen Peter Cushing.

My career advancement in motorsport has been like a long-term initiative test, although I'm well ahead of dad because I haven't been bombed out yet. I've pulled just about every trick in the book to keep going and invented a few new ones, too. My mate, motor racing driver Julian Bailey, once said that I had two major abilities: 'An ability for getting into trouble and an ability for getting out of it'. He may have a point.

At the time of writing, I am unfortunately still about one million pounds away from my first million and I'm still not World Champion. But I have travelled the world, raced the best cars against the fastest drivers, made hundreds of friends, and have somehow kept laughing.

This is how.

Chapter 1

GROWING PAINS

I didn't like this school either. I generally found lessons too slow,
although I did enjoy drawing, and forging my mother's
signature on sick notes.

I'm sure a few things made headlines back on 3 March 1961 but the big story, as far as I'm concerned, was my birth. Somehow, though, the Mile End Hospital in Stepney East, London, didn't get too excited about what was my very first personal appearance.

Although I was a healthy 8lb 7oz baby, a couple of things escaped my attention. Firstly, being born within the sound of Bow Bells meant I was officially a cockney; and secondly, being born to my mum and dad meant I was officially a poor cockney. The 'poor' bit was the first flaw in the grand plan.

My dad was 'on the brush', which is slang for being a painter. His work was never hung in galleries, but he did paint a few, as well as houses, cinemas, offices... in fact, anything that had a wall. He didn't earn much, but it was his first job after leaving the Royal Electrical Mechanical Engineering division of the Army. It was while serving with REME in the Far East that he'd begun writing to Patricia Smith, the pretty girl from across the road whose only mistake in life was to reply. Knowing the old man, he probably told her he was a Brigadier General while Patricia, who had fallen for him big time, didn't work out that two stripes means Corporal. But that didn't stop her marrying him.

Now I'd like to clear up a couple of points here. Firstly, my age: those who have doubted my previous declarations will see from my birth date that they were actually right and that I have indeed been lying about it all along. Secondly, as my mum and dad were married before I was born, all those who have called me a bastard are technically wrong.

Over the next few years, dad continued to paint England and we left the council estate in Dagenham when a two-bed bungalow in Stanford-Le-Hope, Essex, proved affordable at £2,700. My proud parents immediately celebrated by giving birth to my sister Lesley and having me circumcised. This left a lasting impression.

One of my first memories is of being in a warm bath and having the bandages removed from the end of my baby todger. I screamed in pain and I screamed at the blood, which mixed with the water and made it look like I'd had a major haemorrhage.

At two years old, my bed – still the bottom drawer of a side unit – was getting a bit small for me and my swollen willy, but the re-shaping allowed me to pee correctly and dad had drawn a giant Batman on my bedroom wall as a present.

He was working away from home for much of the time, so for long stretches mum had the task of trying to keep me under control and caring for Lesley, who was in leg irons because of a serious hip defect. It wasn't the world's easiest job.

Mum recalls the time I burnt the skin off my face with coal tar vapour fluid and then chased other kids down the street shouting 'Monster!' She remembers that I crashed my three-wheeler bike, lightly scratching my head; and when I called at a neighbour's house crying for help, the lady opened the door and her Alsatian dog attacked me. I remember associating mum with the smell of TCP antiseptic. Whenever I took a beating she was like my own accident and emergency unit, although unlike most paramedics, she was often tempted to beat the crap out of me herself.

If mum was my nurse, then dad was my victim. I once nearly killed him when he was changing the timing gear on his Hillman Husky. I was already fascinated by cars, so I climbed in and, while his head and hands were firmly in the engine bay, I turned the key and started it up. If he hadn't, at that very moment, stood up to get a spanner, he would have never smoked again, mainly because he wouldn't have had any fingers left to hold a cigarette. I was pulled from the car at high speed just in time for smacking practice.

I gave him another little surprise when he returned from Birmingham. It was freezing cold and pouring with rain, and he was wrecked from working 18-hour days, but as he entered the lounge he was willing to see my new trick. Mum gave me the cue and I ran across the room, jumped, bounced on the sofa, got the angle wrong, took off and went straight through the window. Strangely, he wasn't impressed. The replacement window wouldn't fit in or on the car, so dad and his mate got soaked as they walked to get one. Mum, as ever, brought out the TCP. No wonder dad wasn't around much.

In 1966 England won the World Cup and I started school at Giffords Primary in Corringham, Essex. It was a five-minute walk from home and just around the corner from where dad had started his own company. The school was small and looked like a temporary structure, but it definitely had one thing right – it had Julie Cox. Julie was a beautiful child model who starred in cream cake TV commercials as well as mail order catalogues, where she enhanced the 'fashion for five-year-olds' section. While the other boys played football in the playground and talked about Bobby Moore, I stayed close to Julie and discussed international issues such as which one of us had the blondest hair. I already felt something toward her but I didn't know what.

However, as mum pointed out, rubbing myself up and down the chair leg was probably connected. Fearing that I would soon do myself some damage, my parents moved us to a small, four-bed house in a village between Laindon and Billericay in Essex, but I knew one day I'd return for little Miss Cox. Dad's contract painting and decorating business was doing okay, even though the office was only a small maisonette above a Chinese restaurant which, from late afternoon, smelled of prawn balls.

My new place of learning was the Laindon Park Junior School. It was an old brick church building with only 100 pupils and its limited facilities included a netball, a football, a rounders bat and a large climbing frame strategically erected over solid concrete by someone who hated children.

Aged six, I was the new kid on the block and, in a way, I continued to feel like one until I was 11 years old and left the school. I began to realise that it wasn't just Giffords School I didn't like: I didn't like this one either. I generally found lessons too slow, although I did enjoy drawing and forging my mother's signature on sick notes. I was convinced that teachers like the dreaded Mrs Lowe were some kind of vampire bat. Mr Hawes, though, was a good laugh and I had a crush on Miss Jacqueline, but knew our 20-year age gap was a barrier to making a new start together. So I chose my classmate Tracey Willets to replace Julie Cox in my affections. Something must have been missing, though, because I no longer gave the chair a hammering.

Maybe my mind was on space travel. I followed every stage of NASA's Apollo programme in detail, back when the world was fascinated by each death-defying mission. I was inquisitive. Could we one day reach the speed of light? Would we colonise Mars? And if we did, could I take Tracey with me? I read everything about rockets and the solar system, and I thought the three Rs were Nebulas, Quasars and Pulsars. Britain's Gerry Anderson was on the scene and captured this mood of adventure with his incredible range of TV shows – *Thunderbirds, Captain Scarlet, Stingray, Joe 90* and so on. America, meanwhile, produced *Lost in Space, Time Tunnel* and, of course, *Star Trek*.

I bought in to the whole thing – the danger, the excitement and, of course, the speed. Sitting in front of our new, revolutionary colour television, screaming such things as 'set phasers to stun!' I realised the future was now clear. I was going to be an astronaut.

However, it was at about this time that it dawned on me: I was going to be a very short astronaut. I was sure my lack of success with Tracey had a lot to do with being four inches shorter than she was, and she wasn't exactly Amazonian. I didn't really have a problem with my lack of height. I was mostly a bubbly, outgoing kid who was polite to everyone, but the bubble soon burst if someone tried pushing me around. I never backed down from a fight and I suppose I had a nasty little temper, or maybe I was just fiercely competitive. I guess a psychiatrist might say I was 'over-compensating' for something or other, but considering some of the lads I fought, I'd diagnose it as 'over-stupid'. For someone of my age – and especially my size – I was very confident, but I had only a few friends. Sadly, though, I never really felt we were on the same wavelength. It sounds cruel, but there was no 'get up and go' with them, and if mum and dad had decided to move us away, it wouldn't have bothered me as much as missing *Star Trek*.

When I finally left junior school, my only regret was that I'd had to go there in the first place. The Laindon Comprehensive School was going to be a whole different story, with 1200 pupils and the incredible concept of different teachers for different subjects. However, I arrived to find my application had not been processed. I was sent for an assessment to the deputy headmaster, Mr Birch, who took one look at me standing in my new uniform and announced: 'You look like a smart young fellow. We'll put you in the top band'. I'll always remember that. I was pleased, of course, but also irritated because I could see how it could work the other way for a kid wearing hand-me-downs. This was my first lesson in first impressions.

In our form class, they sat me next to a strange-looking kid who used to raise his heels too high when he walked, making him look like he was trying to peer over some imaginary wall with every step. I knew I wasn't going get on with anyone who failed to realise this looked stupid, so by the end of the first day I changed seats because I wouldn't make it through the week without punching him. That's when I met Antony Rogers.

Tony was my best mate all the way through school; we were kindred spirits and became inseparable. We formed a club, with just the two of us in it, and christened ourselves 'The Mutts' because we admired Muttley, who was Dick Dastardly's sidekick in the *Wacky Races* cartoon. We caused a truckload of mischief without getting caught; being in the top academic group served as great cover. We superglued windows shut, doors together and blackboard rubbers to desks, and we stole the record player when our English teacher wanted to play a recording of Shakespeare. In Chemistry, we learnt how to make a potassium bomb, which we used to destroy a toilet, and Physics taught us how to make a nuclear bomb, but we couldn't find any weapons grade plutonium.

Biology, of course, taught us about reproduction and we used to giggle about the varied ways our gorgeous classmate Debbie Brown could help us do the 'practical'. Just to make sure we were on the right track, Tony and I once escaped from home late at night and sneaked into Debbie's garden to peer through the gap in her bedroom curtains. Lucky we had the defence of being young at the time. To this day, though, I always close our home curtains properly, just in case some other little Mutts are doing the same to us.

Other hobbies included hiding with a mirror by a road on a sunny day and reflecting the sun into the eyes of unsuspecting drivers. We also used to play 'Knock down ginger' (banging on people's front door and running away) around Laindon's Pound Lane estate, which had a high density of headcases; capture would have meant certain death. I guess our favourite scam, though, was The French Act. We would cycle to nearby Basildon shopping centre and pretend to be lost Parisian tourists. Using a heavy accent, broken English and any French words we'd ever heard, we would ask people who looked in a hurry for directions to Scotland, and then take about 10 minutes of their time doing it. For us it was top-class amusement, watching them try to work out which way Scotland actually was and then to communicate their best guess. We'd stay with this recipe for mischief all

day and, with increasing confidence, we'd include in our conversations, a few 'Eiffel Towers' mixed with a couple of 'Charles de Gaulles' and then add a sprinkle of 'Jean-Paul Belmondo', lightly peppered with a bit of 'French Resistance'. Once or twice we outstayed our welcome when we mistakenly approached a previous victim and, of course, there was the one who answered us back in fluent French. Suddenly remembering that Scotland was 300 miles north, we remounted our bikes and peddled away.

Our bikes meant a lot to us. We went everywhere flat out – through housing estates, shopping centres and even down a dry ski slope – and no Mutt Mission was complete without a big accident. It was so much fun. We had the lives of a hundred cats, albeit wounded ones.

However, there were other ways to suffer injury and there were plenty of candidates ready to make it happen. The surrounding area of Laindon School wasn't an area of pure natural beauty and maybe this adversely affected some of the kids because a few of our intake made psychopaths look compassionate. There was a distinguishable 'food chain' comprising academics, above average, average, hard nuts and sub-human. It was a good idea to commit to memory just who was in which category, especially the sub-human group. There were quite a few fights, normally spontaneous and held in the playground but sometimes with advance notice and drawing big crowds – especially when our elite force of lunatics went head to head with local rivals from the St Nicholas School, just down the road.

I never experienced too much trouble myself, probably because I could make most people laugh and do chimpanzee noises. However, there was one time when a particularly well-known nutter decided I wasn't that funny and we had a big, well-supported fight. Well, every dog has its day and that day was mine because I beat the bookies' odds, I beat the daylights out of him and I was never invited for a punch-up at school again.

In 1977, I was 16 and some bloke called James Hunt was the reigning Formula One World Champion. I didn't follow motor racing at all but I did spend a lot of time playing 'Monopoly' with Tony and talking rubbish about which multi-national business we were going to run. These conversations were normally at their best after we had finished our third bottle of stolen cider and would include money, fast cars and something nasty to do with Debbie. It was during one of these IQ reduction sessions that Tony produced a brochure from the Jim Russell Racing Drivers' School. I wasn't interested, especially as I was about to throw up, and the subject wasn't raised again.

By now, I'd discovered that I quite liked cider, and lager, and bitter, and I grew to become very fond of them, so I gave up the astronaut idea and chose a different mission: to seek out new forms of drink and to boldly go where many had gone before... straight down the pub.

In my spare time, though, I became a member of the Air Training Corps and had my very own Air Force uniform and a bugle that I couldn't play. I had passed all seven O-level exams at school and planned to take my A-levels, then go on to University and join the Royal Air Force as a fighter pilot – or become a bartender – but the plan changed after my first year in sixth form. I got bored with school and left to work for a company called Alliance Shipping, owned by our new next-door neighbour, Gary Waller, who was only 26. I looked up to Gary, and not just because I was short. He was bright, funny, and totally ruthless. This guy was in the fast lane and, apart from my dad, I'd never met anyone like him. Listening to them talk about life and business, together or individually, was like taking a degree in deals. This was interesting stuff but I still didn't know what I wanted to do. I was frustrated and anxious to get my teeth into something and I just knew there'd be no stopping me once I'd found it. Shipping, however, was definitely not the answer.

Chapter 2

STAYING UP LATE

I didn't even know girls gave signs. They could have had an illuminated badge that said 'Free Sex Right Now, Just Ask!' and I'd have said 'Wow, where d'you get that badge?'

Nobody seemed to want a 17-year-old would-be company chairman armed with six months experience as a shipping clerk, two months experience as a copy proof-reader and three weeks experience as a trainee accountant. Looking at this stunning record, potential employers might have thought I wasn't ready to give the commitment. The 'recognising authority' bit still seemed a particular problem for me and I surmised that commerce wasn't ready for me and I wasn't ready for a boss. Yet every interview I went to I was offered the job, so the first stage of my newly developed 'work avoidance programme' had to be to stop going to interviews. The second stage was college.

I enrolled full-time at Basildon College in Essex and chose A-level courses in Law, Economics, Sociology and Art. The course normally took two years, but I figured that if I failed the exams I might be able to stretch it to three. There were girls everywhere and I thought about ditching the A-levels to take a secretarial course. This place had a lot of potential: I sensed my time had come. My nose stopped producing spots and my body at last remembered how to grow. I shot up by about four inches and went from being a trainee dwarf to my full five feet eight inches. Okay, we're not talking Charlton Heston, but it stopped people asking me after eight o'clock at night if I'd lost my mummy.

With this new-found height, I could now see over a steering wheel, so I took my driving test. However, the examiner felt I still had some growing up to do and failed me for 'going off test route, lack of Highway Code knowledge, and speeding'. I remember being pretty disappointed and hoping I'd read about him in *Shark Attack Gazette* or something.

One month later, though, I passed and bought an old Mk 1 Escort that suffered from a problem called 'Galloping Skin Rot'. This disease was peculiar to Fords painted in the 'Silver Fox' colour and was an automotive version of alopecia. The symptoms began with the Silver Fox actually falling off the car, to reveal large patches of the primer beneath. It looked horrible but I tried to tart it up a bit by spraying the wheels metallic silver, and put plastic extended wheel nuts on it to make it look racy. The alopecia was obviously contagious, though. The chrome finish fell off the nuts and the wheels turned rusty. By the time I'd finished this and my special dashboard modifications, the bloody thing was a mobile disaster.

So there I was, once again a student, but this time I was armed with a driving licence and my £100, 90bhp, mangy piece of crap. Yet, believe it or not, my life had just changed dramatically for the better.

Bob Tappin and Russell Keen, known as 'Tapps' and 'Keeney', were also studying Law and Economics, along with what looked like a master's degree in flat-out entertainment. They were both ace footballers who had also returned to education after a year out, during which Bob had been a professional for Birmingham City and Russ an apprentice for Chelsea. It didn't take long before we joined forces and the three of us became a focal point of a much larger group, whom we corrupted into our way of thinking.

We did virtually whatever came to mind, which normally started with drinking ourselves just short of a coma. In class, our lecturers often knew we were still drunk from the previous night's adventures but they turned a blind eye, although they did ask if we could lay off the lunchtime binge... or at least take them with us. We decided to compromise: if we'd had a really bad session, we just didn't return. The thing was, we could get away with it because the three of us, individually or together, could talk people into anything.

One time, Tapps saw some rugby shirts he thought we should have, so we developed a plan. We told the principal that we needed a student union and that this union should have some funds, to buy kit for a rugby team we would form, to play other colleges. He agreed. We got the money and then went to Basildon and bought a load of shirts for this phantom team, all different colours and designs for us and our mates. Needless to say, none of us went remotely near a rugby game. As ever, there was no malice. It was just another stunt, a laugh, and it just had to be done – like the time we arrived at a party where there was no drink. To keep our entertainment on track, we organised a whip-round and took the money. It was like an initiative test, but the bright ones found us in a pub, drunk, two miles away.

It was all so new, different and exciting. In stark contrast to all this laddish behaviour, though, I was desperately naïve when it came to women. Sure, there were plenty I fancied and many of those I would go out with as friends, but I could never read the signs. In fact I didn't even know girls *gave* signs. They could have had an illuminated badge that said 'Free Sex Right Now, Just Ask!' and I'd have said 'Wow, where d'you get that badge?' There was the beautiful French lecturer, for instance. She was about four years older than me and agreed to go out on a date. We had a lovely evening together and I drove her home late at night. We parked outside her place and she suddenly moved close. With her badge flashing wildly, she asked if I wanted to come inside for a 'cup of coffee'. What did I do? I said: 'No thanks I'm not thirsty.' Truly, I did, and those words have haunted me ever since: 'No thanks I'm not thirsty.' What a prat! For some reason she became quite busy after that and then she started seeing a mate of mine, who obviously was bloody thirsty.

I was very nearly 18 when I had my first official girlfriend: none other than my childhood sweetheart Julie Cox. Julie had matured from a beautiful kid into a stunning teenager who was great fun to be with. I used repeatedly to draw her portrait in Art class. In fact, I knew her face so well that I could draw it even when she wasn't there. Once I realised that, two things started to dawn on me: firstly, I was in a serious relationship; and secondly, I didn't want to be in a serious relationship. Julie was terrific and we were very close but I was worried about settling down before I had something to settle down from. I didn't do a particularly good job of letting her down lightly, but there again who does have the answer to that?

I had learnt a lot from this experience and applied my new-found insight to Art class. Drawing portraits was fun but there was something more important at work here: having a beautiful girl posing, all to myself, provided an excellent opportunity to chat them up. Soon after, I launched a 'model recruitment campaign'. It was easy. I'd see a girl I fancied, ask if she would sit for me and then later we'd have a cup of coffee. Some of those portraits took three hours! The plan proved a great success, but the trouble was all the drawings looked like Julie.

Drawing also took me in another direction. Simon Cummins, a friend at college, was very interested in motor racing and used to show me a great magazine called *Grand Prix International*.

GPI was full of wonderful photographs of Formula One cars, which I started to draw. I was obviously getting better because not one of them looked like Julie. After a while I began reading about the teams, the cars and the drivers. I watched races on TV and talked about it all the time. I had finally found a sport I liked. This was 1979 and the big names were Alan Jones, Nelson Piquet, Jody Scheckter and Gilles Villeneuve. These guys were great – totally flat out. What a life!

It was around this time however that my own life expectancy wasn't looking too good. I was getting into a few fights – the result of one was hospital treatment, unfortunately on me – and I was also a complete nightmare on the roads. I became known for scaring the hell out of my passengers with my 'Highway into the unknown tours', and general opinion made sharing a jail cell with Charles Manson look like a safer bet. Occasionally I ran out of talent and several cars went to that big scrap heap in the sky, but more of that later...

At this point, a few things happened all at once. Dad was doing okay – not mega but okay. He decided we should go on an expensive holiday, so we went to Antigua. As soon as we arrived, dad went on his rent-a-crowd routine and pretty soon we knew everyone in the joint. We had a great laugh but two members of our newly formed drinking club were senior executives of an American oil company and dad's big break came about a millisecond after one of them said to him: 'Hey, Dennis, you ever thought about painting oil rigs?' Dennis, of course, lied through his teeth. He convinced them that not only did his company have the capability to do it, but he had actually been planning to set up in just that line of business and that he had developed a *secret treatment* that prevented freshly shot-blasted metal from rusting. So, a deal was struck. It was going to be dad's finest hour and I recall how he took me warmly by the throat and told me to stay away from the bloke's good-looking daughter because if I screwed this up, he'd drown me.

On returning to England, daddy went into Tasmanian devil mode. He conned, borrowed and cajoled, plotted, planned and schemed. He risked everything he had and didn't have, and amazingly brought to life a corrosion control company with the equipment and personnel capable of shot blasting, scaffolding and spraying oil rigs. He used his initials to christen it 'DJM Construction' and had meanwhile impressed these guys with a sample of metal that had been blasted then coated with the DJM secret formula (better known in chemical terms as hair lacquer). Unbelievably, he got away with it. There are very few people who could have possibly put that deal together and even fewer crazy enough to try. Our holiday friends awarded DJM lots of contracts in the North Sea and, in little more than one year, dad was a multi-millionaire.

The immediate benefit of having a rich dad was that the lovely guy bought me a little Triumph Spitfire sports car, which was a valuable tool in both girlfriend recruitment and my road terror campaign. I remember travelling everywhere with the roof down, listening to ELO's 'Out of the Blue' and the Bee Gees' 'Saturday Night Fever'. But mostly I enjoyed listening to the little 1300cc engine being revved to destruction, the poor tyres screaming for grip and my passengers begging for their life. At 18 years old, I was a happy kid who thought that things don't get a lot better than this.

Apart from driving, my other hobby was playing the keyboards and I started demonstrating instruments as a part-time job in a shop owned by my mate Bob Rouse. Bobby was a great laugh and a real wheeler-dealer. I was always impressed with Bob's superb talent as a musician and he had always been a big fan of my car control. One day, this short fella with thick white hair walked into the shop and proceeded to have a hushed chat with Bob while smiling and looking in my direction. He came over to speak to me and said: 'What do you want to do?'

I looked at him and thought: 'Who the hell are you?' Maybe someone had heard me play and he was from the Noise Abatement Society.

'I'm gonna be a Formula One racing driver,' I joked sarcastically.

'Well, you'd better come with me then,' he said. 'My name is Les Ager, I'm an instructor at Brands Hatch and Bobby here tells me you are the best thing since sliced bread.'

My life was again about to undergo a major change of direction.

Chapter 3

OIL RIGS TO RACE TRACK

I knew that one day I was going to be a racing driver and, more than that, I was going to be a Formula One racing driver and probably World Champion.

Bobby let me have the afternoon off, not least because he was the person who'd arranged Les Ager's 'chance' visit to the shop in Grays, Essex. We took the Spitfire and Les sat in the suicide seat, feeding me directions to Brands Hatch. As always, I rammed the accelerator to the floor with all the delicacy of a wounded hippo but this 58-year-old was totally cool. I couldn't believe I'd failed to scare him and assumed he was nuts, senile, or had spent some time in a sensory deprivation tank. We arrived and Les checked me in to what the Brands Hatch Racing School call 'The Initial Trial'.

This was a trial with a difference, though, because there was no briefing, no restriction on laps, no rev limit and no charge. He really wanted to see if I lived up to Bob's vivid description. So there I was, wearing a safety helmet and fireproof overalls, strapped into a race-prepared Talbot Sunbeam and ready to drive on a world-famous circuit, with a real-life instructor. Oh boy, was I excited!

It transpired that I was too excited and I completely messed up my first attempt. I'd over-driven the car and nearly put us into the guardrail a couple of times, but, somehow, I kept it on the track. Then we changed seats and Les showed me what could be done with some experience but without the death wish.

Within two corners I was convinced that he had totally lost his mind. The crazy bastard was pitching this car sideways at 90mph into the daunting Paddock Hill while *talking* to me at the same time. I was terrified. Now I *knew* he'd spent time in a sensory deprivation tank, and it was also clear to me that Bob's introduction was planned revenge for all the times I'd frightened *him*. If this was penance then oh God, I'm sorry, I won't do it again, anything, just please make this old git stop.

He did, and I composed myself, then had another turn at driving, immediately forgetting about my heartfelt chat with the Almighty. This time it flowed; I was ahead of the car and loving it. I was going faster and faster and Les kept shouting louder and louder: 'Oh you lovely boy!' After we finished, my new friend took me to meet everyone in the pit lane, including John and Angela Webb, who controlled Brands. Les told them all that I was the best natural talent he had ever seen. Then he sat me down and told me that I *had* to start racing.

As we drove back to Grays, the decision was made. I knew that one day I was going to be a racing driver and, more than that, I was going to be a *Formula One* racing driver and probably World Champion. Yes – Jones, Piquet, Scheckter... McCarthy. I liked the sound of it. There would be no half measures. Les said I was great and I *felt* great. Something deep inside had clicked. It was exciting, challenging and fast. It was like meeting the most beautiful girl in the world and having a secret affair: it was dangerous but I was infatuated and totally prepared to risk my future in pursuit of a career that had all the ingredients I wanted.

I'd definitely been bitten by the bug, but after scratching the itch with a few more lessons at Brands I realised that this particular virus was bloody expensive. I needed money, preferably lots of it, and certainly right now. To compound the problem, I also needed a few quid to repair the Spitfire after a bit of McCarthy 'stunt driving' went badly wrong. I had brilliantly reversed flat out toward my mate Steve Osman's Mk 2 Cortina and just to *really* scare him I left it very late to brake. Well, he was scared all right. I'd left it so late that I backed straight into him and, hey presto – one destroyed Ford and one injured Triumph. I'll always remember the look of disbelief on Steve's face just before the impact.

Most of the damage was covered on insurance, which was just as well because I needed every bit of help in attracting the attention of a girl I had seen and seriously fallen for at college. Unfortunately, I was having zero success getting anywhere near Miss Karen Waddilove but my chance came one night when I arrived with college mates Tapps and Keeny at a party – and there she was, dancing. Before I made my move, the boys and I played a drinking game which caused me to swig an entire bottle of white wine down in one go, and I rapidly launched into self-destruct mode.

The room started spinning and falling like a fairground roller-coaster and I was battling to stay on. Having temporarily won my fight against gravity, I decided that now was the perfect time to approach. By the time I zigzagged over, I could see two of her. Then, in a language similar to English, I asked the one who wasn't transparent for a dance, but she didn't seem to understand me. I staggered away and told Tapps, who was now in his own orbit and totally fluent in Drunkeneese: 'I can't get Karen so I might as well settle for Tracey,' who was my girlfriend at the time. The trouble was, I'd been trying to focus on the carpet as I spoke and didn't realise that Tracey was standing right next to me. Like Tapps, she understood every word, but she didn't laugh quite as much. Her look said: 'This is over sunshine.' I passed out, which is probably the smartest thing I could have done. Karen soon went to work for the British Government in Washington DC but, like Julie Cox, I never forgot her.

With yet another girlfriend deciding to leave me, and my potential replacement choosing to flee the country, I concentrated on funding my future career in motor racing. Dad was an obvious target but he looked at me with his well-practised 'You're a bleedin' idiot' look and said 'No'. I was desperate for funds so I convinced him to let me go out to the oil rigs. The business was essentially applying a paint coating system to these installations to prevent the external structure, including the legs, decks, machinery and operating systems, from corroding. Dennis definitely liked the idea of me working and agreed to my plea, so long as I continued studying for my exams. I didn't know what I was letting myself in for.

Over the next two years I was stuck for two, sometimes three weeks at a time, on various platforms in the North Sea, working between 12 and 16 hours a day, shot blasting, spraying, scaffolding, cleaning, lifting and lugging. It was back-breaking, soul-destroying work in tough conditions. It was usually so cold that it was like the Ice Age – and the guys I worked with had an IQ straight from the same period. They probably thought the Economics and Law textbooks I read, while sitting alone in the evening, were a collection of evil spells. Occasionally I toyed with the idea of asking one of their brood for a lock of hair, just to unsettle them.

I hated them and they hated me – and they especially hated me when I punched one of them across the deck after an argument.

Combining the rig work with college wasn't ideal but, after two years, I finished college and passed A-level exams in Law, Art and Economics. Along with my certificates though came the end of an era and time up on full-scale mayhem. I knew life wouldn't be quite the same but, there again, I didn't want it to be. I was utterly focused on putting money together for racing.

That goal pushed me to continue offshore work. And believe me, you need a goal, because anybody who actually likes it out there should immediately be locked up in a high-security prison, or at least turned into a frog. With nobody to talk to, I'd get so lonely that, after 20 days, I started throwing bread to the helicopters: 'Here birdie!' It was a strange existence that couldn't have been further from my life at college or the exciting world of motor racing I dreamed of. However, the rigs hardened me, mentally and physically, and I believed that would help prepare me for the battle ahead. If I could put up with all that, then nothing was going to stand in my way.

By my 20th birthday I was, against the odds, still alive and without a criminal record. I was still driving everywhere flat out and my record of destruction had again led me to smash the Spitfire, then a Triumph Stag, a Ford Fiesta (twice) and, believe it or not, a little Fiat 126. However, the most bizarre accident was in a Ferrari 308, which was being driven by my lunatic cousin Gary Denham.

Gary was doing very well for himself when he bought his dream motor and he immediately came over to take me out for a spin. So there we were, approaching sub-light speed, along a B-road in Danbury, when I spotted a car in the distance waiting to turn right. I kept quiet for a second or two, hoping maybe he'd also seen it, but he hadn't. So I screamed: 'Gary, brake. Brake! Braaaake!' He did as requested but the car locked up. As we slid toward a collision, I screamed again: 'Come off the brakes, go left. Come off the brakes... ' But it was too late. Gary looked like a parachutist who'd pulled the ripcord and nothing had happened. Then... bang!

We went in hard. The front of the Ferrari was destroyed and the other car was pushed across the road. I turned to Gary and said: 'Should have come off the brakes, Gal.' He then got out, walked over to his victim and opened his door. The poor bastard sat there, stunned. He didn't know what the hell was going on: he'd only been trying to turn into his own driveway after a hard day at work and he'd been so very close to making it.

Gary looked in, smiled, produced a card and, in a manner more suited to meeting someone at a party than at a crash site, said: 'Hello, mate. My name is Gary Denham. I'm with Denham Motors and we specialise in accident damage. Don't worry about this – we'll have it repaired for you within the week.' The guy just stared at Gary, probably thinking that anyone who can come out with that must be nuts, and I leaned against the remains of the 308, laughing in disbelief.

The Ferrari, even a damaged one, was about as close as I was getting to Formula One. My longed-for track time was still only the Brands Hatch lessons and a Jim Russell course that included two Formula Ford races at Snetterton (one of which I won, wearing a borrowed helmet and a leather jacket). By contrast, a New Zealand driver named Mike Thackwell was the same age and had already made his grand prix debut for the Tyrrell Formula One team. I was painfully aware that the clock was ticking. I needed to get going immediately but I needed more money and a lot of help.

I had a pretty good history of talking people into things, or indeed out of them, so maybe I could first help myself. At school I'd had the girls do my homework for me and then convince the teachers not to punish me for an assortment of crimes which, funnily enough, included getting the girls to do my homework. At college, the principal had kept me on, even though he had a file on why I should have been put to sleep. While dad was abroad, I could regularly con mum that all the people who told wild stories about me and his new Jaguar XJS were only joking because I didn't even know where he hid the keys (breast pocket of his navy blue jacket, in the wardrobe). My communication skills had also been handy during kerbside seminars with the Essex Police on the benefits of road racing. Last but certainly not least, a lot of girls, for some reason known only to themselves, found me cute and I could now chat them up almost telepathically.

This was all very well, but it was now time to go commercial. If I wanted help, I'd have to tell my story to anyone who'd listen – then tell the same story but louder if they didn't listen. So I talked to virtually everybody I knew and then nearly everybody I met, whether on a train, in a pub or someone's office. If they couldn't assist, I'd ask them for a contact. My barrage of phone calls and mail-shots to big name companies in London made carpet-bombing look like an exact science, and when I took my show on the road, I made double glazing salesmen look like social workers. I was selling Perry McCarthy and I was selling motor racing.

I trawled dozens of local industrial estates, knocking on doors, chatting to the receptionist and getting them to wangle a five-minute meeting with a director. I applied maximum pressure, but even though I often managed to get my foot in the door, my pitch was rejected with depressing frequency. As professional sales people had told me, I had to think of it as a numbers game: the more approaches you make, the better the odds.

After several months, the grind began to pay off and a lot of people, blessed with an active imagination, massive optimism and, often, a sense of humour, dug in, became part of the Perry team and helped me. Russells the jewellers, Tarn Print and Design, Adpol polythene bags, Image Perception Photography, Laidlaw Ford dealership, Alan Burrows Ltd and Essex Colour were among the first to realise that they'd been fortunate to survive in business this long without me, and late in the summer of 1981 I had some real sponsorship which, with my rig money, meant I could at last get started.

From reading *Autosport* magazine I knew any would-be grand prix star needed to race in Formula Ford 1600 and I had already been to watch a couple of these races. Some Brazilian bloke called Ayrton Senna da Silva seemed to be doing pretty well driving for Van Diemen. So thinking that this car must be great, and not realising I was actually watching the best driver who ever lived, I thought: 'I need a Van Diemen'. I called the factory owner, Ralph Firman, for advice. He suggested talking to Jubilee Racing, a team who used Van Diemens and needed another driver.

Based in Rayleigh, near Southend in Essex, Jubilee was only 10 miles from my parents' new home in Little Baddow. Within a few days I met team owner Stuart Veitch, who signed me to drive for the last two races of 1981: the final round of the 'Champion of Brands' series and, unbelievably, the extremely competitive Formula Ford Festival World Cup.

So forget university, forget shipping and forget the RAF. I was now officially in motor racing and I couldn't imagine anyone coming into the sport in quite the same way. I'd had no karting background, no family involvement and only a recent interest. However, unrelated events – such as going to college and drawing Formula One cars, playing the piano and meeting Les Ager and our holiday in Antigua which led to working on oil rigs – had all combined to pull me toward a life on the track. But whatever route had led me in, I was now hell bent on making it work. From that moment, my fate was sealed tighter than a cat's wotsit.

When I flick through the photos of my first race with Stuart Veitch it brings a smile to my face. I was young. I had a head full of hair and my naïve expression made Shirley Temple look aggressive. I bet the other drivers dismissed this kid who smiled at everything – they probably thought of me in the same way that Willey E. Coyote imagines the Road Runner as a cooked chicken leg. But I was so happy to be there I couldn't help but act like a child with a three-month pass to Disney World. I don't think I've ever lost that sense of wonderment. However, critics sometimes confuse style with intent, and my intent was the same then as it's always been – I wanted to win.

I was thrilled to have the number 27 on the side of my Jubilee Racing Van Diemen because 27 was, and still is, famous for being Ferrari driver Gilles Villeneuve's number and that guy, for sheer balls alone, was the cream of the crop. He was my hero, so was it an omen? Well, yes and no. I qualified on pole position and won the qualifying race, but in the actual final of the Champion of Brands meeting I crashed. However, Stuart was encouraged and thought I might spring a few surprises in our next race, the 1981 Formula Ford 1600 World Cup.

It was a nice thought but, in reality, it wouldn't have taken much to spring a surprise. Given that virtually nobody had heard of me and those who had seen my debut might have noticed me slam into another car, then simply staying on the track would have been new.

Ayrton Senna da Silva hadn't seen my debut but he sprung his own surprise by retiring from the sport. I know these two events weren't connected but it meant I wouldn't have a chance to use my vast experience to get in his way. I did, however, meet another rising star. Julian Bailey was a front-runner and race winner for Stuart, and this would be a great chance to learn from an established 1600 driver. Well, come the race, Ayrton's replacement, Irishman Tommy Byrne, won the Festival and, to my surprise, I crashed again. I clearly hadn't learned enough from Julian, but our meeting was the start of a life-long friendship.

I spent that winter telling everyone that I was destined for the top, including all the local newspapers. And believe me, I was well into the local bit. To maximise my publicity and help generate sponsorship, I told the Basildon papers that I lived in Basildon, the Chelmsford papers I lived there and the same with Southend, Brentwood, Billericay and even Colchester, which was 25 miles away. I was on a roll and the McCarthy promotional campaign had started.

My mate Ian Shepherd, who was an art director, designed a letter heading, called in favours to have stationery printed, and organised a studio shoot with ace photographer Malcolm Hulme. I then wrote my first multi-page sponsorship proposal (detailing my press coverage and offering promotional returns), which was typed by a secretary friend and passed over to some bird in a print shop who regularly made hundreds of copies and smuggled them out. Now armed with a fairly professional package, I once again went forth to raise backing and knocked on more doors than a Jehovah's Witness.

I stayed with Jubilee Racing and FF1600 for the 1982 season and together we entered the prestigious Dunlop Autosport 'Star of Tomorrow' Championship. Julian continued as the works Lola driver in a different series. Senna, meanwhile, returned from Brazil, decided to give it another go and progressed to Formula Ford 2000.

We kicked off in March but by June I had been sent off. I was out of money and out of racing. In just six rounds I was finished. I was generally thought to be the fastest and I'd underlined this with two pole positions, but I was also highly erratic. I had developed a close working relationship with the barriers – head on, at various speeds, at different corners, on different circuits, in testing and in a few races. I was practising my crashing technique and I was getting pretty good at it. My collection of local newspapers were intrigued and their headlines began to develop a pattern. Before the race they'd shout: 'Champagne Perry is bubbling'. Then afterwards, it was something like: 'Perry runs out of fizz', 'Perry goes flat' or 'Perry goes pop'. The story became all too predictable – I'm sure some journalists saved their time by preparing a crash story before I'd actually crashed!

The increasing number of people I knew were entertained at

length by this and I came in for a lot of good-natured teasing, but some of those accidents were actually quite bad. However, I was extremely lucky that year, unlike some of the boys in grand prix. I'll always remember being at Brands Hatch when a radio announcement reported that Formula One's hero Gilles Villeneuve had been killed while qualifying his Ferrari at Zolder. Like everyone else, I was shocked.

The bravado with which the guy drove gave every indication that it *could* happen but you somehow never actually believed it would. When it did, it was unbelievable. For millions of fans worldwide, the loss of a hero like Gilles was like telling a kid that Santa has retired. A couple of months later, Formula One newcomer Ricardo Paletti was killed at the start of the Canadian Grand Prix. Then at Hockenheim, Didier Pironi – Villeneuve's team-mate – launched into the air and sustained terrible leg injuries that forced him to retire from the sport. Our speeds in Formula Ford were different but the lesson was learned. I really had to stop crashing for financial and health reasons.

I started gearing up for a return to the track with an all-out assault on the 1983 Formula Ford 1600 Championship. Another year had passed and I had no proper job, no trade, no real career and my friends thought I was crazy. My dad thought I was just a bum and he convinced his mates of the same, along with anybody else he knew or indeed met. On holiday, he'd still find a German and tell him how he'd been bombed out twice, but now he'd add that he had an idiot son. After only 20 minutes they'd be sitting like old buddies with matey-boy, freshly converted, saying 'Mein Gott, Dennis, is he a Dummkopf or vot?'

I was beginning to get irritated by some of the criticism, but I knew part of it was justified because the oil rig money had long since evaporated and I was both in debt and under pressure. My motor racing gamble had to start paying off fast and I needed to prove a point.

I continued my search for sponsorship but, with very little money for expenses, even the search was proving tough. A little episode with Wang Computers underlined the problem. I'd been chasing them for quite a while and one day I talked their marketing manager into coming out for a lunchtime chat. My budget for this power meeting was £10 and I'd calculated that would be sufficient for the cost of our sandwiches, plus a couple of pints. However, I hadn't figured that there would be another mouth to feed.

It was great news to find on arrival that Wang's marketing director would be joining us, but he was a threat to my wallet and I was seriously worried about my lack of cash. Anyway, they had a place in mind and I was praying it was a some dingy back-street pub. They directed me as I drove across Isleworth and as we pulled up outside the best bloody restaurant in the area I thought about making a run for it. I knew that, like most of the stuff on the menu, I was dead meat. I put an instant plan together and hoped that I might just be able to bluff it out.

As we sat down, I told them that I was due at Silverstone the following day and while they ordered *steak à la overdraft*, they were surprised to hear that I never ate or drank the day before testing. I was surprised to hear this as well because first of all, I didn't have a car to test and secondly, I was starving. For the following hour and a half, I sat there and talked about the upmarket image of motor racing, while trying to keep my eyes off their food and hoping they couldn't hear my stomach rumble. They listened to my sponsorship pitch politely, but then it came to the moment I'd been dreading – it was time to pay.

I'd already worked it out as £20 for the two of them and I tried not to look like someone who was suffering from haemorrhoids as I held my hand out for the bill. I readied my plan. I'd get them out to the car ahead of me, hand over my 10 quid, and then secretly leave my tacky watch as a deposit for the rest.

The marketing director, though, cancelled the transaction by holding up his hand, shaking his head and pursing his lips. He took the receipt and then, smiling like my benefactor, slowly patted me on the shoulder, saying: 'No, no, Perry. This is *my* treat!'

'Wow,' I thought. 'Thanks for the glass of tap water.' After I dropped them back at their office, I made a beeline straight to Kentucky Fried Chicken and sat there giggling as I attacked my drumstick. The Wang deal never came off though. Maybe just as well because I'd already had nightmares about a circuit commentator shouting something like: 'Look, there goes the little *Wang car*!'

After several more months of sponsor hunting I managed to attract a small budget from Lee Cooper and Tarn Print, but my situation was looking bad and my old man knew it. He wanted me in the business. How could I ignore his multi-million pound company for this? But he also realised I would not be put off, so he put a deal on the table. He'd sponsor me through DJM Construction, to the tune of 15 grand; in return, if I didn't win the championship I was to stop racing, never mention it again, and work for him. It was a clever initiative but a big gamble for both of us. He didn't want me to race and I didn't want to work for DJM, but we shook hands and both took it seriously.

In my first test of 1983, I continued the good work I'd been doing the year before when I drove my brand new Van Diemen straight into the wall. Then, after Jubilee Racing repaired the damage, we entered round one of the Dunlop *Autosport* Star of Tomorrow Championship and I spun off the track. Well done, Perry: one down, nine to go. In the second race, I was leading by a country mile on the Brands Hatch grand prix circuit when, with just a few laps remaining, the radiator hose came loose, the engine overheated and I stopped.

This was really bad. After all my work, all the time on the rigs, all the crashes of last year, all my dreams of winning, and all the crap I'd taken from everybody, I just couldn't believe it. No, no, no. I leaned my head back against the pit wall and stared at the car in disbelief. I was close to tears. Maybe dad was right: maybe I *was* an idiot.

To make matters worse, John Robinson had now joined the series. John had been chosen as a Brands Hatch star driver and people in the know rated him very highly. He was going to be tough to beat... but I did beat him. In the following race, the two of us dropped everyone else and fought like cat and dog. Lap after lap, we banged wheels, locked our tyres and slid around the Castle Combe track in Wiltshire as if our lives depended on it – and really our lives, at least the lives we wanted for ourselves, did depend on it. Toward the end, we hit hard at about 100mph and John took off over my wheels, went into the air and then landed next to the wall, thankfully uninjured.

His race was run and I won. Yes, yes, I'd won! My career had been holding on by a thread and now I'd shown I really could do it. I was delighted but I knew there was a long way to go. For his part, though, John was pretty unhappy. In fact, he was massively pissed off but we went on to become close mates both on and off the track.

So success at last – I had gained my first win. A little while later, though, I lost my team manager when Stuart Veitch and I parted company. Stuart was annoyed about a silly incident in testing and I don't blame him because, with my car in a controlled drift at 90mph, I was pretty dumb to steer with one hand and wave to a track marshal with the other. That kind of thing could have caused an accident. In fact it did, because I lost control and crashed head first into the pit wall. I remember lying in the car, stunned, when I saw Stuart leap over the pit wall and run down the side of the track toward me. Good bloke, I thought, he's coming to help me out. But when he arrived in front of me, it became obvious that he wasn't there to congratulate me. Almost foaming at the mouth he shook me by the shoulders and started screaming: 'I can't take it any more... That's it – we're finished!' It was a fit of temper and I don't think he meant it, but I took him up on the offer and moved to Dennis Rushen of Rushen Green Racing.

I stayed with RGR for the rest of the year and continued my head to head battles with John. It was rough stuff and must have looked like some kind of suicide pact, but we dominated the championship and, between us, won every remaining race.

The final round of the championship was at Brand Hatch and I was leading by only four points. The papers were giving me a big build-up and my adopted home towns of Billericay, Brentwood, Basildon, Southend, Chelmsford and Colchester expected the best of their gifted son. There was a general air of excitement, even from those who had previously thought I was wasting my time, but my team manager Dennis Rushen, who is brilliant on the psychology of racing drivers, had trained me to cope with it. He was already used to success and he expected me to win. He had run Ayrton Senna the previous year when Senna blitzed the Formula Ford 2000 series and was once again involved in that championship with Julian Bailey, who was fighting with Mauricio Gugelmin – another driver who subsequently made it to Formula One.

For good luck, my close mate and fellow competitor Peter Townsend lent me a set of race overalls that he had mysteriously acquired from current World Champion Keke Rosberg. My dad, meanwhile, rented a hospitality suite by the start/finish line, where he, his mates and my mates got seriously drunk in readiness for our little wager and the biggest race of my life.

The day that promised so much started with a big scare. On leaving the pit lane for qualifying, my engine cut out and the guy behind slammed into the back of me. I wanted to punch his lights out but firstly, it wasn't his fault and secondly, there was no time. My team and I hurriedly wheeled the car back to our pit and Dennis Rushen quickly realigned the damaged rear wheel. There were only a few minutes of the session remaining when I went out on to the circuit, but on my final lap I pulled it together. Peter Rogers claimed pole position and, having set exactly the same time, I lined up next to him on the front row of the grid. Johnny-boy had endured some kind of handling problem and was starting in sixth.

At the start of the race the green lights came on and I said goodbye. I drove around the outside of Pete at Paddock Hill Bend and ran like hell before John could battle through. I imagined him somewhere behind, in a frenzy and chewing through his own tongue at seeing me vanish into the distance, and I didn't want to be *anywhere* near him. After a few laps, I'd broken free from the pursuing pack and John had an incident with another car. Dennis Rushen punched the air as he held out my pit board telling me JR was out – and that meant I was the new champion! I crossed the line to win the race, followed by future touring car star Tim Harvey. On the podium, circuit commentator Brian Jones gave me the garland and through all the noise and excitement I could first hear and then see my old man shouting from the grandstand opposite: 'Well done, boy! You've done it!'

It had been a great year. I'd won six out of 10 'Dunlop' races and gained another four wins in the BP Superfind series against 'Fast' Peter Rogers (in deference to another Peter Rogers who was 'slow') and eventual BP champion Graham de Zille who, on the odd occasions when Robinson and I turned up to their events, thought we were both mental.

Dad had backed me and I doubt if I would have done it without him. I'd won our bet and he'd lost, but that evening, in the midst of wild celebrations back in our new home village of Little Baddow in Essex, my old man couldn't have been happier. Given the amount we all drank, I guess the landlord was pretty happy as well.

So I was now a champion. I hoped the next title would come soon but, for the time being, at least I'd given Rosberg's race overalls one last championship, because as I was blasting around Brands, Nelson Piquet had taken Keke's crown to become the new Formula One World Champion. The following day, the London *Evening Standard* drew a parallel between our victories and I was thrilled to be mentioned in the same context. Yeah, well done, Nelson, but watch out because I'm on the way!

Chapter 4

OVER AND OUT

The car turned upside down, barrel-rolled across the track, dug into the ground, and was then catapulted high into the air.

At various points in the season, several more girlfriends had made the decision to find a boyfriend who had a future, or one who might at least live until he was 25. These girls obviously didn't realise that I, the newly-crowned Dunlop *Autosport* Star of Tomorrow Champion – yes, me, part of the winning British team in the Formula Ford World Cup, a multi-race winner in the BP series, and recipient of my local *Evening Echo* sports personality of the month award – was going to be an international motor racing superstar!

Trouble was, industry didn't realise it either. I just couldn't land a big sponsor and my total budget for 1984 was about enough for a day trip to the Donington motor museum. I had visions of being an exhibit there, standing in the Didn't Make It section, with a cardboard sign round my neck saying: 'Got any money, please, mister?'

I had planned to graduate to Formula Ford 2000 with Rushen Green and I needed a break but dad, who had now sobered up, reconsidered that I was a bleedin' idiot after all and made it clear the break wasn't coming from him. In about November, though, Ralph Firman at Van Diemen called and invited me to test their new stealth-like Formula Ford 1600 at Snetterton along with John Pratt who, in company with Andrew Gilbert-Scott, had been one of my British team partners. It proved to be a good test and we were both very quick. Ralph knew my financial situation was three light years away from the works team's requirements, so he kindly offered to lend me a new car for the year if I raced for a team called Motor Racing International.

The season was approaching fast, so I agreed. Now I had a team and a car, and Dunlop had just stepped in to provide all my tyres for free. Furthermore, my mate Peter Smith at Tarn Print stayed onboard and, once again, ignored his overdraft to pledge a couple of grand. It was still nowhere near enough, but then I got a call from the head of Brands Hatch, John Webb.

I arrived at his office spot on time. I already knew Mr Webb; in fact everyone knew Mr Webb. He was a very intelligent bloke and British motor racing owes him and his innovations a debt of gratitude, but he was also bloody difficult, talked like his teeth weren't connected and, oh boy, did he like to drink!

I walked in. 'McCarthy, what d'ya want to drink?' I knew what he meant, but it had to be a trick. For God's sake, it was only 10am. Do I have one or don't I?

I threw the dice: 'I'll have a tonic water please Mr. Webb'.

He glared at me. Ooops, wrong answer! 'Tonic water! Tonic water!' he bated.

'Oh, with a gin in it,' I added quickly.

'That's better, boy. Large one?'

'Of course, sir!'

This continued until 12.30 and, by the time we met his wife Angela and other co-directors for lunch, I was on warp drive heading for Alpha Centauri. We were now getting on really well and 'Webby' liked my jokes. In fact, they all liked my jokes, and the more drink they fed me, the more jokes I told and the more they all laughed. Hell, drink *and* sponsorship. I could see us all being close friends but then, of course, it happened. It had to happen, really.

I'd already been in and out of about 10 foreign accents, while mimicking different people and trying not to drown in gin, when I fatefully began the actions and started a new joke with the intro, 'There's this cripple girl, in a wheelchair at a disco...' They stopped laughing. 'Oh my God,' my poor drunk mind was silently screaming at this major screw up. Mr Webb, of course, was partly disabled and I'd just done the equivalent of stuffing two grand into the jaws of an alligator and then poking him in the eye for fun. I could see my sponsorship and my season evaporating before my eyes. I had no choice. Stay with it, Perry.

They never even saw me flinch. I continued the joke, delivered the punchline ('Thanks for bringing her back home. Most of them leave her hanging on the railings!') and then waited for their reaction. The half a second it took them to burst out laughing felt like three years. I'd survived – just. 'Webby' gave me the money and I now had enough to start 1984. Not many drivers' careers have relied on the outcome of a joke...

A few weeks later at Brands, I christened my freshly-built car by banging wheels with a promising young newcomer who had inadvertently got in my way during a test session. There was no damage but I was delighted to learn that I'd scared the living daylights out of him, something of which he still reminds me. Well, I was just being friendly. It was my way of saying welcome to motor racing to Mr Mark Blundell, a guy who I was to get to know very well.

Eleven years later, Mark was again nervous – when I was best man at his wedding. McLaren, the Formula One team he signed for in 1995, had delivered one of their 240mph road cars 'to get us to the church on time' but I nearly crashed it during a rather fast, pre-ceremony test drive. Having survived that, and a potential £650,000 bill, we arrived at the altar,

Mark and Deborah said 'I do' and I handed over the ring. Then we went outside for the photos. The photographer, however, barked orders as he roughly pushed and shoved Mark and Deborah into position so I grabbed him and promised to knock him out if he continued. Meanwhile, Mark, who was trying to keep the peace, gave me one of his 'I don't believe you've just done that!' looks and made me promise to stand still and smile. I was more than familiar with that look, because it's one we've used on each other, in many situations and in many places around the world.

One time at Le Mans I was on stage with a microphone and busy entertaining about 300 guests on behalf of MRI, a motor racing tour operator. I had told them that my best mate Mark Blundell would be coming over and the crowd were thrilled when he arrived to be interviewed live before them. I knew our close relationship and banter would work really well, and I was smiling to the room when I opened the interview with: 'So, Marky, it must be all of three days since I've seen you!'

Mark, however, looked back stone-faced and, with the smallest of smiles that only I could see, said: 'What are you talking about, mate? I don't remember that.'

With a sense of panic, I persevered and prompted him: 'When we went out the other night!'

He looked back at the audience and shrugged his shoulders as if we'd never even met before. 'Sorry mate, I think you've got the wrong bloke.'

I was no longer in any doubt that the bastard had decided to set me up and I was left continuing to prove we were great friends, while the evil sod continued giving out blank looks. I could sense some of our spectators had fallen for it and now thought I was a total nutter. I was giggling with embarrassment and, covering the microphone, I leaned over and whispered to Mark that he was a complete... well, I can't actually include the word here. But with expert timing, he turned to the crowd and indignantly demanded to know: 'Is there a proper interviewer here?'

He tortured me like this for a full 20 minutes and not once did he crack. After we finished, we stepped outside and he was bent over in hysterics at the grief he'd caused me. That's typical Mark. He loves a laugh and especially if it's at my expense, but that's often revenge for something I've probably done to him – such as the time I had him close to booking a flight to Paris for a non-existent TV interview with a non-existent TV company.

He likes those stunts because he is one of the lads, but he also likes the good things in life and acquires them from the proceeds of his team retainer, his land deals, his property deals, his car deals and... well, you get the point. Marky-boy enjoys a deal. In this respect, he takes after his father Danny, but another trait he's inherited is loyalty and doing the 'proper' thing. Mark is a man from the old school where your word is your bond, and he doesn't take too kindly to those who break agreements. Mark's speed and determination in a racing car, though, ensured from a young age that his career would also be 'proper'. However, it would include far more dangerous things than banging wheels with me in that test session back in 1984.

That year, my new team, Motorsport International, was run by Barry Chaplin, who was a mate of Ralph Firman. The engines from Scholar were tuned by Alan Wardropper, who was a mate of Barry's, and after our first qualifying session at Brands, I wasn't a mate of either Barry or Alan. I'd qualified fourth but I still wasn't happy with the car set-up and I thought the engine was down on power. In fact, I think I said it was crap.

Barry then started telling me off about being ungrateful and tried to make me apologise to his friend Alan. I felt he was like some out-of-date headmaster and I wasn't too wrapped on that idea even when I was a kid. I told them not to hold their breath waiting and that should include our mechanic, who I thought had cocked up. For God's sake, this was supposed to be professional motor racing: if I've got a legitimate gripe, I expect my team to listen to it.

Anyway, the race approached and I was on the grid, waiting for the start, when suddenly the mechanic's wife stood in front of the car, wagging her finger at me and telling me that I'm spoilt, that her husband is a good man, that...

'Jesus,' I thought. 'Ralph's signed me to the bloody Adams family. I bet this never happened to Nelson Piquet!'

She eventually left the grid when I looked at her with narrowed eyes and started revving the engine. This situation was just unbelievable. I was right about the car, though, because Dave Coyne and John Pratt cleared off at a rate of knots and I finished fourth. It was obvious that our team relationship was destined to last about as long as a chocolate fireguard, but when it did finish it was in a way I didn't expect.

I was still upset with them when we got to the next race at Oulton Park in Cheshire, so I stayed in the same hotel as my mates Julian Bailey, Gary Brabham (middle son of Formula One triple World Champion Sir Jack) and Tim Jones (son of circuit commentator Brian). We had a couple of beers, got a little rowdy and then for some reason, probably because he's Australian, we pinned Gary down and sprayed shaving foam all over his head and face. We couldn't stop laughing when the landlord looked around and demanded to know what was going on.

Brabham, with his head looking like a ball of white candy floss, scooped two handfuls of foam out of his eyes, peered through and said: 'Nothing going on here mate!' To our amazement the fella just said: 'Well, that's all right then.'

The following day was far from all right though. Coyne and Pratt again disappeared into the distance while I was holding third place, with third gear missing, and trying to keep John

Booth, the champion of Oulton, behind me. After a while Boothy made a run at me going into Old Hall corner, the right-hander past the pit straight, and it ended in disaster.

John hadn't made it by me and, as I turned in at 100mph, my right rear wheel rode over his left front. The car turned upside down, barrel-rolled across the track, dug into the ground, and was then catapulted high into the air. The huge g-forces flung my arms outside the cockpit and, as I went upward, I could see the sky. I somehow had time to think of Julian, who'd received a badly broken arm in a crash at Snetterton, and I instinctively fought to pull my own limbs back inside. The car was already in the process of disintegrating but the landing impact finished the job and totally destroyed what was left. This final blow succeeded in knocking me out.

A wheel went into the crowd, thankfully missing everyone, and then a fuel spillage ignited. The track marshals were superb, though, and had the fire out very quickly. They lifted me from the pile of junk that, 10 seconds earlier, had been a racing car, and packed me off, unconscious, by ambulance to hospital.

It had been a spectacular and violent crash and I remember every bit right up to touch down. My next memory was being rushed on a trolley toward the X-ray department with a beautiful nurse looking over me. The pain in my back was intense and, as I was trying to piece everything together, the nurse thoughtfully explained that I'd been in an accident.

'Really?' I said. 'I didn't *think* this was the winners' rostrum!'

She laughed. I had mild concussion, a broken bone in my back, a sprained wrist and bruising to my legs and around my eyes. I had been very lucky, but later that night I got even luckier when the nurse returned. We talked about my pain and then we had a nice kiss 'n' cuddle. Brave little soldier wasn't I?

Dad, on the other hand, wasn't quite so affectionate. He'd had no idea about his *bleedin' idiot's* new adventure until the following morning, when he was sitting down to breakfast in a hotel in Holland and noticed a large picture, on page five of *The Sun*, capturing me mid-flight and en route to the wall. See, dad, I told you I'd be famous. One thing nobody read about, though, was that during my trip to hospital, my own team manager Barry had started helping John Booth to realign the wheel on his car in time for the restart! So much for loyalty.

It was goodbye, 1984. My budget and my car had been scattered across Oulton Park. The only thing left intact was the rev-counter and even I knew we couldn't rebuild a car around one component. I was in no state to drive for about three months but – go ahead, call me spoilt, call me ungrateful – at least I wouldn't be driving for Motorsport International! I did, however, need to find a way to get back on track.

Over the previous two years, I'd been keeping in touch with the Toleman grand prix team, which was owned by Ted Toleman, an industrialist from Brentwood, Essex. I'd regularly visited their offices to meet their commercial manager Chris Witty, who gave me advice on various topics. I had also met the company and team managing director Alex Hawkridge, who was to become a great friend and mentor. To me, this was some kind of progress because, through them, I had developed a contact with Formula One and that made me feel as though I was getting somewhere. I knew I shouldn't get too excited; it was only contact of a *sort*. It was a bit like fancying a girl who asks you for advice on which pair of knickers she should wear for her boyfriend. But what the hell, at least they knew you existed.

While I was recovering, Chris invited me to Zolder for the Belgian Grand Prix as an award for surviving Oulton. Nearly everyone in racing knew about that shunt courtesy of *The Sun*, plus a stack of magazines including *Motor*, whose sports editor Russell Bulgin offered to drive me to the race. I needed to make this trip work from the start, and I talked to Russ about the magazine backing me when I returned to the track. By the time we arrived, we'd developed a plan that Motor would have a small space on the car in return for publicising my exploits. This coverage would in turn be good for both me and for a sponsor.

I didn't know at the time that I was paving the way for a big deal. We arrived in the Formula One paddock and I entertained a lot of people with the motor-drive photos of my crash. I remember showing every frame to Renault driver Derek Warwick, who enjoyed putting funny captions to them, but Toleman's new signing, Formula Three champion Ayrton Senna, just viewed them in stony silence, then winked, said I was 'lucky', and walked off.

At that time, it was fantastic just to talk to these guys whom I so admired, and it was great that they were talking to me just like another driver. I wanted to be with them, so my next stop was the TAG Williams motorhome, where I planned to find and speak with Mansour Ojjeh, the wealthy sponsor of Williams and owner of the giant Techniques d'Avant Garde company. With my back injury it was a bit difficult to walk but, driven by optimism, I limped over and knocked on his door.

It was a long shot but this was actually quite sensible compared to some of the stunts I'd already pulled. He wasn't available, so I left a copy of my crash video with a note asking for help. Well, I never heard from him, but it was *almost* a brilliant move because years later in Monaco, Charlie Crichton-Stuart, who worked at Williams, told me that Mr Ojjeh had been captivated by the video and played it over and over again. He had said he did indeed want to help me, but somebody in the team (not wanting to see their sponsor have other interests) talked him out of it. Charlie's story made me feel like I'd won the football pools but forgotten to send the coupon off.

Back at home, 'Webby' was two grand down after my air display at Oulton. He said he was very unhappy about me not racing and that I was 'a complete bastard for ripping him off' – obviously his term for surviving. I organised a publicity stunt to show good faith, when reporters Lee Horton and Dean Morse did me a big favour by spending a day at the Brands Hatch race school and producing a full-page feature in the *Essex Chronicle*.

Sadly, though, Mr Webb had made up his mind. He had obviously forgotten that he liked my jokes and told me he could make me or break me and that he'd decided he was going to 'break me'. I wasn't too happy about this nonsense and in a heated exchange I told him to give it his best shot. He never quite understood that I wasn't exactly delighted with breaking my back either. And neither was I thrilled with being on the sidelines, yet again.

Chapter 5

WHAT IS A
WADDI LOVE?

*There was something very different about this girl.
I thought she was beautiful and she possessed a look and
manner of sheer elegance.*

I was feeling pretty depressed and arranged to have a beer
with my art director mate Ian Shepherd, in Basildon town
centre. You have to be depressed to go to Basildon town centre
but my mood swung to red alert when I bumped into Bob
Tappin's ex-girlfriend – and she just happened to be walking
along with Karen Waddilove, the slim, 5ft 7in girl with clear
blue eyes whom I'd been smitten with at college. I'd never
forgotten her and now here she was, just returned home from
America.

This was a major stroke of luck but I couldn't believe my
timing. Four years ago I'd made a play for her when I was very
drunk. Now, with bruising around the eyes from my forced
landing at Oulton, I looked like a badger. Even so, my senses
were tingling like it was the start of a race, but I tried to stay
cool and seized the opportunity. I told her I was no longer at
college. Christ! What an opener! She'd have to be an imbecile
to think that I *hadn't* left by now, and I'd have to be a moron
to be into my fifth year of retaking exams. I smiled and quickly
added that I was now a racing driver; I was recovering from a
crash and would she like to join me for a drink?

It's funny how one seemingly innocuous decision, at lunchtime, in a shopping centre, can prove to be a major junction in one's life. She said yes – and I can now imagine some long-dead game show host looking down on her and saying: 'Ooops! Sorry, my love. Wrong answer. You've just lost a nice secure life, a fridge-freezer and a trip to Miami. But you do get to take away with you an injured racing driver with the career prospects of a lemming.'

However, if Karen Jane Waddilove, or 'KJ', had heard that voice, then it wouldn't have fazed her one bit. She was adventurous and her job (with a hush-hush government department) had certainly not been routine. My gut feeling at college had been spot-on. There was something very different about this girl. I thought she was beautiful and she possessed a look and manner of sheer elegance. I was infatuated. I know it sounds corny, but that afternoon I was in love by the time we'd finished our third bottle of Mad Dog 20/20. Sorry, Karen, I mean, by the time we'd had a long chat and a glass of wine.

Just about all my other girlfriends had ditched me but it had never bothered me, and that's exactly why they'd ditched me. However, I'd now found somebody who I didn't want to be without. Karen and I saw each other every day for three months and were engaged in February the following year. Our party was a big occasion and Formula One drivers and close friends Mark Blundell, Julian Bailey and Johnny Herbert helped us celebrate. We danced to a band playing modern jazz and I told her how happy I was.

She was happy too, but Karen was, and is to this day, no push-over.

Across the years, we have faced many and varied pressures, times that would have seen others say 'see ya later sucker' – but not KJ. Sure, she goes ballistic every now and then, but for me that's just one of the ingredients that make her a sexy lady. She's always had a strong mind and an opinion about nearly everything, especially my behaviour, but if anyone was ever going to understand me then it's KJ. To this day, 19 years and three daughters later, I'm still in love with her.

So, from August 1984, I was no longer trying to reach the top by myself. I now had the best team-mate anyone could wish for.

Chapter 6

MONEY, MONEY, MONEY

*I wanted to be moving toward Formula One for Christ's sake,
but at this rate I'd be 78 by the time I got there.*

Seven months had passed since I'd smashed up the Van Diemen and, as I hadn't been working regularly, I'd also caused a bit of damage to my overdraft. My bank manager wanted the outstanding £3,000 repaid and told me that I had one month, after which I should go out and sell the BMW 316 I'd arrived in. I agreed and this seemed to keep him satisfied, although he might not have been too happy if he'd known it wasn't my car. Anyway, I had four weeks and I was forced to develop a Get Out Of Trouble Plan that I'm not particularly proud of. As they say on TV, don't try this at home.

I found £4,000 from a sponsor in Europe, who liked the idea of seeing his company name on a Formula Ford 2000 racing car for three races. However, the going rate with most teams was more like £5,000. I eventually chose to do a deal for one race, which cost £1,200. So I was back in business while, incidentally, a lad called Damon Hill was just starting in it.

In qualifying I was greatly encouraged to run second fastest in wet conditions but I then slipped down the order as the track dried. After the session, though, I nearly slipped off the entry list when my old friend Mr Webb remained true to his word and tried to have me and my team excluded. The reason? Because my team-mate had stuck his fingers up at Gary Brabham while on track! Nice try, but it didn't work.

In the race, I was careful not to stick my fingers up or make nasty faces at anyone and I finished ninth. It wasn't a bad effort considering that I had been out of racing nearly all year and, sure enough, I received mentions in *Autosport*'s report, which I sent to the sponsor; and that's when I had the idea for my Get Out Of Trouble Plan.

I was desperate to start putting things together for a full return in 1985, but I really needed to straighten my life out first, so... basically... er... how can I put this? Well, I guess it's fair to say that after paying the team, I kept the remaining £2,800 of sponsorship in my account, which paid off my debt. Of course, I *know* I should have explained to my sponsor that I wouldn't be driving in the extra two races, but knowing that no sponsor is going to take too kindly to that, I kind of... forgot.

Instead, I made several photocopies of the *Autosport* report I had legitimately been in and then carefully cut out my name and glued these 'Perry McCarthy' tabs into the two new reports and results, over another driver whose name was the same length as mine. I then photocopied these 'adjusted' versions and held my breath as I sent them out to the sponsor. He was delighted with my coverage and I felt very guilty when he congratulated me on my great performances. He never realised that he was the only person in the world to know that I'd finished the last two races of the Formula Ford 2000 Winter Championship – on the podium.

I felt bad about the whole thing but, at 23, I just couldn't think of another way that would get me out of trouble and keep my dream alive. I didn't forget about my wrong-doing, though. Two years later I set the record straight by placing that same sponsor's name on a better, faster, car.

Over the winter, I ignored a possible career as a forger and instead went back to work for my dad. I was charged with assembling the high-pressure water blasting machines that we used to clean large areas of grease, oil and dirt on the rigs. It was a job for a brain-damaged chimp but it did allow me some freedom again to go out searching for sponsorship. In the past, we used to buy these water blasters, but having been a millionaire for about three years, the old man had now gone into his world domination phase and started buying various companies who used to supply such equipment.

By a peculiar coincidence, this was also the beginning of his lose-everything phase, a programme that accelerated seriously after he'd decided that owning a corporate jet was an absolute necessity. I remember thinking he was losing it *before* this. Then he bought a couple of donkeys, like the company whose accounts had been dreamed up by someone who must have been on acid. To top that, there was his £500,000 investment in an impossible oil reclamation project, which probably originated from the same guy, or at least the same drug.

So now with the Hawker Siddeley HS125 jet purchase, I begged him to reconsider and shouted: 'Why the hell are you doing it?'

Guess what he said? Dad nostalgically reeled off: 'Son... we come from the East End... we 'ad no money... and I was bombed out twice.'

I didn't quite see the logic and said: 'Well, what's that got to do with it?'

Then, looking deprived, he said: 'Well, we never 'ad a jet!'

I carried on walking around industrial estates, putting money together and feeling more and more alienated from my family. Was I changing or were they? I mean, even Stevie Wonder could see that the business would soon be worth about £20. And as far as they were concerned, I was still nothing but a dreamer.

I was actively discouraged from continuing and I remember it was around this time that dad read me the riot act and shouted that I was a bum who was going nowhere. This really upset me. Nobody seemed to feel that my work and determination deserved any merit and dad had obviously forgotten that, only a year ago, he'd cheered from the grandstand as I won the Star of Tomorrow Championship. The only thing his lecture achieved was a bad feeling between us and I took a mindset that began to apply to everyone: 'If you're not interested in me, then I'm not interested in you.'

As a parent myself these days, I can now finally understand their concerns. Kids are a worry and you want the best for their future. The world is a hard place for someone who dreams. However, that winter I found a few grown-ups who liked my particular dream, and I did more deals than Cool Hand Luke. I found several firms who each chipped in a few quid, but then my scouts struck gold when they told me of a company in Basildon who had a picture of a racing car in their foyer. That picture was to prove very expensive.

My tip-off was the automotive design engineers Hawtal Whiting, and it was a good one because I could neatly dovetail them into the *Motor* magazine deal I'd arranged after my Belgian Grand Prix visit. Within days, I met a very nice chap called Ken Edmondson, who listened and smiled. He liked the idea, he liked the *Motor* connection and he liked me. He suggested five grand for 1985 and I suggested I'd take it, but he also added that if I played my cards right, Hawtal Whiting might just be my ticket to the top.

I remember once asking Guy Edwards, the multi-millionaire master of motor racing sponsorship, what the secret was for finding sponsorship. He replied: 'Four letters, and they are: "W", "O", "R", and "K".' I think Guy appreciated my tenacity and in further meetings he kindly spared the time to talk about the necessity of a good presentation and long-term planning.

The lesson was learned and my new plan was to stay in Formula Ford 1600, use the year to catapult into the 1986 Formula 3 championship, and then totally dominate, just as my friend Johnny Dumfries had done throughout 1984. For this to work, though, I would need cubic industrial-strength money, so I thought about my future presentation and set to work on a 12-page glossy brochure capable of impressing the hell out of everyone up to and including President Reagan.

Such a production would be hugely expensive but I don't work like that. I did some research and then met with several local companies. I convinced Walker Roast Advertising to design it, Delta Paper to supply the paper, and Tarn Print to print it – all of which was cost free – in exchange for their names on my racecar. Lee Cooper jeans stayed onboard and then I set up a contra-deal with Crest Hotels to get free accommodation. Finally, my Ferrari-smashing cousin Gary Denham talked Volvo dealership South Hill Garage into supplying me with a road car. The local newspapers announced this fact with a picture of me flying through the air at Oulton Park and carried the headline: 'Would you lend a car to this man?' Cheers guys!

Now with the badges of 11 different companies all over me and the car, it looked like I had more money to spend than a Third World country. The truth was that I had only 12 grand and, even back in 1985, that was nowhere near enough. What I really needed to do was win the high-profile 'Racing for Britain' scholarship, which had been set up a few years earlier by an enthusiast named Steve Sydenham. Steve had a dream of helping under-funded drivers and his efforts had already made a difference to the struggles of recent British Formula One drivers Jonathan Palmer and Martin Brundle. The scheme relied on public and corporate donations and, in return for taking out a subscription, members received a host of benefits and discounts – and the right to vote in three different categories for the trainee superstars they would like to see get the cash.

I had my sights fixed on 'Racing for Britain' like a laser-guided missile. Armed with an agreement with two other drivers and a map of the northern hemisphere, I went forth and solicited votes for myself in FF1600, Andrew Gilbert-Scott in Formula 3, and Graham de Zille in Formula Ford 2000. In the meantime they, bless their little hearts, did the same for me.

The score was taken and, now with corporate funding from Systime Computers, the Racing for Britain drivers for 1985 were announced as: Andrew Gilbert-Scott and Anthony Reid in Formula 3; John Pratt in Formula Ford 2000; and in Formula Ford 1600... yes folks, all the way from Little Baddow in Essex... you voted for him, welcome back – Perry McCarthy! It suddenly seemed that talking people to death had been worth the effort, after Steve Sydenham stated that 'the Formula Ford vote had been a walkover'... for *me*. My prize included a loan car from Van Diemen, engine rebuilds from Minister and free insurance from TL Clowes.

There was nothing wrong with canvassing for votes and it was taken as accepted practice because, of course, it increased the fund's reserves. However, they did lose their sense of humour about one particular tactic. A few years earlier, my mate Julian Bailey had won the Racing for Britain 1600 category with the aid of a cunning plan. At that time, Jules had a friend in Norfolk who, in turn, had a lot more friends, and he kindly sent JB a list of their names and addresses. Anyway, unbeknown to this list, Julian then filled their details on to a stack of forms, all of which carried votes for *him*, and sent them through to RfB, complete with the required postal order for £10. Well, he duly won the selection but suddenly the population of King's Lynn were surprised to find a free membership arriving in the post, along with a letter thanking them for voting.

A few weeks later, though, Jules was rumbled when somebody at RfB noticed 'Kings Lynn' was spelled incorrectly on 100 different subscriptions. Their suspicions were confirmed when one of these 'voters' called up to say: 'What's all this rubbish you've been sending me? I've never heard of Julian Bailey.' Steve Sydenham wasn't happy but Julian, by this time, had won three races so they stayed with him. The irony was that the postal orders had cost Jules £1000 but his Formula Ford scholarship was worth only £750.

My own RfB win was great news but, truth be known, my total budget was still only half of what it should have been. However, all those who said I was finished needed to think again: I had successfully returned to racing full time, I had signed for Milldent Motorsport and I had a truckload of supporters willing me on.

My 1985 attack on the British championship was now ready, but there was only one small problem: I didn't want to do it. I just didn't want to spend a fourth year in Formula Ford. A fourth year was more like a prison sentence. I wanted to be moving toward Formula One for Christ's sake, but at this rate I'd be 78 by the time I got there. I was bored with being a 'junior' driver: I wanted to be a star. Why couldn't I jump up a level?

Maybe I was suffering from Post Traumatic Sponsorship Syndrome or something, but my motivation nose dived just when I needed it for going head to head with future stars such as Johnny Herbert, Damon Hill, Mark Blundell, Bertrand Gachot, Alain Menu and a supporting cast of Paulo Carcasci, an on-form Jonathan Bancroft and a psychotic Lindoro Da Silva.

I pulled myself together and got on with the job, but in terms of what I wanted to achieve on the track, the season was a disaster. Paulo and I hit several times, Bertrand and I hit whenever Paulo was busy, and Lindoro attacked me whenever Bertrand wasn't around. My Van Diemen RF85 took a major battering and Steve Farrell, owner of Milldent, had drawn my attention to the increasing stock of damaged parts I had supplied him with. As we didn't have a budget even to test regularly, we certainly didn't have the money for accidents.

The frustration boiled over after a race at Donington when, because of an engine fault, we couldn't run in qualifying and the organisers started me at the very back of the grid, in 26th place. This was all the way up there on the 'Things you don't want to happen' list, especially as my possible saviours, Hawtal Whiting, had, for the first time, booked a hospitality suite and invited about 20 guests to watch their little star. So sitting about 100 metres away from pole position, I was determined to put the record straight.

As the lights went green, I made an absolutely fantastic start. I was out to win, I had everything to play for. It was a drive I'll always remember because, unbelievably, I passed 19 cars on the opening lap and forced my way into seventh position.

That really should have been enough work for one lap, but all I could think about was catching the leaders, and on the final corner I saw yet another gap that was just about McCarthy width. I left my braking to the last microsecond and dived down the inside for sixth. The car ahead, though, turned in at the same time and, braking in a cloud of tyre smoke, I couldn't stop. I slammed into his side. With hindsight, I realised that my braking limit of 'the last microsecond' was probably about a full second too late but, just to make sure it was a *really* bad day, my victim was my own team-mate Tim Jones.

A course vehicle dragged our broken cars back to the paddock like a couple of dead cats and then dumped them next to my team. I knew it was my fault and when I returned to face the music, there was a crowd inspecting the remains of Team Milldent's equipment with the same morbid fascination you see in biology students dissecting a frog.

My team owner Steve, who sometimes used to stutter, was pretty unhappy and in front of our audience told me: 'Y-You kn-know P-Pe-Perry, the race is-isn't w-won or lost on the fir-first lap'...

I said: 'Oh yeah, well that's easy for you to say!' Steve was torn between laughing or hitting me, as he chased me all the way down the paddock, shouting: 'You b-bas-bastard!'

I was proud of my wisecrack but feeling bad for the team. I liked Steve and my mechanic, Malcolm Oastler (who was to go on to become a top Formula One designer) and they did a good job on a tight budget. Above all, though, I was deeply concerned that this crash, here of all places, might force my sponsors to think again about the 'future star' bit. As I approached Hawtal Whiting's hospitality suite I felt as if I was making my own way to a firing squad but when I walked in, blow me down if it wasn't smiles and sympathy all round. They obviously understood the will to win. Okay, some of them thought I was crazy, but even they thought my opening lap was amazing. They were still on my side and I was still in.

Throughout the season, we were usually close to the ultimate pace but, as in all motorsport, 'close' is the difference between winning and losing. Sure, I had some excuses – racing drivers are famed for their excuses – but we had genuine problems. We weren't testing, which meant there was little opportunity for me to practise against more experienced drivers or experiment with mechanical changes to make the car faster. But I think the biggest problem was that my frustration at not graduating to Formula Ford 2000, or even Formula 3, was causing me to make too many mistakes. A general pattern emerged: qualify top six, collide with someone, spin to the back, mount a big recovery drive and finish about top six again, then have a couple of beers and return home in complete silence with Karen, which could actually be more frightening than crashing in the first place.

So, if the dream had been dented, I reasoned it was still better than the nightmare of the oil rigs. I returned to the North Sea for one last time and to a job where DJM Construction was under heavy scrutiny. On arriving, I could see a few things were wrong and I was convinced the behaviour of a couple of our blokes was going to cost us the contract. In a heated argument, I lost my temper, punched the ringleader across the deck, took command from the manager and sent him and his mate home on the first available helicopter.

I did all this without back-up, I did this in front of about 12 blokes who didn't like me, but I did it because they were setting my old man up for a fall. As far as I was concerned, I'd done the right thing, but some others in the company didn't like it and talked dad into rehiring these guys. I was furious. Dad should have supported me, so I sent myself home on a helicopter and then left the company.

At the end of the year, I had a good look at both my life and my stop-start motor racing career. I decided that even though I seemed doomed to prowl the city streets for sponsorship, and then slam the sponsorship I'd found straight into the nearest barrier, I was sure that it was still better than a life of monotony in the North Sea – or anywhere else for that matter. I was a *racing driver* and one who had a real chance to make it to the top. Of course, it had already been hard going but it was stupid to feel sorry for myself because there was still such a long way to go. It was going to take stamina. I'd have to keep trying and I'd need to keep fighting in more ways than one, but my experience on the rigs was good for motivation. It was, and still is, important to remember the times I had clung to a piece of scaffolding, 100ft above the sea, buffeted by freezing winds, trying to erect a temporary platform, on the underside of a deck the size of a car park, which, once finished, I would stand on and shot blast for days at a time.

No, Perry, my boy, motor racing – good or bad – was definitely a lot better than real life.

My tally of accident damage had bust the budget by £4,000 and my team owner Steve Farrell needed the money. I used everything except a metal detector to try to find it, but then my mate Antony Rogers phoned with some bad news. Tony, my old 'Mutt' partner at school, had been nicked for drink-driving and had consequently sold his car. I asked him how much he'd got for it. He didn't need to be a psychic to guess why: 'Four grand. How much do you need?' he quipped.

'Well, Muttley... I need it all.'

'When will I get it back?' he asked, nervously.

I told him straight that I didn't know. So with no security, Antony gave me everything he had, which allowed me to keep my word with Steve.

Even though the results were awful, that whole season in Formula Ford had been geared to making the quantum leap to Formula Three. My new super-duper brochure was finally ready to help with marketing. It needed to be good because I had to attract about £120,000 for my target of a drive with a top team.

Why so much money? Okay, let's say you've been crazy enough to become a driver. Assuming you've already qualified for the correct licence, you would need to join a team of proven personnel capable of providing and tuning competitive equipment. Like any professional business, they will calculate the costs involved in trying to help you win. The budget they quote will include such things as workshop overheads, engine rebuilds, tyres, fuel, entry fees, travel, accommodation, insurance, staff wages, capital depreciation and their own profit, which they tend to hide or at least keep really quiet about.

If you have personal money, and lots of it, then that's great. You just hand over the loot and go racing. If your mum, dad, grandfather or great auntie has the dosh, then a severe amount of creeping might help separate them from it. If, however, you are like most of the planet and aren't loaded, then you will need a rare creature known as a sponsor. The sponsor is shy and elusive, ranking just below Lord Lucan, Glenn Miller, Big Foot, Shergar and the Loch Ness Monster on the 'tough to meet' scale.

Some drivers use agents to track them down but most of these experts are usually expensive, or useless, or both. So most guys are left to try to find a sponsor themselves, and most of them fail, which is why fewer and fewer drivers progress through the ranks. Talent aside, money is motor racing's equivalent of food in Darwin's theory of natural selection. With lottery-type luck, though, you might find a backer. Then, just maybe, they'll give you a full budget and this will allow you to race without compromises.

So why does the sponsor invest? God only knows. It should be because they have identified, or been presented with, an opportunity to place their corporate name on a mega racecar, run by a top team with a star driver, that can be used for a multitude of marketing and promotional programmes. The PR and advertising benefits should be weighed against cost and if the sponsor agrees, it's because they believe their spend is effective.

The truth is often very different, though. It's nearly always because you know the chairman personally, or somebody you know actually knows him, and that chairman likes motor racing. It normally has to come from the top end because almost every company turning over more than £20 is pursued by an army of wannabes, aren't-we-greats and help-us-outs – in plain English, a multitude of sports, a selection of arts and thousands of charities. The poor souls in the marketing departments feel like they've been in the trenches by the time it's 11am and basically they become immune to any call or letter beginning with: 'I have a fantastic opportunity for your company'.

You could hit them with 'Look, I've found Elvis and he's willing to skydive from Concorde, into the middle of the World Cup Soccer final, wearing your company name on his chest, and all for only fifty quid' and they'd say, 'sorry, company policy, we don't sponsor dangerous sports'. I'm not kidding. They just shut off. I guess they have other things to do besides fend off vultures like me and I do understand their position. But I'd still like to strangle some of them.

Most of the time it's personal relationships. Get the decision maker on board, make him laugh, sing to him, juggle, do whatever the hell it takes, but get to him. You know

the adage: 'It's not what you know, it's who you know.' Well, I've added: '... and if you don't know them yet, *get to know them*.'

I've used this philosophy on numerous occasions, such as the time I was chasing a large computer games company. Several months earlier I'd written and I'd phoned but forget it – no way, no interest, end of story – they wouldn't see me. I was bored of taking no for an answer, so I thought: 'How about a bit of star quality?' I called again for Mr Clarke and went directly through to the chairman's office. Now, I'm not too bad at impersonations and I'd already spent a few minutes practising one particular public school accent before I said: 'Yes, hello. This is James Hunt. I would like to make an appointment to see Graham to discuss a young protégé of mine by the name of Perry McCarthy.'

The previously hostile assistant melted faster than butter in a frying pan. 'Are you *the* James Hunt?' she pined.

'Yes,' I said, confidently, and smiled at my mum, who had been scowling at me from the entrance to the study.

'Well, Graham has a gap in his diary next Wednesday at 10am.'

'Super,' I said. 'I'll see you then.'

So, I arrived as scheduled, but alone of course, and after practising my excuses on the heartbroken secretary, I was shown in to see the chairman. Stay cool, Perry. Keep a straight face. Be confident. It might just work. I took a deep breath and said: 'James has been called away on business. However, he sends his regards and has asked me to outline a sponsorship opportunity to you.'

There was an uneasy silence. The guy didn't take his eyes off me. I know that because they, like his mouth, had slowly creased into a grin before he said: 'Nice try, son. Get out!'

Ooops a daisy. I knew the game was up, so I reversed back out the door, giggling with embarrassment, and said: 'Okay. See ya.'

I didn't even have the chance to giggle during another episode in my 'Meet the chairman' campaign. Staying with the computer industry, I'd heard there was to be a large exhibition at London's Olympia centre and I knew Amstrad, the business phenomenon of the 1980s, would be attending. I calculated that the best time to hit would be press day because it was a sure bet that one of Britain's richest men, company chairman Alan Sugar, would be there. I imagined meeting him, having a drink and getting to know him. If he liked me, then I'd be in Formula One within two years, no sweat. Before becoming best mates, though, I actually had to get into the press day. I got my pals Lee Horton and Dean Morse at the *Essex Chronicle* to tell the organisers they were sending their reporter P McCarthy to cover the event and they would like a pass made available. Lee and Dean loved stuff like that – they were completely crazy and we had a lot of laughs together.

So I got the pass, took the train to Olympia and, after a while, spotted Mr Sugar surrounded by a large entourage. He obviously had a lot to do because he went from one group to another one, and then another, and another, and was never alone. I tracked his every move from a distance for ages and began to feel like Stewart Granger in a big game safari movie. I was the poacher, Sugar was the quarry and I needed him on his own.

Sure enough, after about two hours, he made a mistake and eventually split from the pack. It was my chance and I pounced confidently and decisively up to his side. 'Hello, Mr Sugar. My name is Perry McCarthy and I wonder if I can take a moment of your time?'

The guy didn't even break his stride as he growled: 'No you can't. I'm very busy.' And with that he accelerated away, escaping my ambush. I didn't know what to say. I just stood there open mouthed. It had all gone wrong and I had just been badly mauled. End of day and end of plan. Maybe I should have shot him with a tranquilliser dart before I said hello. Rejection is a hard thing to take and regular rejection can make you feel as popular as the Elephant Man. It is nothing less than soul destroying, but if you quit trying, you're definitely out of the game.

New Year arrived – 1986, the year I had dreamed would take me into Formula Three. But by mid-January, I had no sponsorship, my meetings had all crashed and burned and, as always, I was running out of time. I was desperate, but it wasn't my first time and it certainly wouldn't be my last. I needed big backing, and fast. So forget research, company targeting, market compatibility and integrated promotions: I was now sending my glossy brochures out to anybody who could just bloody read.

Day after day I waited and waited for some kind of positive reply. Every morning I'd run downstairs to check the post, but apart from a having different company headings, each letter contained the same message: 'No!' However, one day I received a reply from the international division of a high street bank, who I had met several months earlier and who, on that occasion, had also said no. I was intrigued and, being an optimist, I was excited. I slowly opened the envelope and read the letter that began 'Dear Perry'. Encouraging start, I thought. It continued: 'You may recall that when you last approached us for sponsorship, we were unable to offer support. However, since then we have once again discussed your proposal and... '

'Yes, yes,' I thought. 'They've changed their minds. They're in. I'm going all the way. How much? How much?'

I continued reading faster: '... I am sorry to tell you that we still cannot help.'

Still can't help! There was a loud clunk as my chin hit the floor. No, I must have read it wrong. I went through it again, willing the sentence to change into '... and we'd like to give you £500,000 over the next two years.' But it didn't. This unexpected letter had initially raised my hopes sky high, only to make them nosedive back to earth with a bang. I couldn't believe it. The circuits in my poor little brain had fried and if the author had been near me I would have forced the letter back on him, right up a place where nobody would want to collect the stamp.

From about 500 'green bottles' I had only one left standing on the wall: Hawtal Whiting. I arranged a meeting on a Friday with the directors and, as I sat waiting in their boardroom, aware that this was probably my last chance, I started reading my own brochure. Within it was a diagram of a Formula Three car, divided into prime and secondary sponsorship areas, which were marked from '1' to '5' along with a corresponding list of costs.

I still hadn't decided how much to pitch them for: should I go for '5' and '4' (30 grand); '2' on its own (40 grand); '1' and '2' (100 grand)? Who knows? I needed a £120,000 for the drive and if I could get £30,000 for wages, it'd be like winning the Pools. I had to think fast and, as they walked in, I closed the book, threw the dice, went for broke and prayed as I heard myself say: 'One hundred and fifty thousand pounds'.

At the time, it really looked as though I was finished, but if I was going down, I was going down fighting. During the meeting I went into complete overdrive. I showed facts and figures, talked about image and exposure, and then ricocheted eight miles off course to tell Mr Hawker, Mr Whitecross, and Mr Talbot a host of stories and jokes. I was relieved when they were laughing and delighted when they threw back a few ad-libs. As with their manager Mr Edmondson from the year before, they liked the idea and they liked me. It had been a good day, they were successful and humorous, and I had really enjoyed meeting them. Mr Hawker told me he would call with a decision on Monday.

Once back home in Little Baddow, I was paralysed with anticipation. Throughout the weekend I could think of nothing else. Formula Three is a crucial step on the motor racing ladder and most drivers in Britain – in fact, in Europe – never make it to that level. A break like this would be against the odds. Julian Bailey said he'd eat his crash helmet if I got it.

Bob Hawker, managing director of Hawtal Whiting, left it until 5pm on the Monday to make the call. Bob has a wicked sense of humour and I can imagine that he must have been smiling from ear to ear as he kept me hanging in the breeze with questions like 'How are you?' and 'Have you had a good weekend?' Although I'd played it as Captain Confidence during our meeting, I'm sure he knew my life was hanging on his next words...

'We've had a chat Perry and... ' he paused for effect. 'And... we're coming with you. Come in and see us tomorrow and we'll sign.'

I hadn't breathed for two minutes but then, very softly, I managed to say thank you and replaced the handset back on the lovely phone that had delivered this absolutely fantastic news. I looked out the window and just smiled a big smile. I'd done it. I had bloody well done it! I then called Julian Bailey and asked him if he'd like his crash helmet served plain or with jam.

A few weeks later I was just as happy when I returned Antony's four grand. As a little present for risking everything to help me, I also bought him a holiday in Austria.

Chapter 7

HOUSTON, WE HAVE IGNITION

The Reynard was a sophisticated piece of engineering and the increase in power and grip over Formula Ford made me feel like I'd been strapped to the back of an Exocet missile.

This was a big deal, probably the biggest one-car deal Formula Three had ever seen, and for a number of reasons it had come just in time. Over the past few months, Karen's behaviour had started to change. We could be having a normal everyday conversation about Keke Rosberg or turbo engines when, suddenly, the word 'house' would come from out of nowhere. I'd try to ignore it and get back to interesting stuff like boost pressure, but I knew I was fighting a losing battle.

We could be on our way to meet friends in a pub, but Karen would find an excuse to lead us past an estate agent's window and peer through with a glazed look in her eyes. At the age of 25, her home-starter hormones had kicked in and during the run up to the Hawtal Whiting deal, I was being dragged unwillingly to see any property falling inside the 'I've only got £20' end of the market.

Although I loved her, this moving-in together business had some serious downsides. Okay, I definitely liked the idea of being in our very own bedroom and making love 80 times a day, but I wanted it to be in a *nice* bedroom. I'd become used to living in a beautiful home with log fire and lovely grounds; a home where my mum would get up at one o'clock in the morning to cook bacon and eggs for me and my mates after we got back from the pub. And while we're on the subject, would Karen look after me like mums do and protect me from the realities of domestic life? I mean, who would do all the washing and ironing? In fact, what was washing and ironing? And what about the bills: how does all that stuff work? Personally, I just paid £10 a week to the nice lady in the kitchen, and then in a process I never dared inspect too closely, everything just happened magically.

Resistance however was useless. Firstly, Karen had a bee in her bonnet and secondly, my traitorous parents had decided to move to Spain and sell the property that had been my never-never land. I must be the only kid around whose mum and dad had left home. So I was doomed.

We decided our love nest would be a really horrible terrace house that cost 30 grand and stood right next to a main road. It was a horrific thought and, from our previous viewing, I calculated that at seven o'clock each morning, our heads would be lying six-foot away from a stream of passing juggernauts.

But it never happened. It was like Bobby Ewing's famous shower scene in *Dallas*, because it all proved to be a bad dream once Hawtal Whiting came along and changed the script. Their financial backing, along with my personal sponsorship deal from Lucas, put me on £40,000 a year. So we immediately forgot about the house that could have featured in a road accident story and, instead, bought a beautiful and spacious apartment, at twice the price, in the lovely village of Stock. I then waved *adios* to mum and dad.

Julian Bailey, meanwhile, had made a purchase of his own when he and his brother, Adrian, bought the Lord Louis pub in Stansted Abbotts. On one of my regular trips to see him, we attacked his stock of drink and discussed which Formula Three team I should join. It came down to a choice of two.

I went to see West Surrey Racing, who were regarded as

the best outfit going, but the team boss Dick 'The Guru' Bennetts hadn't exactly done cartwheels when I'd arrived and their number one driver Bertrand Fabi told me privately that I would need to push hard. Conversely, Robert Synge, owner of Madgwick Motorsport, was pushing hard for *me* and he had chosen to stay with the new Reynard F3 car for his team. I've always had a lot of faith in Reynard racing cars, and especially Adrian Reynard himself. Adrian has a brain the size of a small planet and even though nearly all the other teams had ordered Ralt chassis, I believed in him and his latest car. So I signed with Madgwick as team-mate to last year's championship runner-up Andy Wallace. I had known Andy since my first year in motor racing and he was very fast. A.WOL, as we call him, was destined to become a great friend and, in later years, stand up for me by fighting my corner.

We announced the agreement with a press launch in London but some of my mates also had news. In Formula Three, Damon Hill signed for Murray Taylor Racing (courtesy of a secret backer), Martin Donnelly signed for Swallow Racing and, later in the year, we'd all be joined by Johnny Herbert and Julian Bailey. Meanwhile, Mark Blundell had moved into Formula Ford 2000, where he would spend an entire year at war with Bertrand Gachot.

My first Formula Three test was at Snetterton circuit in Norfolk and the experience of driving it was like staying up late and drinking with the big boys for the first time. The Reynard looked like a small Formula One car. It was equipped with aerodynamic wings, a full carbon fibre monocoque, slick racing tyres and a 160bhp, 2.0-litre Volkswagen race engine. It was a highly sophisticated piece of engineering and the increase in power and grip over Formula Ford made me feel like I'd been strapped to the back of an Exocet missile. There was so much to learn but, lap after lap, my times came down. It was a good day but it was soon tragically overshadowed with news that Bertrand Fabi had been killed in a violent testing accident at the Goodwood circuit. Poor Bertrand; he was so bloody young.

The 1986 Lucas British Formula Three Championship burst into life at the Thruxton circuit. I saw little of the Hampshire countryside however as I spun to the back in pouring rain. I rejoined in 35th place and drove through the field in blinding spray to finish 15th. I got a lot of praise, then made up for it in the following race at Silverstone when I crashed into Graham de Zille on the first lap. Back to Thruxton for round three and my 10th place finish was described as the 'drive of the race'.

Armed with a bit of confidence and with my engineer, Yorkshireman Paul Haigh, telling me I was great, I surprised a few folk in the next race on the Silverstone grand prix circuit. Again it was raining in qualifying, but this time I was second fastest to the Brazilian Maurizio Sandro Sala. It was a shock to the pit lane because there I was, just out of Formula Ford, right up front with the established Formula Three stars. Eddie Jordan, who later became a Formula One team owner, was running Maurizio at the time and came over to congratulate me. Wow, this was *the* Eddie Jordan I'd read about, coming over to call *me* a star. I felt great. In fact I felt so great that,

in the race, I stalled on the grid and was hit by another car. I felt terrible.

Still, I'd thrown the cat among the pigeons and I wondered if I could do the same at Brands Hatch? It rained yet again but, guess what, I was fastest in my group and lined up on the front row of the grid next to my team-mate Andy Wallace. It was a one-two for Madgwick and I'd shown my speed at Silverstone was no fluke. Rival team boss Murray Taylor told me that Damon just could not understand how I was so fast in the rain. Damon was watching me and I was watching him. Friendship to one side, we had graduated together and we knew we'd be compared, so we were highly competitive. In the race I slipped back but I finished sixth to collect my first point in only my fifth race. My drive had impressed motor racing journalists David Tremayne from *Motoring News* and Marcus Pye, who wrote in *Autosport*: 'The progress of F3 newcomer Perry McCarthy has been astonishing... '

It was a terrific compliment and, yeah, I thought I was good as well. But this was re-enforcement from important sources and told me I wasn't wasting my time. I needed it, especially after the disappointments of the previous year. Even established grand prix stars – the idols of motor racing who earn several million dollars a year – need to feel and be *made* to feel that they can really do it.

Oscar Wilde once said: 'I can dine out on a good compliment for a month' and after our testing performance the following week, *Autosport* laid on a feast when they reported that I was fastest in both the wet and dry conditions at Donington. There was no doubt about it: the McCarthy motor racing plan was bang on target. I was now a front-line Formula Three racing driver, I was getting noticed and, if I carried on like this, I would be well on the way to a life in Formula One.

There was, however, just one tiny little problem. After the test, I started to lose feeling in my lower right leg. I sat by the pit wall and I looked down at my foot that now repeatedly failed to move when told to. Try as I might, there was just no response: it wouldn't even lift. Obviously I couldn't drive like this, and if whatever was causing it didn't heal, my career would be over. I tried to think back to recall if I'd ever upset a witch doctor, or opened some sacred crypt or something, because I was becoming convinced there was a curse on me.

The man who might be able to do something for me was both head of neuro-surgery at the London Hospital and

Formula One's chief medical officer. So, two days later, I went to see Professor Sid Watkins. The 'Prof', as he is affectionately known, is a great character and he somehow made me laugh while pushing needles into my leg for electro-conductivity tests. The results, however, were depressing. A cord nerve, which runs below the knee to the foot, is responsible for carrying motor impulses: mine was damaged and had virtually shut down. We figured it had been caused while racing and testing when my leg had been constantly banging into the Reynard's front bulkhead seam. Sid told me it could take years to repair.

I couldn't believe it. I just could not bloody believe it! I had to fight. I had to get back in that car. There was no way my leg was going to stay damaged for years on end. I went to the West Ham United football team for regular physiotherapy and made several more visits to the Prof.

It was during one of these sessions with the Prof that I became thankful for small mercies. Sid left the room to answer a telephone call and when he returned, he looked concerned and said: 'Elio's been killed at Ricard.' He was talking about the Italian Elio de Angelis, who was driving for the Brabham Formula One team and had been testing in the south of France. Shortly after that, Formula Three driver Dick Parsons was killed at Silverstone.

Three races passed before I returned to the cockpit for testing at Silverstone. It was raining and I was one second faster than anyone else, but it was a false dawn because the following two races were dry and I couldn't put the right amount of pressure on the brake pedal. The situation was depressing, but in the next race I faced trouble of a different sort. And just for good measure, I got Damon Hill involved.

The Formula Three world was ferried to Holland for round 11, which was held at Zandvoort. The weather was fantastic and we all had a few days to sunbathe on the beach, which was full to the brim with girls who didn't know what bikini tops were. The whole lot of us sat there giggling because just when we thought we'd seen the best looking girl in the world, along walked a better one. We all put in an appearance at the circuit for qualifying and then Damon and I returned to the hotel, where we started chatting to a couple of young ladies who worked there. Doing our bit for Anglo-Dutch relations, we asked them if they would like to join us for a drink. We had a nice evening at a local bar, they were good company, and that was it. Honestly.

The following day our girlfriends, Karen and Georgie, flew out together early and arrived at the hotel. Karen came to my room and we left immediately for the circuit. In the meantime, Georgie had gone to Damon's room and as she walked in, who should pass by pushing a towel trolley and sweetly sing: 'Good Morning Damon'? Yup, one of the girls from the night before. Bad timing or what! Damon then came under intensive questioning from Georgie and he eventually cracked and told her the whole story.

I hadn't seen Damon all morning, so up to the start of the race I didn't know anything about this episode. I was sitting in the car on the grid, with three minutes to go, just staring ahead and concentrating as the mechanics started to leave the area, when... Bang! Something hit my crash helmet. It scared the hell out of me and I looked up to find Karen leaning over the cockpit, looking a trifle upset. She said: 'I've just been speaking to Georgie and she's told me all about you bastards taking those girls out. Just wait till you get back!'

Ooops! Cheers, Damon. Well, I got back ninth and I tried to break the ice by relaying the heart-rending story of the ex-family of ducklings who had wondered on to the track and been used as an apex by about 15 cars. I pumped the duck story for all it was worth and Karen started mellowing. Eventually, about four hours into our drive away from the circuit to the south of France, she forgave me. I never did ask Damon how the rest of his day went.

We made the journey south because my team had entered me in a round of the French Championship, which was a support race to the French Grand Prix. It was my first time at the Paul Ricard Circuit but Formula One driver and now TV commentator Martin Brundle helped out by driving me round the track in his rental car to show me the racing line. It was a fast circuit and in the race I was fighting with Jean Alesi and Eric Bernard, but I fell back to fourth and then hit a back marker on the last lap, finishing seventh. It had been a good race, but Karen and I were about to have another one, and this time it was with the world's fastest driver.

After watching the grand prix we left the circuit, hoping that we were pointing toward England. However, I've got the directional sense of a lemming and, as always, we got lost. We found ourselves out on some back country roads but we also found two lonely souls, whose motor scooter had broken down. It was Lotus Formula One star Ayrton Senna and his Formula 3000 mate Mauricio Gugelmin. We stopped to help but within a few minutes a car arrived for them, which they commandeered, leaving its driver stranded with the scooter.

I pulled away from the scene first but Ayrton was tormenting me by driving about one millimetre off my rear bumper. Seeing that Nigel Mansell had beaten Ayrton that weekend, I thought: 'Let's see if I can make it two–nil to England.' I floored the accelerator and, over the next three or four minutes, gave my little Volkswagen Scirocco more revs than a food mixer. It was maniac stuff; I was locking the brakes for corners, throwing the car sideways and several times going completely off the road and on to the verge.

Ayrton, meanwhile, was doing exactly the same. My efforts to stay ahead were like waving a piece of raw meat to a sabretooth tiger and it was obvious that Ayrton was hungry. I kept looking in the mirror to see if I'd made any ground but, no – don't be stupid, Perry – there was no way I could lose him. He was, as Mark Blundell would say, stuck to me 'like a bogie on yer finger'.

It was great fun. I was having the time of my life, Karen looked like a kid on a roller-coaster and my mirrors were full of Ayrton and Maurizio laughing. We were now hurtling toward a town at around warp seven and I could see a queue of traffic stretching from behind a totally blind corner. Ayrton's next move came as no surprise. I knew he'd do it, I told Karen he'd do it, and sure enough he did it. We screeched to a halt behind the line but Ayrton was waving as he overtook the lot of us around the outside, off into the twilight zone and, for all he knew, into the path of a juggernaut. Unbelievably, he got away with it. He really was a crazy bastard!

Back in the UK, I was in my second Formula One support race in as many weeks. The nerve damage still hadn't completely repaired but I learnt how to drive by lifting my whole leg up and down to get my foot on and off the throttle. This was like icing a cake with a shovel, although it was a damn sight better than not racing.

I qualified fourth but in the race, filmed live on BBC TV, I was fighting furiously for second with Gary Brabham. In fact, it was just after Murray Walker told the world 'Perry McCarthy just keeps getting better and better' that Gary turned in and took my front wing off; without front downforce, I slammed into the barriers. Dear old Murray!

There wasn't too much damage, though. I was saving the really big accidents for the following week.

The Zytek engine company had been developing the previously uncompetitive Saab engine and wanted an on-track evaluation. A unit was put into one of last year's Reynards and

I was asked to carry out a test on the Silverstone grand prix circuit. It didn't quite go to plan.

Long before Silverstone was reconfigured for safety reasons, the old Club Corner was a very fast, very ballsy affair and could just about be taken flat out. On my approach to this notorious right-hander I was in fifth and accelerating flat out. Then, being the observant fellow I am, I noticed my left front suspension had collapsed just before the apex. Seeing a wheel rise above cockpit height and feeling the car hit the ground is always a pretty good hint that something is wrong. To confirm my theory, the catch-fencing was coming toward me at high speed.

I was heading straight for a large wooden pole that supported the fence. My instinct told me not to brake but instead try to alter course with the remaining front wheel. I made it and hit the wire first, but with my speed at 135mph, I proceeded to flatten another four layers of fencing en route to slamming into the wall. It was a big crash and a nice blow to the head cracked my helmet.

I pushed away the debris that had come into the car and got out, stunned, with blood streaming from my nose, lip and hand. I walked away furious with the car and I was delighted to see that it, too, had suffered. In fact, the thing was destroyed – all except for the rear wing. So I returned, climbed up on the sidepod and stamped on it, just to complete the job.

Exactly one week later I was back in my own car, at Snetterton, and the team wanted me to test some new development rear suspension. Again, before circuit alterations, the old Russell chicane was one of those flat-out corners, and with no run-off area it was regarded by all as doubly scary. Again in fifth and again flat out on acceleration, I turned for the sharp left-hand entry and 'click!' I actually heard it break. The right rear suspension collapsed. With the barriers less than 10 metres away, I had just enough time to close my eyes as the car smashed into them, this time at 140mph.

I took another blow to the head and my brain said 'thank you and goodnight' at about the same time as the car took off and flew into the air. I landed about 60 metres away, unconscious and still strapped into what was now another complete pile of junk. A few minutes later, somebody gave me smelling salts and I woke up to find a crowd standing behind Adrian Reynard, who looked shocked as he held my shoulders and asked if I could hear him.

It was good to see him and I held his gaze as I quietly said: 'Adrian'.

'Yes,' he said, tensely.

'Adrian, come nearer. Come nearer,' I murmured weakly. His face was now 10 millimetres from mine. 'Adrian!'

'I can hear you, Perry.'

I could see he was nervous. 'Well, Adrian' I piped up, 'I don't think much of your new effing suspension!'

The team worked their little socks off to build a new car for me and I suggested that as I was spending a lot of time in the air, perhaps they should fit an altimeter. They ignored me and finished their task in only four days, just in time for the biggest race of the year: the Cellnet-sponsored Formula Three Super Prix at Brands Hatch. It was to be the biggest test I had ever faced.

Having taken two serious blows to the head in the past 10 days, I was slightly concussed as I left the pit lane for qualifying. My brain wasn't working properly and I was confused. I felt like a 10-year-old who had drunk three pints of lager and now had to solve a quantum physics question. I did one slow lap and came back into the pits, scared. I really didn't know what was going on. I had completely lost it and I rammed my hands between my legs so the team couldn't see them shaking. I had to think.

I didn't say a thing to the mechanics but I'm sure Paul Haigh knew I was in trouble and he made sure everybody just left me alone. I shouldn't have got back in the car so quickly. I'd had two massive accidents – neither one my fault – and now I needed to put it all on the line again. The concussion was making it difficult to think and this had shaken my self-belief, which had always been my biggest asset. I sat there trying to fight the fear that had gripped me; I was frightened of the car and of the speeds; I was frightened my career could be over.

I had to get back in control.

I sat there just asking and answering the same question to myself: 'What do you want to do?'

'I want to be a racing driver.'

'Well, racing drivers are fast. If you go back out, you will have to be fast.'

'What do you want to do?'

Over and over again...

'Close the accidents out. They do not exist. Focus. Concentrate.'

It's difficult to explain, but it was as though the enduring picture in my mind had now been broken into a jigsaw. Over the next 20 minutes, I sat still and alone in my car, gradually putting those jumbled pieces back together. With five minutes of the session remaining, I was feeling stronger and I signalled Paul to start the engine. I did about four laps and then recorded the fastest time to set pole position. Paul was so pleased he had tears in his eyes. I then went on to win the heat from Ross Cheever, come second to Andy Wallace in the semi-finals, and finish fourth in the final.

I still had a pretty good headache but it was a terrific result and the team had done a great job building a new car for me so quickly. I was also quite proud of myself for beating back that terrible fear and, from then on, my confidence in those situations has never wavered. Ayrton Senna once had some pertinent words to say about fear and they went something like this: 'Sure, I have fear. Fear keeps me alive, but you have to squeeze that fear down, to control it.' As always, Ayrton was spot on. Any driver who says he never gets scared is too slow, too safe, lying or clinically insane. Fear is part of your life but you have to be its master.

By this stage of the season, Andy Wallace was the master in Formula Three and dominating the championship that he would later win. Andy was always very talented but technically he was a good guy to listen to and learn from. After a while, I started to understand that it's not just about wrapping your balls round your neck and going for a time: you had to do that *and* set the car up. So I carried on learning but in the remaining races I also learnt how to crash with Maurizio Sandro Sala at Brands (he later apologised) and Julian Bailey at Silverstone (I later apologised), but I came fifth at Snetterton and Zolder (Belgium) and second to Andy at Spa (Belgium).

My debut season had been dramatic. I had overcome injury and survived two enormous accidents and a year of living with Karen, who back then could change moods faster than I could change gear. However, on the up-side, I was generally the fastest in the rain, I was in the top group in the dry, I was beginning to understand the importance of car set-up and the press were behind me. I was one of four Formula Three drivers to win a prestigious Cellnet award, presented to us by Nigel Mansell, and after shaking hands with him, I was delighted to see the circulation returning to my fingers in only four days.

I was looking forward to the new season but life can change quickly. Fewer than 10 months ago, most people thought I was a washed up Formula Ford driver: now I was being talked about as one of the favourites to win the 1987 British Formula Three Championship.

Chapter 8

THE RAT PACK GO RACING

I had to do something, because people in Formula One were already looking at Johnny Herbert and I needed them to look at me.

Journalist David Tremayne was the first to use the term 'Rat Pack' and it was one that stuck. The pack consisted of Damon Hill, Johnny Herbert, Julian Bailey, Mark Blundell, Martin Donnelly and me. We were all good mates and nobody had a bad word to say about the other – well, apart from the time Julian and Martin started fighting after they'd crashed at Brands. But that was in the past. The six of us often got together when we weren't racing and we had a bloody good time.

It was around this time that we developed nicknames for each other. We called Johnny Herbert 'Little 'un' for obvious reasons and Damon was 'Secret' – short for 'Secret Squirrel', because he rarely told us what he was up to. Julian was 'Grumpy', mainly because he could be very grumpy. Mark was 'Mega' because he liked mega cars, mega watches and would shyly call himself a 'Mega bloke'. And Martin Donnelly was called 'Yer Man' because he always used this Irish term as a prefix to anybody's name. When we referred to Johnny Dumfries (an associate member), we'd abbreviate him to 'The Earl' in deference to his title of The Earl of Dumfries and it was The Earl who tagged me as 'Mad Dog'. During a special meeting at the end of the season, I presented 'The Rat' to 'King Rat' – a trophy of a rat mounted on a plaque awarded to the most accomplished driver of the year.

Back in 1987, Grumpy Rat signed to drive in Formula 3000.

The rest of our main core, though, were going head to head for the Formula Three championship title.

PR man Tony Jardine put together a great press event for me at the Kensington Hilton which was attended by, among others, John Watson and Murray Walker. John, as an ex-Formula One driver, gave his views on me and the championship but then Murray, who had only been invited as a guest, kindly jumped up to the microphone and did a major number for me. Thank you, Murray. Anyway, we announced that I was staying with Madgwick, Hawtal Whiting were staying with me and, since Andy had graduated to F3000, Warmastyle Radiators transferred their backing. To cap it all, I was chosen as Volkswagen's new works driver. On paper, we were looking very good indeed.

I should have kept that bit of paper. Unbeknown to any of us, this would be a year of engine wars. In the past few years, nearly everyone had used VW motors and the most successful tuner was John Judd. This year, however, Alfa Romeo and Toyota were on the scene, as was another Volkswagen tuned by a German concern called Speiss.

The first three races showed that we'd chosen the wrong engine. We were underpowered and I was very disappointed. I felt that Judd's new contract to work with the Williams Formula One team for the following year might have compromised development work on my programme, so we went to see Magnum Racing and eventually agreed that they would be my new tuners.

It seemed to do the trick and for the next race I put the car on to the front row next to Johnny Herbert's. I led away and stayed in number one spot ahead of Johnny for 22 laps around the Silverstone circuit. However, the little so-and-so got by me on the penultimate lap and we finished Little 'un first, Mad Dog second. I blamed it on a backmarker and we still laugh about that race, although thinking about it, he always laughs a bit louder than me.

Maybe this new engine was my return ticket but I wasn't celebrating just yet, mainly because I didn't feel too good. The following morning I woke up early with a serious pain in my side. I wondered if Karen was knifing me because Johnny had won, but no. It was coming from inside so maybe she'd used poison. I put up with it as long as I could, then yelled at Karen to get me to a hospital. They diagnosed acute appendicitis and operated immediately.

Nine days after being discharged I was back in the car at Brands Hatch for qualifying. I had a gearbox problem and, on lap four, one particular shift didn't go in, which over-revved the new Magnum wonder unit and blew it to pieces. I had set a time of ninth fastest for the qualification race. I ended that encounter fourth but the physical strain of driving a racecar finished me off. Some of the stitches had burst, which coated the inside of my race overalls with blood. Paul Haigh saw the mess and made me withdraw from the main race.

We reverted to the Judd engine but the Brands disaster was followed by the Thruxton disaster, which incidentally preceded the Zandvoort disaster (broken gear linkage). And let's not forget the Donington disaster, when yet another engine failure took me out of second place. Why was my season turning into a nightmare? Or more accurately, why had my nightmare turned into a season?

I went back to the mess that we called home. Karen and I had now sold our apartment in the village of Stock, which was only two miles away from Johnny's place, and bought a much larger house nearby. It was, the estate agent said, 'in need of some repair'. They weren't kidding.

There was method in my madness although, considering how much work was needed, I had to keep reminding myself about the method bit. Property prices were soaring and we had made £25,000 on the apartment in just one year, so I was pretty certain we'd make a lot more from this project. It would take a year to finish but, in the meantime, a burst pipe had soaked the lounge ceiling, which collapsed on to the lounge floor. Karen and I looked at the rubble, looked at each other and started laughing. It summed up the year.

The house had to wait, though. I needed to pull my championship assault together and to do that, I needed a touch of Italian. I needed Alfa Romeo.

I flew to Italy and signed a deal with Pederzani tuners to supply me with Alfa engines for the final six races. I was praying this would get me back to the front, especially as I'd borrowed 10 grand to pay for it, which back then was the equivalent of 25 weeks on an oil rig. I had to do something, though, because people in Formula One were already looking at Johnny Herbert and I needed them to look at me.

Somebody was looking at me thoughtfully, though: Bill Blandford, who owned Warmastyle. I'd always liked Bill. He was fun and had been generous to many drivers, including our mate Russell Spence. However, this was business and he wasn't happy with our reliability problems. Bill sent me a letter that, while charming, made his sentiments crystal clear. I travelled to North Yorkshire to see him in an attempt to save the deal while, on the same day back in Essex, Karen was having a pregnancy test.

Standing in his office, I sensed I was losing. Considering my mortgage and loan repayments, this was not a good idea, so I just kept talking – about everything. I rapidly explained how I'd taken the initiative, borrowed the money, got the lightweight Alfas, had my appendix out so I was also lighter... er... had measles as a child and I hadn't enjoyed school... I thought that if I kept going, at least there wouldn't be a gap in the conversation for him to say: 'Sorry, but it's over.'

I knew I was still in trouble when suddenly the phone rang and it was for me. Karen had got the test result and was so excited that she'd called me at my sponsor's office to say that it was positive and she was expecting a baby. I was delighted and immediately told Bill our wonderful news. I honestly hadn't planned the call – not even I'm ruthless enough to use the news of our baby to get some sympathy. Hang on a second... no, I'm not, but it had changed the mood nonetheless.

Suddenly I was once again a struggling young racing driver who had borrowed money to turn events around and was now about to support a family. Being the smashing fellow he was, Bill made the decision to stay on board and I breathed a sigh of relief. I've had some close shaves in my career but this time I reckon I had just been saved by an embryo.

We went to Oulton Park and I qualified second fastest, but in the race I was fighting for the lead with Martin Donnelly when an electrical fault switched the stupid engine off and I fell back. The Cellnet team had just developed one of the first driver/team radios and Damon Hill gave the system its race debut when he shouted the words 'Perry's broken down!' He should have added '... again!'

I was down but not out. The electrics suddenly clicked back on and I charged back through the field to finish fifth and set a new lap record. Our speed was encouraging but deary, deary me, goodness gracious, damn, drat and blast – another win down the drain.

I wasn't always alone with this type of thing. I remember Damon having a problem at Silverstone and I also remember about 100 different spectators asking him why he had stalled on the grid. It was torture as he explained, time and time again, that he didn't stall: there was an electrical problem and the engine cut out. This was driving him crazy. After a while Damon grinned at me. Holding a large spanner he whispered:

'The next person to ask gets hit with this.' At that very moment, a spectator edged along and said: 'Here, Damon, why'd you stall on the grid?' We both looked at the spanner, the spectator kept smiling, I started laughing and Damon gritted his teeth and then explained. If spectators were trying Damon's patience, then unreliability was testing mine.

At the Brands grand prix circuit, it was raining and I was in third place, closing on Martin and Damon at two seconds per lap. I was within striking distance when the left front wheel came up, the car hit the ground and, well, you know the routine. 'Yes folks, welcome to another round of Suspension Failure where we send Perry McCarthy out in a car and all you have to do is guess which wheel will collapse, on what corner will it happen and how fast will he be going when he hits the wall.' Well, the winning contestants said: 'left front wheel, Paddock Hill Bend, 130mph.' I stepped out unhurt but I was pissed off.

The big win that went on the missing list, however, was my fault. The best of Europe's Formula Three drivers converged on Silverstone for the biggest race of the year and the winner would take home the title of European Formula Three Champion. I qualified on the front row, then made a pig's ear of the start. I dropped to seventh before fighting my way back to battle with Germany's Bernd Schneider for second place. With time running out to catch the leader, I tried an all-or-nothing manoeuvre, which ended as 'nothing' right in the gravel trap – just after Murray Walker once again told BBC viewers how good I was.

We then went to Spa in Belgium, where Little 'un wrapped up the championship and, after one more race, I was pleased to see the back of the season.

I'd proved my point with the Alfa Romeo engine and, then again, when I smashed the Silverstone lap record while testing for the Reynard works team, but it was all too late. I had to start thinking about next year. However, for my old friend

Peter Rogers, there wouldn't be a 'next year'. I remember that, the morning after our Oulton Park race, it was Damon who made the difficult call to tell me that Pete had been killed. I listened in disbelief. Fast Pete had been fighting for second place in a Formula Ford race at Donington, when his Quest and Alain Menu's Reynard touched on the way into Redgate corner. His car left the circuit, cleared the gravel trap and then crashed head-on into a tyre-lined concrete wall. He should never have been in that bloody race – he was too good for 1600 – but despite a couple of class B outings in Formula Three, he never had the budget to make the deserved jump up the ladder.

Apart from the cruel disappointment and frustration that lurk below motor racing's glamorous veneer, we'd once again been brutally reminded of its dark side: the raw danger of high speed. I'd already seen in the past that it could turn around and bite, when Villeneuve, Paletti and de Angelis were killed. And then again, closer to home, with the deaths of Bertrand Fabi and Dick Parsons in Formula Three. But for me, this was different. Peter was a friend of mine. He was a good-looking lad who was a product of his family: a perfect gentleman with a great sense of humour. It was a horrible episode. I will always remember my old mate Pete with affection, but as a racing driver I had to lock away the loss in the back of my mind. Motor racing is an intoxicating sport, where speed is the drug and no matter what the possible consequences, I couldn't stop. None of us could.

The Rat Pack was now gearing up for the next battle en route to the holy ground of Formula One. In 1988 Little 'un was going into Formula 3000 with Eddie Jordan and Mega was doing likewise with Middlebridge Racing. Yer Man and Secret Squirrel were staying put in Formula Three while Grumpy had become the first Briton to win a Formula 3000 race and was now talking to Tyrrell. As for me, Mad Dog, I was thinking of changing my nickname to Mad As Hell Dog or Barking Mad Dog. Mechanical failures and engine problems had wreaked havoc on my season and possibly my future.

I think I would have won at Donington, Oulton and Brands – if only the car had held together. I know I would have won the European Championship – if only I hadn't cocked up the start. And I'm sure I would have won at Silverstone – if only Johnny hadn't overtaken me!

Paul Haigh had given me the confidence to believe totally in myself. He called everyone 'flower' or 'petal', and he would somehow rationalise the 'if onlys' of motor racing by sitting me down, giving me a cigarette, and saying: 'You're all right, petal. If ifs and ands could make tin cans, there'd be no need for tinkers.' I understood, but just hoped that the teams in Formula 3000 understood that if only this little tinker had the equipment, he could – and would – win. A chap called Nigel Mansell had won only once in Formula Three, so there was hope for next year.

During the final seconds of 1987, I may very well have toasted 'hope' when Karen, Johnny and I raised our glasses to cheer in the New Year. However, what I do remember is Karen moving closer, all set for a romantic embrace, but as the clock struck 12, Johnny dived in between us, held my head tightly and kissed me full on the lips.

Jesus, what chance did I stand? My first kiss of 1988 had been from the guy who had beaten me to the Formula Three championship.

Chapter 9

WAR IN EUROPE

We all knew that success in F3000 could lead directly to grand prix stardom and, with this in mind, desperation set in.

I once saw a great film called *The Right Stuff* about the start of America's manned space flights. It showed that even though the space race received massive public support, NASA actually needed money from Congress more than it needed the goodwill of the people. One line summarised the relationship perfectly: 'No bucks, no Buck Rogers.' It's also true of motor racing. Maybe our version is: 'No sterling, no Stirling Moss'.

Toward the end of 1987, sterling was in trouble and so was the Stock Exchange. Billions of pounds were wiped off London's stock market value on 19 October, or Black Monday as it was known. People were worried, companies were scared and the recession kicked in. My sponsors Hawtal Whiting and Warmastyle, with an eye to the economy, cut back on spending and top of their cutbacks list was me. They had given fantastic support, but my plan to move immediately into Formula 3000 now had the life expectancy of a Klingon who'd upset Captain Kirk. I was boldly going where many racing drivers had gone before: back to the sidelines.

I tried everything to attract new backing, including sitting in the bar of the London Hilton Hotel, making a £5 cup of coffee last for two hours and striking up conversations with people who looked rich. I hadn't come this far just to be forgotten, but the economy was getting worse and I wasn't the only one trying to survive.

One particular day I was prowling around a large industrial estate and saw a building I liked the look of. It's simple McCarthy logic: nice offices cost a lot; to pay a lot, its occupants must earn a lot; therefore, they could sponsor me. I walked in and noticed their reception had a fish tank in the centre. I allowed myself a smile because Bob Hawker from Hawtal Whiting used to say that any company with a fish tank in its foyer was doomed to go bust. I re-focused and told the receptionist that I would like to see the managing director to discuss sponsorship. After a call, she told me he was very interested and I was shown in to see both him and his finance director.

They greeted me like a long-lost pal, sat me down, gave me coffee and I started getting worried. Things didn't work like this, especially with me. Once the pleasantries were dispensed with, the MD looked at me like a kid on Christmas morning and said: 'We'd love to hear about sponsorship. Tell us how it works.'

I was smiling but also highly suspicious as I warily began to explain it to them: 'It's a form of marketing and the money you give me is used to... '

'We give to *you*,' he interrupted. Then, with a look of horror, he put his head in his hands and explained he thought I'd come to sponsor them. They stayed silent and deflated for several seconds; it was a bit embarrassing actually and then they looked at each other and said things like: 'What are we gonna do?' 'I don't know, I thought this kid was our last hope.'

Then they burst out laughing, It was, of course, a wind up. Bob was right about the fish tank – these boys were in trouble and teasing me had just been a bit of entertainment, which had put the reality of another bad day on hold for a while. As I was an expert on bad days, I appreciated this black humour and laughed along with them, but after they'd finished telling me about the state they were in, I realised I'd probably been lucky to get the coffee.

Eddie Jordan, meanwhile, was having better luck. EJ secured Camel cigarette backing for his new Reynard Formula 3000 after Johnny Herbert won the first round of the championship in Spain from Mark Blundell. These two had blown the rest away but, the month before, the entire Rat Pack got blown away when we went to Julian Bailey's pub and celebrated the birth of my first daughter, Poppy. We had a great time and that night six future Formula One drivers, including one World Champion, slept where they dropped. The following day, Johnny, Damon, Marlboro's David Marren and I made a flying visit to see Karen in hospital, where we stayed for about 10 minutes, said goo-goo-ga-ga to Poppy, and then went straight back out to play again. Karen has never seen the funny side of that.

Although we didn't know it then, 'Poppy Night' was the last time we would all meet at the Lord Louis pub. Over the past two years, the Lord Louis had tripled in value and Julian, with his brother Adrian, had three good reasons to get out fast. Firstly, they were selling at the market's peak; secondly they'd found somebody willing to buy it for that money; and thirdly Julian had a chance to go into Formula One with Tyrrell. Although substantial, the pub money wasn't enough to finance Tyrrell's sponsorship requirements, so JB had brought his Formula 3000 sponsor Cavendish Finance into play. Paul Carnill, who owned the company, was doing very well. Between them they offered to pay the half a million pounds Ken Tyrrell was looking for. It was brave.

I was delighted because Julian, along with Markie, is my closest mate. Julian, Jules, JB, Grumpy or, as his dad calls him, Julie, is an enigma. He's incredibly funny and can be totally outrageous, such as when we were in Zolder and Jules (after a good few drinks) decided to take over the hotel kitchen before coming out to serve food with no clothes on. He can also be infuriating and if he's in the mood will deliberately bait me. Like an idiot, I normally bite. If anybody else goaded me in the same way I'd punch them, but Julian knows that, which makes it even more fun for him. He'll take it to the limit and then bring it back again because he enjoys playing mind games, especially with me and his partner Deborah.

Jules can magic a deal out of fresh air. He'd already proved his talent in a racing car as Formula Ford World Champion in 1982 before going on in 1987 to become the first Briton to win a Formula 3000 race. Like the rest of us, Jules wanted to join motor racing's elite. Both he and his brother thought nothing of selling their business because it was now or never for joining Tyrrell. Julian, no stranger to risk, was about to gamble everything and, in so doing, became the first member of the Rat Pack to sign as a Formula One driver.

JB had been out of Ken Tyrrell's office for about two minutes when he called to say the deal was done. It was fantastic news but during the season it proved to be an uphill struggle for him and his team-mate Jonathan Palmer. Julian was getting no testing and the car was uncompetitive. I remember it raining in Monaco and, while standing by the pit wall with Ken Tyrrell, I could see even a man of Jonathan's experience had little confidence in a bad car.

Ken, however took, no prisoners and when Jonathan returned, he was relentless in his goading and teasing: 'Why are you lifting [off the throttle]. I could hear you lifting. Yes, you were – you're like a little girl. Are you all right?'

I felt sorry for Jonathan but it was very funny. All the time JP was saying indignantly: 'Okay, Ken. I've got the picture. Thank you very much. Yes, I've got the point.' In the end Jonathan just walked off. Ken wore a mischievous smile.

By the end of the year, though, Julian's own smile had long since evaporated. He had qualified for only six races and was now back on the outside of grand prix. That kind of disappointment either destroys you or it makes you harder. JB looked for a deal elsewhere and survived, but one of our pack was lucky to be *alive*, after a crash in F3000 destroyed both his season and his feet.

Formula 3000 had, from 1985, taken the place of Formula Two on the motor racing ladder and this new series used a stockpile of Formula One's redundant 3000cc Cosworth grand prix engines. Many liked the idea, but thought it wrong to change the category's name. We could all see the '3000' link but surely Formula Two was the best clue as to the sport's pecking order. I remember Damon offering his own interpretation: 'Formula 3000 is called Formula 3000 to confuse those people who don't know about motor racing, and to make those of us who do, look like idiots trying to explain it.' He was right, but the trouble was that it did have to be explained to potential sponsors. Given that a one-car budget for the season was seven hundred grand, I think we should have called it 'Formula 3000 pounds a day'.

I was pestering the daylights out of several F3000 teams but it was the same old story: they needed money and I didn't have any. The championship itself was razor-sharp competitive but those lucky enough to be there normally had only one shot. We all knew that success here could lead directly to grand prix stardom and, with this in mind, desperation set in. Some drivers behaved like a pit bull terrier on steroids.

By round two, the action was already getting rough, and on the Vallelunga circuit in Italy, Johnny was concussed after being shoved into the barriers. More drama followed during round five at Monza, when home boy Massimo Monti collided with Frenchman Fabien Giroux and the Italian was launched over the barriers, through an advertising hoarding and his Ralt car was then cut in half as it hit a tree. Miraculously, Massimo emerged unscathed but Fabien wasn't so lucky. With two badly broken legs, his career in single-seater racing cars was over.

Giroux's countryman, the jovial Michel Trolle, also suffered terrible leg injuries and the same career fate, after he crashed in free practice for round seven at Brands Hatch. This, however, was just the start of a terrible weekend.

The race itself, on 21 August, was stopped after an accident between Roberto Moreno and Gregor Foitek. They were okay, but halfway around the restarted first lap, Foitek continued as he'd started and made contact with Johnny. The result of this new collision was complete carnage, setting off a chain reaction involving 11 cars. Foitek broke his wrist, Olivier Grouillard badly bruised his legs and Little 'un was in big trouble, still strapped into his seat with his bloodstained legs protruding from the remains of the mauled Reynard. It had been a massive crash at more than 150mph and news spread immediately.

I was at the Oulton Park track in Cheshire when someone from the circuit office came running to tell me that Johnny was fighting for his life. I felt sick as I jumped into my borrowed Renault 21 Turbo and aimed for Kent, but within a mile of the circuit police stopped me for speeding and 'dangerous driving'. Me? Dangerous driving?

I was annoyed at losing time, so I kept my mouth shut, took my ticket and then put my foot down hard. If I'd been stopped at any point after that, they wouldn't have bothered with a ticket: I would have been sent straight to a salt mine in Siberia.

I made it to the Sidcup hospital very, very quickly and, on arriving, I saw Johnny's parents Bob and Jane with his girlfriend Becky. I was apprehensive as I approached but I could read their body language and it gave me cause for relief. They explained that both feet had been smashed but his life was safe. His left foot, however, had been hanging on by only a few threads of muscle tissue and the surgeons had now done the best they could to save it. Johnny's chances of walking again, though, were not looking good and his driving career looked non-existent. I stayed to see him but he was drugged to the eyeballs and didn't recognise anyone. From what I'd been told at Oulton, though, it was good just to see him breathing.

Before I left, I stopped to see how Michel Trolle was doing, but he was still unconscious and it looked bad. I drove home just hoping they'd both be okay. It was upsetting to see one close mate, and another guy I liked, badly injured. As for the other one, well, this was the second time Johnny had suffered from dicing with Gregor Foitek, so I didn't drop in for a chat. Three days later, though, Foitek's team manager Mike Collier wanted to have a chat with me.

Mike, from GA Motorsport, had run Julian in 1987. We had always got on very well together, but with Foitek injured, Mike needed a replacement for the Birmingham Super Prix on Bank Holiday Monday, which was just five days away. He knew I was damn hungry and he offered to put me in the car if someone could donate a few grand toward his expenses. A 'few' actually meant £8,000 and although it was peanuts at this level, it was still a chunk of money. However, Julian's sponsor came to my rescue. Paul Carnill generously wrote a cheque, wished me luck and gave me a chance.

It was ironic that my longed-for break into the International Formula 3000 Championship had come about as a result of Johnny's crash, and I found myself returning from a nine-month break to drive with three times the horsepower of a Formula Three car and on a circuit I didn't know. As I powered on to the track for official qualifying, I was armed with a one-year-old Lola and only 20 laps of testing at the Pembrey circuit. But what the hell. I was now a '3000 driver and I was going for broke.

We broke all right. The differential blew up and the escaping oil then started a small fire, so we missed the session. Just what I didn't need. It could be repaired but the big concern was rain. With no timed laps to my credit, I hadn't made the cut. If it rained in the next session, the cars would be slower – while I needed to go faster. The Lola was repaired and guess what – it rained. After all, this is the Perry McCarthy story...

The fastest guy in the dry morning session had been Olivier Grouillard, but there was no way I could even think about challenging him in these conditions. Instead, my target was Jean-Denis Deletraz, the slowest to have qualified. Championship leader Roberto Moreno, whose earlier time had qualified him third, was now fastest in the final session. Even in this light rain, he was only one-third of a second slower than Deletraz's earlier dry mark.

Since I'd had no morning time to fall back on, I had to go faster than Roberto, and then some, to beat Deletraz and qualify for the race. I gave it everything I had and slid my 450bhp car within millimetres of these unfamiliar concrete walls at speeds of up to 170mph. I just had to get this car into the race.

I was flying and stunned the team by going second fastest, only nine hundredths of a second off Moreno, but then on the following lap I stunned myself. The rain was coming down harder but all I needed was another 0.37 seconds to qualify, so I held my breath and took even more risks. As I passed the start/finish line, I began to line up for the Pye chicane, but I didn't make it. I had marginally brushed my left front wheel against the inside wall that we use as an apex. With very little grip, it was enough to change my corner exit plans. I went head-first into a concrete block and the impact broke the car in two. Ooops.

Apart from being winded, I was lucky to escape with only bruising to my legs and feet, but it hurt. I was helped back to our garage, from where I could see Mike Collier sitting on the pit wall. He was smiling at me as I slowly hobbled towards him. With each painful step, I toyed with different explanations as to how and why I'd actually arrived back in the pit lane without his car. However, Mike already knew his Lola had ceased to exist because he'd seen the whole thing happen on the TV monitors. He was leaning back and looked relaxed, with his hands behind his head, and waited until I'd made it all the way over before he said: 'Well, son, at least you've got the good grace to limp.' That was typical of Mike and his humour. He believed in me and my speed had really impressed him, but he was still quite pleased that I'd taken a hiding in exchange for wrecking his car.

I was devastated not to qualify, but I wasn't alone because 40 cars were trying for only 26 starting positions. It was a real pity about that differential problem but I was delighted to be second fastest, to Moreno of all people, in the final session. The car and the power suited me but Gregor Foitek had now recovered and resumed his place within the team. So no more GA Motorsport, but I wanted to drive again as soon as possible.

From the start of the year, I had dramatically increased my training programme. I've always been quite strong (probably from my work on the oil rigs) but now I was very fit as well. Our home in Billericay, Essex, also looked healthier since we'd finished the renovations and the purchase had, as expected, proved to be a good financial move. We had previously borrowed against the house to finance its own modifications and we had also borrowed to pay for the Formula Three Alfa Romeo engines. Furthermore, since we'd had no income for the past year, we could still borrow to pay for our living costs. In fact, we were getting really good at borrowing and we even borrowed a bit more to pay for the interest on our borrowings.

Anyway, we had a new valuation carried out and, placing our spiralling debt to one side, we had about £70,000 worth of equity – and I had a plan.

I knew that racing car manufacturer Ralt had been impressed by my efforts in Birmingham and I knew the factory team were once again changing their driver line-up. The works Ralt team was the most successful outfit ever in both Formula Two and Formula 3000 and, at this level, they were the equivalent of Ferrari. However, their new high-tech RT22 chassis was something of a dog and nobody seemed to want to drive it. In fact, very few *could* drive it.

In the past eight races, three different teams had entered these cars and from a combined total of 40 chances, Ralts had qualified outside the top 20 cars 30 times, including 20 non-qualifications. Frenchman Eric Bernard was the only driver to have scored a good result, including a brilliant fourth place in Pau. However, in the fifth round at Monza, he too failed to qualify. Like most other Ralt drivers he was not satisfied with the car and had now abandoned ship to drive for Reynard.

Bad news? Not at all. This was my chance and I wasn't going to lose it. I met with Ralt's owner, Ron Tauranac. My job was to get this drive and I went in faster than a retriever on a downed pheasant: 'No problem, Ron. I'm your man. I'll drive it'.

Strangely, I knew I'd succeeded when Ron looked at me sternly and said: 'Now, have you got anybody looking after you, because if we're abroad, and you crash and get hurt, we're leaving you there. We can't mess around talking to doctors and that. We're coming home; I've got work to do'.

I was still smiling but now in amused disbelief: 'How incredibly kind of you,' I thought to myself. Ron, whose Brabham F1 cars had won World Championships, certainly didn't suffer from being over-sentimental. I knew I was in, but we had to talk about his budget requirements or, in my case, how much of my house it would take. Like Mike Collier, Ron kept the money down and heavily subsidised me. I then wrote a cheque for £30,000 and, converting that back into my oil rig exchange rate, it came out as 16 hours a day, for 525 days straight. But think happy thoughts. I was now the new works Ralt driver for the final three races. Karen had a few thoughts of her own and gently reminded me that we now owed a total of £215,000. I never felt the need to calculate what this meant on my rig exchange rate as I had hoped to see the children before they left college.

Still, fortune favours the brave. I wasn't going to let a little thing like no income, big boy debt and one child (with another on the way) influence me. I had not only made another comeback but I had also taken the giant leap into International Formula 3000 and signed for a famous team. I had wanted this so much and was convinced that I was well and truly on the way to the grand prix jackpot. Like a slot machine, if you pulled my arm down, my eyes would spin around and come up as F1.

I drove to France for my first test and met with the team manager, Alan Howell. I really was a works Ralt driver, I told myself excitedly. Then he thoughtfully told me: 'We've got a really good driver in the other car.' Cheers, pal. What I didn't know was that Alan, being the bastard he was, had said this deliberately to get me mad – and it worked. My team-mate was the Dutchman Cor Euser and Alan's quip had made me determined to beat him.

Between us, we had replaced Ralt's previous drivers, the Brazilian Marco Greco and the Swiss Mario Hytten. I knew Marco from the Madgwick F3 days and he came to see me when I arrived at the circuit: 'Perry, which car did you get?' he asked.

'Well, Marco, it's funny you should mention that because I had my first row with Ron about it. I remember you telling me at Silverstone that Mario's car was faster than yours, so I said to Ron "I want Mario's car" but he went ballistic about there being no difference between the two. However, eventually I got it, so thanks for the tip.'

Marco slapped his hand on his forehead and exclaimed: 'Oh no, Perry! We swapped cars after Silverstone!'

Oh shit! I'd been in the team five minutes and already out-manoeuvred myself.

All the teams were present for the test on the Le Mans Bugatti Circuit so it was a good chance to see exactly how far off the pace we were, but as we went out onto the track, it started raining. 'So, they've got a really good driver in the other car, have they?' I seethed. 'And that makes me a complete tosser, does it? Well, here goes!'

By the end of the morning I was fastest – not just faster than Cor Euser but fastest overall. Alan put his arm around me and couldn't stop smiling. From that point on, we became firm friends and the works Ralt team, including Ron Tauranac, were totally behind me.

In the race, Cor beat me after Gary Evans drove into my side, which sent me into retirement, but afterwards we went to Belgium for round ten at Zolder. The car was pretty bad in the dry and, by the end of timed practice, I was the only driver to have qualified a Ralt for the race. However, my old mate David Hunt, better known as 'Wadda' (think about it!), would have reason to regret that. Wadda Hunt and I got on very well and we had a lot in common, such as the ability to work hard and attract sponsors, the ambition to follow his brother James into F1 and our habit of smoking.

Ten minutes before the race start, we leant against the pit wall, had a chat, had a laugh and enjoyed our last cigarette before we were strapped into our cars on the all-British eighth row of the grid. As the lights went green, we charged toward the first corner with Damon Hill and Johnny Dumfries hot on our heels. Suddenly, in the middle of a tight bunch, Andrea Chiesa hit me and I ricocheted over to the right and into the side of 'Wadda'. It was a hard knock. The impact ripped off his left front wheel and then pushed him into the concrete pit wall which, in turn, ripped off both his right side wheels. David now had no brakes and no steering, because he had nothing to brake or steer with. He continued like a high-speed bobsleigh, skimming over the next 100 metres of tarmac before ploughing headlong into another wall.

Poor David was getting a bit bored with walls but he couldn't complain because this was light relief compared to his shunt in the Birmingham Super Prix street race. There, his car had spun, reversed off the track at 120mph, hit a kerb, taken off over the barriers and slammed high into the side of a Tesco supermarket wall. By the time it bounced back toward the track, it was in kit form and the wheels, gearbox, engine and chassis had all arrived as a separate delivery.

My own race at Zolder was also finished because the contact had punctured my right rear tyre and damaged the suspension. I walked back to the pits thinking about this lost opportunity. I was thinking about the house and the money we'd borrowed against it, so when Alan Howell asked me what happened, all I could say was: 'Alan, I've just crashed the dining room.' Then I slumped off to find Wadda and together we had another cigarette.

If the car was bad at Zolder then it was a complete nightmare at the Dijon circuit in France. I never thought a racing car could be possessed until I tried to qualify for the final round of the championship. The fast downhill right-hand curve leading on to the pit straight is taken flat out in fifth gear but the car was rebelling. It didn't want to go flat out, it didn't want to turn right, and I don't think the bloody thing even wanted to be on the track. It was a battle of wills and with my past life flashing before me I was only just winning.

Damon, who was driving a Lola, had followed me through a few sections and later told me that, from where he was sitting, I looked nothing short of frightening. Karen has said the same thing about me when I wake in the morning but there were others at the track who knew what Damon meant. My friend, the motor racing insurance specialist Tim Clowes, explained that more and more people were gathering by that corner, waiting and expecting to see me have a major accident. They weren't alone. I was surviving purely on instinct.

The risks paid off, though, and once again I was the only Ralt to qualify. I was just about two seconds faster than my team-mate, who had even tried my car. Looking back, this maybe wasn't two seconds more talented; it was probably two seconds more rash. To have pushed that car, on that circuit, *that* hard was the sign of a desperate man, but there again, I was desperate. I was more than aware that, over in England, the bank had invited me to pop by for a chat when I got back (well, actually, they'd insisted on it). So as ever it was 'put up, or shut up'. With an eye to 1989, this was my last opportunity to impress.

During the race, I wondered if I would actually see 1989, because there were several times when I was more scared than the priest in *The Exorcist*, but I never stopped trying. The chequered flag fell after an hour and five minutes and my fight for control over who was actually steering the thing was finally over. A car like that is tough to drive and I was exhausted. I had never worked so hard for 16th place in my life but I had won my own battle when Ron Tauranac said he wanted me as a fully funded works driver for the following season. The dream of racing in Formula 3000, without having to find money, was fantastic but about a month later he must have realised what he'd said and promptly sold the company.

Ron Tauranac and I had an unusual relationship. There was great mutual respect but we would always find something to argue about. One particular row about aerodynamic settings actually started while we were 30 metres apart in the pit lane at Dijon. We were both still shouting with every step we took toward each other, which did nothing to solve the problem but at least it entertained everyone else within a 100-metre radius. But Ron loved our confrontations because he was born to argue. I could see his eyes light up when the prospect of an argument arose and, being no stranger to a row myself, we were made for each other. He could win whenever he wanted to, though, because all he had to say was: 'Do it my way or you don't drive the car.' That threat will beat a racing driver every time.

Four years earlier, Toleman team boss Alex Hawkridge had used a similar tactic with Ayrton Senna during the Brazilian's first year in grand prix. Alex had signed Senna to a three-year contract but, mid-way through the year and without the notice his contract demanded, the Brazilian signed with Lotus for the following season. Alex was very annoyed and decided to teach him a lesson. He figured the only thing that could get to Ayrton was to keep him out of a racing car. So Alex suspended him for one race and replaced him with Stefan Johansson. The psychology was spot on because, even though Ayrton planned to leave, the thought of someone else driving his racing car left him distraught. So forget money, forget everything: racing drivers want and need to race. It's fundamental to the breed – and it can be used against us.

With Ron selling Ralt, I was back on the endangered species list. My debt mountain made me more vulnerable than Chin-Chin, the giant panda. Things were looking very bad. The bank rejected my idea of putting their name on my overalls as a way of freezing the interest, and we were about three millimetres away from putting the house on the market when we received a couple of early Christmas presents. I had carried some corporate names on the Ralt in the hope that my friends who owned those companies would sponsor me, and I got lucky. Paul Carnill of Cavendish, David Berger of British Motors and Tim Clowes' insurance concern all sent me cheques that, in total, amounted to 20 grand. It came at exactly the right time.

Across the winter months I continued to keep the bank off my back and, dreaming of Formula One, I charged after a drive. I began to empathise fully with the phrase: 'You know, doctor, it's a crazy idea but it just might work.'

Johnny Herbert, meanwhile, had made quite a recovery from the terrible leg injuries he sustained in the F3000 crash but, unfortunately, not a full one. However, Benetton's F1 team manager Peter Collins had such faith in Johnny that he signed him as their new driver, even while he was still undergoing treatment. It had looked like an inspired gamble when, in his first race and hardly able to walk, Johnny scored a brilliant fourth place in the Brazilian Grand Prix. Subsequent races though showed that he was having big problems applying heavy brake pressure and this was costing him time on the track. During this period, Flavio Briatore, MD of Benetton Formula, was keeping a very close eye on his progress.

So was I. Since 1984, Johnny and I have been very close mates. For several years we lived only two miles apart, so we spent a lot of time together during the week and at races. He is great fun to be with and would happily back me up with any mischief that came to mind, which normally had something to do with driving like hooligans, practising handbrake turns into my driveway, wheel spinning in Billericay high street, and ramming each other on the M25.

Nearly everything we did degenerated into laughter, especially when we played golf or trained together at a gymnasium in

Chelmsford. After a workout, I'd have a cigarette but Johnny, a non-smoker, would do everything he could to stop me and this often led to us rolling around and fighting on the floor. One time, a new receptionist watched us on her security monitor while we were busy bouncing off the gym's walls and wrestling each other into headlocks. Thinking it was a real fight, she called the manager over. He took one look at the screen and said: 'Oh, don't worry. It's just those lunatics McCarthy and Herbert. They try to kill each other at weekends, then they come down here and start again.'

I suppose people thought we were nuts but, as close as I am to Little 'un, I often haven't got a clue about what he is thinking. John is emotionally a very deep guy, although most of the people in racing and the public often miscast him as laid back and happy-go-lucky. He is both of those, and his imperturbable attitude is endearing, but the cheeky cherub veneer shrouds huge reserves of determination, ambition and confidence. He knows exactly what he wants, where he is going and how good he is. He just keeps it all inside, and he needed every one of these attributes after his terrible crash.

Johnny went through severe pain for months as he bravely fought to recover and get back in a car. I went to visit him most days in the Sidcup hospital and the X-rays of displaced and fragmented bone looked just like a map of the Caribbean. After extensive treatment, he returned home gaunt and frail. He spent many evenings with Karen and me. Although we knew he was in pain, he never complained, but then getting any kind of information out of Johnny is like pulling teeth.

I don't think he deliberately keeps things secret. It's just that he doesn't think to talk about them, such as the time in 1987 when he was late arriving at the Spa circuit in Belgium. I said: 'Where have you been? Somebody has just come out with a crazy story that you tested for Benetton at Brands yesterday, and that you were quicker than Thierry Boutsen [Benetton's F1 driver].'

'Oh yeah, that's right,' he smiled. 'I didn't have time to tell you. It was all a bit last minute.'

And that was it. He didn't go on about how great it had been or what a thrill it was to beat Boutsen. Or how Nigel Mansell demanded to know who was driving the car. That was typical Johnny. However, in early July 1989, we were driving along and he was very quiet, which is normally the only way I can tell something has upset him. 'I'm out,' he said with a little smile. It had taken him about an hour to force those words, which were probably as painful as his injury. I knew exactly what he meant and I was really choked. Flavio Briatore had brought in Emanuele Pirro to replace him at Benetton and Little 'un would have to start fighting once again to get back into Formula One.

That same week in Formula One, Tyrrell and their driver Michele Alboreto parted company because of a sponsorship problem with conflicting tobacco companies. How about that, huh? *Conflicting* tobacco companies. I couldn't get one of them to back me – and I was among the few drivers who smoked! Anyway, Jean Alesi replaced him in the French Grand Prix, but his F3000 commitments meant he'd have to miss both Belgium and Portugal. My ex-Ralt boss, Ron Tauranac, called Ken Tyrrell and told him that I was the man for the job.

I was invited to see Ken and during our long chat I was tempted to say that I didn't care what bloody cigarette company they had: if it helped out, I'd smoke 40 a day. I was now tantalisingly close to my goal of becoming a Formula One driver. However, having gained a release from Benetton, the decision finally went to Johnny. Well, chin up. If I'd got that close once, then I could do it again. It was a great confidence booster that somebody like Ron believed in me enough to push me forward and that Ken had taken the idea seriously. But with super-stardom back on hold, I had to concentrate on returning to F3000.

From the start of the year in which Johnny bounced into, then out of and then back into grand prix, my best chance of getting back in Formula 3000 was with the Roni Q8 Petroleum team. My old pal from Toleman, Chris Witty, was co-ordinating the deal, but he was being chased by every guy with a crash helmet. He did, however, want me. The drive was very heavily subsidised by Q8 and instead of 700 grand, all they needed from me was £100,000, which was about £100,000 less than the offer they'd given to anybody else. The trouble was, it was £80,000 more than I could get hold of, so once again the season, and Q8, started without me.

From possible Formula One hero or slightly more possible F3000 hero, I was actually back to confirmed zero. I made sure I wasn't forgotten though. I was bumming my way out to races, just to be seen in the paddock, and I was regularly in phone contact with several teams, whether they liked it or not.

Mid-way through the year, John Wickham became the first team manager to give me a break. He had previously owned the Spirit Formula One team and had been responsible for bringing Honda back into grand prix in 1983. More recently, though, we had been friends from when he ran Mega Blundell in F3. He was now heading the Japanese Footwork team in F3000 and his driver, the tiny Ukyo Katayama, was having a tough time with their unique 'Mooncraft' chassis. They were looking for a replacement and those tested included Andrew Gilbert-Scott, Gary Brabham, Damon, Ukyo himself and me. I ended up fastest of the lot. John wanted to sign me, after choosing to ignore one particularly wild lap at Snetterton when, after smashing across the chicane exit kerbing at 150mph, I was actually airborne as I went past his pit.

He regularly faxed Japan to promote my cause and I called him every day, sometimes twice a day, to see how the cause was going. I was hell bent on getting that drive and I must have driven poor John crazy with my tactics, which included dropping by the factory unannounced: 'Hi, John. I thought I'd pop in as I was just in the area. Okay, I had to drive along the A12, then round the M25 and halfway down the M4 to be in your area, but I thought I'd just see how it was going!' Eventually, though, the decision came back and the Japanese owners chose Damon. Footwork was a massive commercial concern and the son of a former World Champion was, in their eyes, a good marketing point. I understood that, in fact I'd had nightmares about it, but I was very disappointed. Even so, I was pleased for Damon and when I called to congratulate him, I knew he was feeling bad for me. It was just a shame one of us had to lose, and it was a real shame that person was me.

The Leyton House March 3000 team had also developed their own car. Once again I was invited to carry out several tests and once again I was fastest. However, no sterling, no Stirling Moss. And it was exactly the same story when I tested for the CDM Reynard team at Silverstone.

It was good to be in demand for testing and it was good to be faster than their race drivers. But having to watch others actually race the cars was very frustrating. It was a bit like pulling the best looking girl in the world, taking her back to your hotel room, going to the bathroom to freshen up and then finding you can't get out because the door has jammed.

GA Motorsport team manager Mike Collier had stayed in touch with me and suddenly an opportunity presented itself. With only a couple of days to go, Mike asked me to race his Lola at Brands Hatch in the final round of the British F3000 Championship series. As I had no clashing Formula One commitments I grabbed the chance. I also grabbed a hospitality suite from a mate of mine and immediately invited my bank manager as a way of pacifying him.

I qualified third for the race but I made a start every bit as bad as the one that cost me the European Formula Three crown. On the way back through, I overtook Paulo Carcasci around the outside of Paddock Hill Bend and then had the problem of the hitherto charming Marco Greco. Marco pushed me off the track at 150mph, in exactly the same place that Johnny had crashed the year before. Now, having just missed the Pilgrims Drop bridge support, I was furious. 'No Marco, if you want to play, this is how to do it.' I'd re-caught him by Druids hairpin and I launched down the inside. While we were side by side in the tight right-hander, I turned left in to Marco's car and he went flying off the circuit. I finished second and, in so doing, scored the best result of the year for a Lola chassis. I was pleased, Mike Collier was delighted, my bank manager thought I was a star, and Karen smiled while breast-feeding our new baby daughter, Frederica.

I then had a few beers with Gary Brabham, to help him celebrate winning both the race and the championship, but I was still mad at Greco. I told him straight that our final contact was deliberate so don't mess with me. However, this had again been a one-off race and I was back out of a drive, although I was destined to meet my Brazilian mate again later that year.

RCR team owner Roger Cowman didn't know what he was letting himself in for when he was quoted in *Motoring News* as saying: 'What I really need is a hard-charging driver like Perry McCarthy.' This was the final link in a peculiar chain of events that saw me back in the international championship.

I'd first met Roger the year before, on the grid at Zolder, when his driver David Hunt and I hid our lit cigarettes from a track official by passing them off to 'Rodge'. He was to remember me for more than that, however, when 15 seconds after the start I hit David, and Roger's car was well and truly stubbed out. Smoking and destroying his car must have made a pretty good first impression.

The second time I met him was in the paddock of Vallelunga, Italy, just a couple of months before the *Motoring News* article. On that occasion, I'd heard he was having problems collecting payment from a driver. Sensing an opportunity to replace the driver, I started shadowing Roger, and everywhere he went, I went. The poor bloke was having a miserable weekend, with his own driver apparently trying to con him, while another driver was now stalking him. The money was finally sorted out but, perhaps fearing more problems, and seeing me still stuck to his side like a Siamese twin, Roger officially entered my name to the governing body as his emergency reserve driver. It didn't mean much at the time since it was really just a safety precaution for RCR. However from that moment on, I began to watch the team's progress like a hawk. Eventually the two sides divorced – I was trying to place myself in Roger's custody, but he still needed someone with money.

It was then that Sicilian Dominico Gitto arrived with backing from his family. However, in his first race he failed to qualify, and in the second he was involved in a start-line crash. His father said maybe Dominico should run a restaurant instead. He dragged Dominico away from racing and took him back home.

So Roger was now all set to sign yet another driver, the Austrian Pierre Chauvet. Pierre had agreed to provide them with £100,000 for the final four races of the international championship, but there was just one little problem. The governing body FISA (now the FIA) had a ruling about driver changes and Roger Cowman Racing had used up its quota for their one car. Under the regulations, the only driver they could now use was their nominated 'emergency reserve' – me.

You can imagine how poor Roger felt. He'd just been forced to put me, who had no money, in his car and at the same time to wave farewell to £100,000. Nowadays I can bait Roger with this at will, and he'll bark back that I'm a bastard who cost him a fortune, at which we both start laughing. What rotten luck for Roger that the regulations could be so dumb. And what fantastic luck for me.

Again in fluke circumstances, I was back. Roger worked miracles to keep me, his car and his team on the track with a budget that wouldn't run a Formula Ford outfit. Very few people could have done that. Our first race together was the Birmingham Super Prix, the scene of my Formula 3000 debut the previous year. Looking back, I think I must have told some jokes against Birmingham at some point in my life, because the place is like a curse to me. Roger's Lola was bang on the pace in free practice, and with no testing I was immediately 10th fastest. Come official qualifying, though, the curse struck. The engine was misfiring badly and we were constantly in and out of the pits. We hadn't set a time so, just like last year, it was all down to the final session. I was revved up but unfortunately the engine wasn't and, on my first run, the car broke down on the back of the circuit. I was sure our misfire was the result of the fuel management system receiving an incorrect voltage, therefore it was probably a battery fault. I wasn't giving up, I had to fix it and I had to qualify, but I didn't have much time.

I was cursing as I ran half a mile in my thick fireproof overalls back to the paddock. But when I attempted to enter the pit area, a police officer stopped me and asked to see my pass. It was unusual for a policeman to request this: it's normally a security guard. Either way, though, it's a big mistake for anyone to get in my way when I'm in that kind of mood, and at full volume and with colourful vocabulary, I pointed out the error of his ways. Bloody idiot.

He let me through. I saw Roger and told him the story. I then ran all the way back to the stranded car, holding a heavy battery and pulling along a huge compressed air bottle, which was supported on little wheels. It was really tough, but in those situations I just create a mental picture of what I want. And what I wanted then was to: 'Get to the car. Keep going. Get to the car. Keep going. Get to the bloody car.' A mechanic busted a gut to keep up and, once there, we hurriedly took off the sidepod, connected the new unit, plugged in the air (which is needed to start the engine) and bingo! Houston, we have ignition.

The exertion and stress had left me breathless and my heartbeat and body temperature were off the clock, but I screamed back to the pits where the team made a quick check of the system. If the car was okay, then zap! I knew we'd be in the top 10, but I just needed to have that one lap and we had only minutes to spare. I was still trying to control my breathing as I accelerated along the pit lane when suddenly a mechanic from the Italian First Racing team stepped out in front of me. I slammed the brakes on and went as far right as I could. I was only millimetres from the pit wall, but my left front wheel hit him. He went up into the air and came down with his head directly in front of the left rear. If my reactions had been marginally slower then... well, he would have had a severe problem.

I could see he was fairly okay, though, so with the obsession of qualifying the car and my heartbeat bordering on valve bounce, I thought: 'For God's sake, just drag him off, get him out of my way. I'm running out of bloody time!' However, before I could pull away, I felt a heavy knock into the side of my head, compliments of First Racing team's Lamberto Leoni, who was now gripping the front of my cockpit, screaming something in Italian and pointing at his man rolling around on the floor.

'Get out of my way!' I screamed back at him. I raised up my arm and threw a karate chop down on his hand as hard as I could. Trouble was, he moved his hand and my blow made full contact with the rock-solid edge of the car. Aaaargh! I felt like the cat in a *Tom and Jerry* cartoon when he hits something hard, pauses, looks out from the screen and then shatters into a million pieces. I thought I'd busted it, but there was no time to worry. I'd get it sorted out later...

I revved up and selected first gear and shouted: 'Lamberto, get out of my effing way or else you're coming with me!' I was now totally manic. I wanted to jump out of the car and beat the daylights out of Leoni, but I also needed to be out on the track. Decisions, decisions. I dropped the clutch and got to the end of the pit lane just at the very moment the session was stopped. Well, that was it: deal over. We hadn't qualified and I was livid. I was so mad that I didn't know what to do.

My hand was swollen and I wanted to hit somebody – in fact anybody, and preferably right then. It was a straightforward plan: Lamberto was top of the list and once I'd whacked him, I'd break his mechanic's other arm, then throw our flat battery at the cop. Roger had his own plans though. After I got my hand bandaged, he took me away from the circuit and I went back to the hotel where I got drunk in the company of James Hunt.

James was a real hero of mine, a good-looking Formula One champion with what seemed to be a playboy lifestyle. I didn't know him well but we did have a couple of laughs and I'll always remember him on one particular flight back from Italy. Many of the F3000 pack were already onboard when James wandered into the cabin holding some helium-filled, parrot-shaped balloons in one hand, and a lady who looked like she'd

No doubt planning something nasty during this Laindon Comprehensive School mug shot. *(Author's collection)*

Wow! I'm a racing driver! Early days, new overalls, silly grin, and World Championship aspirations. *(Author's collection)*

Working 12 to 18 hours a day on North Sea oil rigs to bring in the money to start racing. *(Author's collection)*

Good Friday becomes Bad Friday on the Oulton Park circuit in 1984. Me and my Formula Ford at 100mph in the wrong direction after touching wheels with another competitor. Result: end of car, end of budget, end of season, concussion and broken vertebrae. Ooops! *(Chris Harvey/Hilton Press Services)*

Left: Karen Jane Waddilove. The girl of my dreams, and together since 1984. *(Author's collection)*

Right: Go, go, go! Formula 3 start at Oulton Park and leading from Damon Hill (7), Johnny Herbert (on our left), Thomas Danielsson, Bertrand Gachot and Gary Brabham (next row behind). *(Sutton)*

Right: My chance to win the race and become the 1987 European Formula 3 champion ended right here with this spin at Silverstone. *(Sutton)*

Left: Pat and Dennis, better known to me as mum and dad. I was better known to Dennis as a bleedin' idiot! *(Author's collection)*

Right: On the podium and congratulating Johnny with champagne! *(Author's collection)*

Paul Radisich, me, Mark Blundell and Damon Hill catch up with the gossip. *(Sutton)*

On the limit in Belgium and closing in to take Eddie Irvine (24). *(LAT)*

I'm nearly there! My first taste of Formula One inside the Footwork, with my manager Roger Cowman looking in. *(John Colley)*

It felt fantastic to be in an F1 car and flat out at Silverstone. *(John Colley)*

This is your life Damon Hill, and I've just handed over Johnny Herbert as a small 'trophy' in recognition of Damon's achievements. *(Fremantlemedia Ltd)*

Left: As usual, my youngest daughter, Finella, gets in on the act while Poppy (the eldest) and I pay our tribute to the Beatles. *Right:* I prayed to God to be surrounded by women for the rest of my life … and this was the answer! Day out at the Tate with my girls. *(Author's collection)*

Sao Paulo, Brazil, and at last I was a Formula One driver. Little did I know that a few hours later my race licence would be taken away. *(Sutton)*

The licence was re-issued for the 1992 Spanish Grand Prix where I managed to impress the world with F1's shortest-ever qualifying attempt! *(Sutton)*

Exiting Casino Square in Monaco. What an incredible experience. If only we could have done more than three laps. *(Sutton)*

Left: The German Grand Prix pit wall where Julian Bailey is pleased to see me still alive after my qualifying session. *(Sutton) Right:* Deborah Tee presenting the T-shirt I designed as a joke protest about the number of laps I was completing. *(LAT)*

Ready to begin qualifying for the British Grand Prix where the team were kind enough to supply wet tyres for dry conditions! *(Sutton)*

Mark Blundell explains the benefits of being issued with a grand prix pass after I had yet again conned the security staff with a variety of stories to let me into the F1 paddock. *(LAT)*

Yes it's true! I was a Grand Prix driver and here's the proof, from Monaco: Back row from left: Gerhard Berger, Ayrton Senna, Nigel Mansell, Karl Wendlinger, Damon Hill, Ukyo Katayama, Andrea Chiesa and Gabriele Tarquini. Middle row: Johnny Herbert, Mika Hakkinen, Christian Fittipaldi, me, JJ Lehto, Andrea de Cesaris, Eric Comas, Ivan Capelli, Mauricio Gulgelmin, Olivier Grouillard and Ricardo Patrese. Front row: Michael Schumacher, Paul Belmondo, Eric van de Poele, Roberto Moreno, Pierluigi Martini, Gianni Morbidelli, Thierry Boutsen, Michele Alboreto, Stefano Modena and Martin Brundle. *(Sutton)*

Trying desperately to qualify in Belgium but narrowly avoiding a head-on clash with a wall, courtesy of a steering rack problem, and in the process waving goodbye to both my F1 career and our home. *(Sutton)*

Testing for Benetton. A proper car run by a proper team. *(Author's collection)*

Driving in the 1997 GT World Championship with the new Panoz, which became known as 'The Batmobile'. But the heat in that car and the noise from the bloody engine could make you lose the will to live. *(Sutton)*

After a year of problems this was the GT result of the season. My pal David and I drove our hearts out to score Panoz's only World Championship podium position of the season. *(Author's collection)*

New crash helmet, yet another return to racing, and at speed with the Panoz during the 2002 Le Mans pre-qualifying event. *(Sutton)*

The 2002 hardback book launch

The author, Damon Hill, Julian Bailey, Martin Donnelly, Mark Blundell. *(Paul Nicholls)*

Below, left: Jeremy and Francie Clarkson. *(Paul Nicholls)*

Right: Me with Ulrika Jonsson. *(Paul Nicholls)*

Dreaming of glory with my team-mates Frank Biela (in car) and Mika Salo.
(Audi Sport)

June 2003: Me and my Audi at warp speed on my favourite circuit, Le Mans.
(Jeff Bloxham)

been around the block a few times in the other. They sat down but James, who had had a couple of drinks and was aware he'd been spotted, suddenly stood up and announced in his public school accent: 'Okay, she may not be much to look at, but she's got great tits!' Nearly everyone I know in racing has a James story and the world was left a duller place when he passed away four years later, in 1993.

I had been very disappointed in Birmingham, but if I didn't find some money soon I'd be even more disappointed because our shoestring campaign would definitely be over. Roger just had to have some contribution to his running costs from me. Our regular phone calls would always end with him saying: 'Perry, find the money.' So, I did. Well, at least I tried. TL Clowes threw in a few bob, a company called Westley Controls gave us a couple of grand and Hawtal Whiting made a donation.

We were still a million miles short of what we needed, so I arranged a meeting with my friend Ivan Mant, who was the promotions manager with my old sponsor Lucas. Ivan agreed to bring along one of the company's high fliers, Mike Littlejohn, and together we had a long chat in the bar of a local hotel. Halfway through, though, I started to feel that I needed to do something to make me different from all the others who wanted Lucas to sponsor them – something that made me stand out as a future star, a good investment, a safe bet.

As I needed a pee, I excused myself and went to the cloakroom. It was there that I had the idea. Another chap was washing his hands and I immediately took the opportunity to put a deal to him. Matey-boy agreed to my plan. I went to rejoin Ivan and Mike, where we continued talking about Formula 3000 and, sure enough, after about five minutes, my new friend came over to our table. 'Excuse me,' he said. 'Are you Perry McCarthy?'

With mock surprise and embarrassment, I said: 'Yes.'

He continued: 'I'm sorry to disturb you but I'm a big motor racing fan and I've been following your career.' I waited for the next part of his script. 'So, Perry, are you still sponsored by the giant electrical and automotive parts company Lucas?'

I had to clench my teeth to avoid laughing. Sure, in the toilet, I'd told him to say 'Lucas' but he'd overplayed his part with the 'giant electrical and automotive company' bit. Anyway, he really started enjoying himself and came out with new gems like: 'I think it's great that a British company like Lucas backs British sportsmen.' It was unbelievable. I must have stumbled across an out of work character actor or something, but now realising that my plan was actually pretty stupid, I just wanted him to go away. By the time he did finally leave,

I was making small whining noises while trying to contain my laughter and it took me a while before I could look either Ivan or Mike in the eye. At the end of our meeting, Mike smiled and Ivan, who knew me well enough to realise I'd set the whole thing up, giggled just loud enough for me to hear. I then kept my side of the bargain and went over to buy my cohort and his girlfriend a beer.

Lucas did indeed come forward with a little bit of sponsorship, which made the difference between going to Spa and staying at home. Qualifying at Spa showed signs of promise but, like the rest of my career, this was dramatic. It was raining and I was second fastest with Eric Comas fastest and Jean Alesi just behind me. I came into the pits for new tyres but Roger had used his last available credit with Avon and wanted to keep our only new set in case it rained for tomorrow's race day. He also said we had to stop, especially as it had now started raining harder.

It made sense but I was totally focused on going for pole position and did something a bit naughty. Roger left me and walked back over to the pit wall, but once he'd gone, I held a straight face and told the mechanics that he said I should go back out. So while he was busy watching the other drivers, the team put on our new set of wets and I went out on to the circuit in a last ditch attempt to take the number one spot.

The first Roger knew of this was when I came past the pits, flat out in a ball of spray, and a rival team manager exclaimed: 'That was Perry!' Roger spun round and checked behind him, only to see an empty garage. Needless to say, he wasn't terribly happy about this and on my next lap, he was furiously shaking a pit board at me, displaying the word 'IN'. If he'd had enough letters, it would probably have said 'AND THAT MEANS RIGHT NOW YOU LITTLE BASTARD!' But his gaze became transfixed and his eyes widened in horror as I entered the daunting Eau Rouge corner sideways and heading straight toward the barriers flat out. The conditions and visibility were now so bad that Roger didn't know if I'd actually crashed or not.

A few minutes later, though, I pulled up back at the pits, where Roger was waiting for me with a face like thunder. He went crazy at me and I was just playing it down nicely when he noticed scuff marks on the left hand tyres that I'd received while skimming along the barriers at 130mph. He started shouting at me again, and once again I had just started telling him it was no big deal when the French driver Paul Belmondo, who I'd overtaken going into the corner, made a special trip down the pit lane to see me.

'Perry!' he said, right in front of Roger. 'I just cannot believe how you held that. I mean, I backed right off waiting for you to have the biggest accident... Well done!' Ooops! Cheers, Paul. Roger looked at me through squinted eyes and I did my very best Lassie faithful pup impression.

Qualifying dried and we slipped down the order to 11th place. I quickly dropped to about 16th when the race started after I made another poor getaway. However, I fought my way back through the pack, which included Damon (who had beaten me to the Footwork drive), Gary Brabham (who had beaten me to the Leyton House March drive), and Naspetti (who had secured the Q8 drive). I then had a terrific dice with Eddie Irvine, who drove for the big budget Marlboro team, and we ran side by side, banging wheels at 160mph. After a couple of near misses, I eventually made it through and started closing on Thomas Danielsson for sixth place. If the race had been one lap longer, I would have taken him, but I finished in seventh, only one and a half seconds behind.

It was a great day for RCR and we had done it with no money and no testing. My performance had been noticed by some important people, including Peter Collins, who had now become the Lotus Formula One team manager. Peter told *Motor Sport* magazine: '[McCarthy] convinced me he had something extra. I watched him at Eau Rouge and he was doing something special in that car.'

It really was a good race but it was certainly going to take something 'special' for us to compete in the next one. Roger had braved it out and yes, we could run on a pittance, but no, we couldn't run on fresh air. We desperately needed some help at the Le Mans Bugatti circuit and that's where I was a very lucky boy. I had a lot of support in the paddock and this was one of those times in motor racing that gives you a warm feeling. John Wickham diverted a new set of tyres away from his Footwork team for me, the Q8 team secretly sent over some replacement parts for our car, while Robert Synge at Madgwick Motorsport supplied all my fuel. If the drivers of these teams had known how their own managers were helping me, they would have gone ballistic. This was great stuff, but I had one problem that wouldn't go away: Marco Greco.

We saw each other for the first time since I'd pushed him off at Brands and Marco said: 'Perry, I am not happy with you. Today I kill you!'

I knew Marco was serious because I remembered him when we were in Formula Three at Donington, bursting into the West Surrey Racing garage, punching a mechanic in the face, then punching Dick Bennetts in the ribs and swinging a torque wrench around in search of Bertrand Gachot. Bertie, however, had seen it all coming and did a Houdini out the back door. Bertrand could be a pest, though. I'd had him by the throat the same year at Snetterton and Mark Blundell had punched him when we were all in Formula Ford.

Anyway, I was in no mood for threats and I said: 'Okay, pal. Let's go into the wall flat out together; let's see who survives. I'll see you out there!' You have to understand that, as a driver, you cannot allow yourself to be intimidated and with my little burst of 'track rage' I'd just turned the tables. Marco is a big bloke, but his expression changed because he knew I meant it.

I didn't really expect to even see him, though, because he was good for midfield and I was going to qualify up front. Well, that was the plan, but sometimes a seemingly unrelated issue can alter things. Bernie Ecclestone, boss of virtually everything in motor racing, had told the F3000 teams that presentation was important and he only wanted to see large 40-foot articulated racecar transporters in the paddock. So Roger left his smart little one at home and rented a monster from the CDM team. On Saturday morning, with good memories of Spa still fresh in our minds, the team started preparing for qualifying using the simple mechanical process of removing the racecar from the top deck of the transporter. The hydraulic tail of the transporter folded down to the floor, then rose up horizontally to the top of the truck, from where the car was wheeled on to this elevated platform. The control button was then pressed to bring the whole lot back to the ground. Simple enough, but there was a problem. A problem that was unheard of, a problem that was too cruel to consider! My car was stuck three metres up in the air because the tail lift wouldn't bloody well come down.

We could see the car, and if we jumped we could touch it, but we couldn't actually get to it. The whole thing was a big tease. It was like holding a biscuit out to a dog and saying 'Rover, sit' and he duly sits, then 'Rover, paw' and he holds out his paw – and all the time the dog is thinking 'just give me the stupid biscuit will ya!' We tried everything but the bloody tail lift was still up there along with my car when qualifying started. Oh, for God's sake, why me? We couldn't believe it: tell me what more can go wrong? Should I have stayed on the rigs? Maybe I should have gone into the city with college mates Tapps and Keeny. Or how about that idea of joining the RAF?

Jesus, this effort was financially strangling Roger and me. 'Give us a break!' I shouted, but then Roger and I looked at each other and started laughing. Eventually we got the only crane on the circuit – the one that should have been in position to assist after an accident – to come into the paddock. Finally our £90,000 Lola was yanked up into the air and hoisted down to earth. 'Houston, the Lola has landed.' But, as they say in B-movies: 'Too late Earthman!' The first qualifying was over and it was back to an all or nothing effort in session two.

The drama continued in the second session. We had gearbox problems and a misfiring engine, and right up to the final five minutes we still hadn't set a timed lap. Roger and his team worked flat out, never giving up, and I just managed to get out in time to do one lap on cold tyres before the chequered flag dropped. We just made it. I'd set a time that earned us the final place on the grid. We had definitely earned a couple of beers.

Race day came and the warm-up session times read: Bernard, Comas, McCarthy, Alesi. It was good, but my teeth were grinding at the thought of where we should have qualified. I mean, if you blow an engine or break a driveshaft you might think: 'Okay, these things happen.' But having the day ruined by a tail lift...

In the race itself I was determined to make up for lost ground and by the end of the first lap I was up to 15th from 26th on the grid. The next position, however, was occupied by Marco Greco and I wanted to get past him quickly. After exiting the chicane, I tried to overtake him on the right, then left, then right but he was weaving faster than a downhill skier. Well, the stupid idiot should have learnt his lesson at Brands Hatch and, just like that incident, I dived down the inside for the right-hand hairpin. Once alongside, I again turned left and sent dear old Marco into the air and crashing into the barriers.

On the following lap I could see him standing on the side of the track, jumping up and down and waving his fists at me. He looked like a cross between Mike Tyson and a block of flats, and it dawned on me that I was going to have to face that nutter when I finished. I thought about staying in the car, turning out the circuit, and driving to Paris at 180mph. The Lola wouldn't have made the journey, though, because the clutch was on the way out and I was losing power from a cracked exhaust. We finally limped home in 14th place and I returned to the paddock where guess who was waiting for me.

There was a bit of pushing and shoving, and quite a lot of shouting. Marco was towering above me and shaking with anger. If it came to a fight, I might be able to hurt him but I'd calculated that he was going to hurt me a lot more.

I looked across for some reassurance from my friend Mike Collier of GA Motorsport, who was about 10 metres away. But Mike, who is even bigger than Marco, just stood there smiling and I cringed at the realisation that Greco was his driver and it had been another one of his cars that I'd smashed up. I braved it out and it finished with Marco promising to kill me in the next race. Ah well, all in a day's work.

Unfortunately, I never got to go for my hat trick with Greco because that was it for RCR. Roger had run himself dry and my house was once again in the balance, but had we proved a point? The Formula 3000 International guide for 1990 reported: 'Each outing has provided further evidence that [McCarthy's] skills remain undiminished. The only factor which keeps him away from the winner's rostrum is a continual lack of sponsorship.'

It seemed as though I wasn't wasting my time and after a lovely compliment like that, it would be downright rude not to continue, wouldn't it? Anyway, I still wasn't a Formula One driver yet.

Chapter 10

THE LAND OF MILK AND HONEY

'Do you realise what you've just done?' he laughed.
'You've just blown away Chevrolet's "Golden boy" by over
a second in his own car and on his home track!'

Crazy things like the tail lift problem just kept happening to me but they were funny and news of my latest adventures seemed to spread far and wide. I guess some things were down to me, though, and not taking 'no' for an answer often lit the fuse to a new story. Take, for example, some of the stunts I pulled to get into a Formula One paddock without a pass.

In 1982, a security guard I knew turned a blind eye as I darted behind the garages at Brands, just before the start of the British Grand Prix. I had to see these cars close up in the pits, and to an impressionable 21-year-old it was like a different world. I saw some of the drivers making their way to their cars and it was as if all the wonderful pictures in the racing magazines I constantly read had suddenly come to life. The howling noise from the race engines made my ears ring and I looked around in awe, thinking: 'Wow! So this is Formula One.'

I now needed a good place to watch the race from, and preferably one where I wouldn't have to keep dodging the pack of security guards that I *didn't* know. I was wearing a Ferrari cap when I stopped by the Italian team and convinced some mechanics that I was with Ferrari's UK division, after which they kindly let me join about 10 others who were standing on top of their racecar transporter. This was great fun. I was close to the action, playing it cool and doing all the right things, when suddenly British driver Derek Warwick, racing the unfancied Toleman car, took a big dive down the inside at Paddock Hill Bend and incredibly passed Didier Pironi's Ferrari for second place. I threw my arms in the air and let out the biggest cheer I could. The rest of them looked at me in silence before a voice said: 'Are you sure you're with Ferrari?' I'd blown it and was politely shown the way down.

I had a more ambitious plan at the British GP at Silverstone in 1987. I was riding around on Julian Bailey's motorbike, just outside the F1 paddock fence, when suddenly I had an idea. I asked a guy at a hot dog stand for two paper plates, which I then placed face to face and held them together with my left hand. With my right hand, I gently rotated the bike's throttle and passed through a crowd waiting beside the entrance for driver autographs.

Riding one handed, I held the closed plates up high and, like a delivery boy, I shouted: 'Pizza for Ayrton. Pizza for Ayrton. Make way.' They parted like the Red Sea and, still balancing the plates, I told the security guard: 'Pizza for Ayrton Senna, mate! Where can I find him?'

He bit. 'Straight down there, mate. He's with Camel Lotus.' I prepared to pull away when suddenly the second guard spotted the two plates had slid apart, revealing only fresh air.

'Oy you – there's nothing inside!'

I'd been rumbled but I carried on: 'Ah damn!' I said. 'He's going to kill me. It must have fallen out.' I looked up to the concerned crowd and shouted: 'Ayrton's pizza's dropped on the floor. Help me find Ayrton's pizza!' Unbelievably, everybody started looking for it and I was desperately trying to stop grinning.

The security guard looked at me seriously: 'Sorry, mate. You can't come in without the pizza!' Well, once he said that, I thought I was going to wet myself with laughter and I rode off. I actually didn't care too much about not getting in; I just wanted to see if I *could* get in.

With my collection of stories to date and other less repeatable tales, it was beginning to dawn on me why the rest of the Rat Pack called me Mad Dog. However, their individual stories were also ongoing, as we collectively followed our ambitions.

During the 1990 season, Grumpy and Mega (Julian Bailey and Mark Blundell) continued from their previous year's adventures as team-mates for Nissan in Group C Sports Prototypes, while Secret Squirrel (Damon Hill) had a drive with the Middlebridge team in Formula 3000. Jean Alesi had taken up an offer with Tyrrell, which meant Little 'un (Johnny Herbert) was out again, so he went to race sports cars and F3000 in Japan. However Yer Man (Martin Donnelly) backed up the F1 race he'd driven for Arrows the previous year by signing for Lotus as their full-time driver, thus becoming the Rat Pack's lone representative in grand prix.

And me? Well, I was off to the place of opportunity, the land of milk and honey. I was going to the United States of America. I had to go because there was nothing for me in Europe. Two of my ex-Formula 3000 team managers, Mike Collier at GA Motorsport and Alan Howell from Ralt, had tried hard to set something up for me but it came to naught. My own efforts had also failed to secure a drive, but my other F3000 team manager Roger Cowman had been in contact with his old mate Julian Randles, who was running the works Spice sports car operation in America's IMSA GT championship. Okay, it wasn't part of the accepted path to Formula One, but it was a recognised series. I wanted to race, the cars were quick and Ferrari still hadn't called me. It was only a last-minute, one-race deal, but it might lead to other things. I was very excited about this unexpected opportunity as I flew out on TWA to Cleveland Ohio.

The IMSA (International Motor Sports Association) GT cars were split into two classes. First there was the big monster, 200mph, GTP division (Grand Touring Prototypes, the kind that raced in the Le Mans 24 Hours). And then there were the smaller, less powerful Camel Lights cars. Spice USA had a car in each category, but for the race on the Mid Ohio circuit, I was being tried out in their Lights car.

It was my first experience in a prototype and the first time I'd been entered in a race that demanded a driver change. So with my new team-mate, the 16-stone Mexican Thomas Lopez, we practised against the stopwatch the sequence of getting in and out of the car. Because of the enormous heat, we were wearing special 'cool caps' inside our crash helmets. These were connected by a long umbilical lead to the dashboard and had small capillaries inside that allowed cold water to be pumped through them, thus keeping our heads cool. Disconnecting these leads was proving the trickiest part of our changeover.

I qualified the car second fastest but then the McCarthy curse struck when I somehow damaged a nerve in my right foot. Julian Randles had seen me limping heavily and was very close to replacing me. I couldn't allow that, though. To prove I was totally okay, I stood before him and jumped up and down on it while he watched my expression. The only way I fooled him was to let out my screams as bursts of demonic laughter, as if I was teasing him. After a few seconds he said he believed me, and I immediately shot off behind the garages and rolled around on the floor almost in tears.

Thomas started the race and then, after 40 laps, he came into the pits as scheduled, but the plan had already begun to go wrong. He had slipped down to fourth position, he had a damaged fourth gear, he was starting to panic, and our carefully thought-out driver change procedure was about to go to pieces.

The car stopped next to our pit but as I opened the door, I found Thomas still struggling to release his seat belts. Dripping in sweat, he was pulling and shouting and I lent in quickly to help, but then 'pow!' the belts sprang back and this bull of a man, desperate to make up lost seconds, was grabbing and swiping at anything, including me, to help him exit the small cockpit. I broke free from his hold but then he got a firm grip on the roof support. He pulled hard and hurled himself out but the radio and thick umbilical leads from his crash helmet were still plugged into the dashboard. Like a charging dog who'd reached the end of his rope, he was pulled back by the head while the rest of him jerked up, feet first into the air, and he crashed down on to the pit lane.

His mind had now gone into meltdown. Forget disconnecting this stuff conventionally, he wanted revenge. As he staggered up, I saw him grab both sets of leads in his hands. 'NO, THOMAS!' I yelled. But it was too late. He ripped the whole lot out with such force that it brought the dashboard sockets with it as well. He was in a rage and I jumped into the car before he decided to go the whole way and turn the thing upside down. I immediately felt around for the release so that I could slide the seat into my own driving position. As I disengaged it, Thomas – now even more desperate to help – wedged his paw behind the backrest and powered me forward along its rails like a rocket sled, after which he slammed the door shut and walked away. The seat had been rammed so far past my mark that my chest was now jammed against the steering wheel. Unable to move, I could only scream 'THOMAS!!' He ran back, detached me from the windscreen, and I went into the next 80 laps starting from fifth place, with no radio, no cool suit, no drinks bottle and no fourth gear. Cheers, Tommy!

Unbelievably, though, we won. But the drama wasn't quite over yet and I was in no mood to celebrate. Every dab of the brake and flick of the throttle across the last hour and a half had felt like a nail being pressed into my inflamed foot. I couldn't back off though, because I had to fight tooth and nail for every opportunity I'd ever had to drive racing cars and, back home, Karen was financially hanging on by her fingertips.

As I came into the pits I didn't have to pretend any more – not that I could anyway. I was almost delirious with pain as the team lifted me out and I screamed: 'Forget the rostrum. Get me to the doctor now!' But Roger Cowman, who was now my personal manager, recognised the importance of winning my first race in America and said: 'You're getting up on that effing podium even if I have to carry you.' Well, he did carry me over and he was right. Everyone thought I was a bloody hero and, once in bed over at the medical centre, the press interviewed me and thought I was 'brilliant'.

This suited me just fine. Back home, though, David Tremayne, executive editor of *Motoring News*, was just getting started. David had been a friend and supporter of mine for several years and believed I should be in Formula One. Even though I was to spend two seasons racing more than 3,000 miles away in America, he made sure my exploits were rarely out of the headlines.

One story David didn't know about, though, was the mistake I'd made at Heathrow Airport on the way to Ohio. As I said, it had been a last-minute call-up and I was in such a rush that I mistakenly parked my car in the short-term car park. On arriving back I was about to have an expensive lesson in the difference between short-term and long-term when, at the pay booth, the attendant asked me for £200. I looked at him in disbelief. I had about 10 quid on me and, what's more, my car was a 12-year-old Vauxhall Cavalier that was worth less than the car-parking bill. I offered him the keys and said: 'You keep it, mate.' But he didn't want it.

Then it dawned on me that even a chap who works in a car park had a better car than me – and, incidentally, we wouldn't even have had that car if Karen's father Jim hadn't bought it for us. Anyway, the guy finally let me out after taking all my details and I'm sure the car we called the Ratmobile was laughing: 'Ah-ha, McCarthy. You've finally spent some money on me!' Actually, I quite liked that old car. Anything that's hand-painted in purple must have a sense of humour, and I reckon it laughed again, two months later, when I had to pay up.

Julian Randles invited me back to race for him, this time at Watkins Glen in New York State, and he promoted me to their works Chevrolet engined GTP car. My new team-mate was the Trans-Am champion Tommy Kendall. However, after testing, it was Nissan's driver and ex-Williams Formula One star Derek Daly who came to see me. 'Do you realise what you've just done?' he laughed. 'You've just blown away Chevrolet's "Golden boy" by over a second in his own car and on his home track!'

I did know and I'd been secretly smiling like a Cheshire cat about it, but after qualifying eighth quickest overall and the fastest of the non-turbo cars, I also knew that here, at the Glen, our 6.0-litre V8 was giving away more than 100bhp to the turbo cars and we didn't stand a chance.

But then the rain came. By the third lap of the race, strapped inside my Spice, with the windscreen wiper on full blast, I had just taken the lead from the works Jaguar team in my first GTP start. I could hear the crowd cheering, because this was the first time in years that a Chevrolet-powered car had led, and I felt totally alive as I pulled away from Davy Jones and the rest of them at two seconds a lap. I knew this must have looked good to my team and all the others in the pit lane. It was sensational.

'Newcomer in GTP beats big works teams... la, la, la.' The dream of recognition, glory, and big offers kept me pushing to ram the point home to everyone. In fact, I was still thinking about the glory while sitting on the garage floor about an hour later after the car had stopped with electrical problems.

The race had been televised, though, and that had hidden advantages. I drove across state to New York City and about five miles from the centre, the police stopped me for doing 110mph. I was asked to get out, which I agreed to do, especially as one of the cops was aiming a gun at me. The other one, meanwhile, kept his gun packed but, with legs apart and his hand hovering over the holster, he looked like John Wayne. I was tempted to say 'Draw, yella belly!' but didn't, mainly because I didn't want to die. Instead I opened the trunk, or boot lid, as directed. They noticed my crash helmet and overalls.

'Hey, you a racecar driver, buddy?' he enquired. That was my opening.

'Yeah, I'm the Chevrolet works driver. I'm just on the way back home from Watkins Glen where I led the foreign stuff like Jaguar, Nissan and Toyota.' I played on the foreign bit.

'Wow, I saw that race... *that* was you!'

So having established that I wasn't the getaway driver for a group of criminals, they kindly decided not to shoot me. I then signed a couple of autographs, they wished me luck, and off I went without a speeding ticket. Television is a wonderful invention.

Leading at Watkins Glen, fresh from our Ohio win had definitely made an impression, especially on Julian Randles. The Spice USA team was running on a shoestring budget against works teams from Jaguar, Toyota, Nissan and Porsche so Julian was under pressure to put drivers in the car who had sponsorship. But he didn't. As long as I could keep springing surprises, he'd keep taking financial risks and he once again brought me back to the USA.

During testing for our next race, though, I was about to prove expensive. Everybody had been talking about my GTP debut at the Glen and, in Britain, David Tremayne was going into publicity overdrive. My confidence was sky high but I needed to keep the momentum going and my driving on the Sears Point circuit in California was, at times, looking as desperate as General Custer's last stand. After I'd overtaken Derek Daly around the outside of the high-speed Carousel corner, he had a chat with my team manager and said: 'Julian, that boy of yours isn't long for this world!' Julian had, in fact, already spotted this and repeated Derek's observations to me. I got back in the car, and assured him everything was all under control.

Just under 10 minutes later I smashed the car to pieces against the wall. It was a dumb mistake and I'd just used up my collection of Brownie points, all in one go. I felt like a slug and, knowing I'd let everyone down, I was still feeling depressed and dejected the following morning as qualifying approached.

One of the team saw me alone, approached and sat beside me: 'Hey buddy, we were up until 3.30am fixing your goddam car.'

'Yeah, I know,' I replied like the slug I was.

But then he put his hand on my shoulder, smiled and said: 'Well, go out and put it on pole – we know you can do it.' I'll never forget that. It was as if 100,000 volts had just recharged me. They *did* still believe in me; they *were* still behind me.

It was time for single-car qualifying, where each of us had a two-lap run with no other cars on the circuit, and I was the last to go. My confidence was back, I was locked on and the wheels were spinning as I left the pit lane intent on making up for my accident. Both my laps recorded an identical time, and that time was one and a half seconds faster than the next fastest qualifier, the South African Wayne Taylor. I had smashed the outright track record and, as I returned to the pits, it was great to see that even the Jaguar team were stood there clapping. Julian flung the door open, dragged me out and we put our arms around each other. We then joined with the rest of the Spice USA crew, who were jumping up and down and cheering, just as they had done in both Ohio and Watkins. They had all worked so hard to repair the car and I'd just delivered, big time. We had pole position. I was so happy and felt totally at home in our small, close-knit team. It really was a good lap and it took a further 10 years for that record to be beaten. In the race itself, though, we again suffered disappointment when the engine blew up and we retired.

My first GTP races had been encouraging but financially I was ducking and diving, desperately turning any opportunity into a money-making venture. By this time, as predicted, dad's DJM Construction business had come to an end and my sister Lesley told me that to avoid more storage charges, he was selling a lot of equipment cheap that he'd had packed away since 1986. She then told me just how cheap. I told her to stop the sale and I put my crash helmet to one side and immediately drove out to Holland, where the equipment was.

I hadn't worked with dad since he'd asked me back a few years earlier to help with a one-off project, which proved to be about the funniest screw-up ever. That was when the Mobil Oil Company had asked DJM to shot blast and paint the legs of its oil tanker jetties, over at their Coryton refinery on the Essex side of the Thames Estuary. Scaffolding was to be the biggest headache in this exercise but the old man had an idea. A mate of his down the pub had a couple of ex-army pontoons for sale, and dad suddenly realised that these huge metal box things could float on the Thames Estuary. His eyes lit up. If they were fitted with our equipment, plus a motor, there'd be no need for scaffolding. We'd simply power up to even the furthest part of the structure, and the operative would then carry out all the work from the pontoon's deck. It was brilliant.

Dad bought them, had them sprayed company blue, had a shot-blaster and spray pump bolted on deck, then fastened a perimeter handrail to the side and mounted a Mercury outboard motor on the back. In the meantime, I'd been sent on some speedboat lessons and gained the required certificate to operate a powered vessel in the Estuary. We were ready and dad proudly stood on the shore with Mobil Oil's contract managers to witness the maiden voyage of this technical innovation.

I knew I was in trouble within seconds because nobody had thought about weight distribution. I set sail with the thing tilted over at 30 degrees and me hanging on to the railings. While this was going on, my old man was pointing toward the jetty using secret hand signals that were about as subtle as a knee in the groin. I was trying, but the light current wouldn't let me anywhere near it. I had no steering and even with the motor running flat out, my pontoon was the nautical equivalent of a supermarket trolley.

Worse was still to come. I was sinking. With water now up to my knees, I'd still only travelled 30 metres but *HMS Shotblast* had decided it was going down. I couldn't stop laughing as I put my arm across my chest, like Admiral Nelson, and saluted dad, who had his head in his hands, while the guys from Mobil stared in disbelief. Unsurprisingly, we didn't get the contract.

So that was the last time. I now arrived in Holland on this new deal and spent two days going through the discarded equipment that I had previously used on the rigs. I loaded it into containers, then had it sent back to England and sold it for 25 grand more than Dad had been offered. My share was £12,000 and, with this, Karen and I had just bought another six months before the wolf would once again try to come salivating through the door.

Back racing in the States, I ran third at Portland, fighting with Juan Fangio III, and then led in San Antonio, Texas. But on both occasions we retired, which made it four non-finishes in a row. It wasn't all bad news. The series sponsor, Camel cigarettes, always laid on some entertainment and the drivers would get together for drinks and a joke, so apart from constantly living on the financial edge, I was having a lot of fun.

My career was going well, the racing was competitive, I was travelling all over America – it was one great big adventure. My new team-mate, Jay Cochran, was a terrific guy and at a time when I had a little more hair, we became known as 'The Beach Boys'. One of the people who coined that phrase was multiple IMSA champion Geoff Brabham who, like his brother Gary, would become a good mate. However, as we prepared for qualifying in Tampa, I had a premonition that another friend was in serious trouble.

In testing, I had been faster than anyone around this half-racetrack, half-street circuit, and as I walked toward the car, I was thinking of nothing but pole position. That was, until I just happened to glance over to a seated Julian Randles and Roger Cowman. I suddenly had the strangest feeling and I just knew that something bad had happened. I stopped and looked at them, then walked over and asked what was wrong.

'Nothing,' came the reply.

I stayed there. 'Yes, there is. It's Martin, isn't it?'

'Yes,' they conceded. 'But it's just a broken leg.'

They were protecting me from the details, yet somehow I knew. As I turned towards the car, I said: 'It's a lot more serious than that.'

I was now in a bad mood and as I lent against the car one of the mechanics put his hand on my shoulder and said exactly the wrong thing. 'Hey, Perry, don't do anything crazy. Think about the car, think about us, and think about Karen and the kids.' I exploded and picked the guy up, put him across the car and told him with my fist next to his face that he should never, ever, talk about my family as I'm about to go out in a racing car.

My first timed lap was pretty spectacular and by the mid point I was already one and a half seconds faster than anyone, but coming into the final corner we ran out of petrol. Our fuel guy had forgotten to do the number one thing that fuel guys have to do: put fuel in the car. I was so livid with anger and frustration that I remained seated and silent in the car for 30 minutes after it was towed back to the pits. It had been a fantastic, maximum-risk lap that would, without question, have won us pole position, but it had been ruined. Jay started the race from the back but crashed soon after and our race was over. In the meantime, though, I was desperately worried to hear that this weird premonition of mine had been confirmed. Yer Man was fighting for his life.

Martin's accident at Jerez, in qualifying for the 1990 Spanish Grand Prix, had been perhaps one of the most violent crashes ever. I know because David Tremayne witnessed it all and told me about it. The front suspension on Martin's Lotus had collapsed in the fast right-hander behind the pits and he speared head-on into the wall at 160mph. The car totally disintegrated on impact and poor Martin was thrown out and along the track like a rag doll. The remains of the Lotus looked like a cheap plastic pen that had been smashed by a hammer, and Martin lay still on the tarmac, 30 metres away. Ayrton Senna pulled over and stayed with him, while Formula One's finest doctor, my old friend Professor Sid Watkins, provided emergency assistance on the track.

Martin was conscious for a short time and, once back at the medical centre, the Prof stabilised him for the air ambulance journey back to England. However, his condition became critical when his body went into shock and he was on life support, because his kidneys, liver, and lungs stopped functioning. I took the first flight home, the day after my race, and spoke with Damon Hill, who told me he'd already been to the London Hospital and that I should be prepared for the worst.

During the long flight I couldn't stop thinking about Martin. We didn't meet each other until our Formula Three year in 1986, although I'd been familiar with the Belfast-born driver's name before that. Martin had always been somebody to keep an eye on because he was very talented and could be a formidable opponent. By formidable I mean hard, so you had to watch yourself. With Yer Man, there was no quarter given and none asked.

One time at Spa, I overtook him as we came out of Eau Rouge. Once alongside, I actually closed my eyes just waiting for contact, but it never happened, and he teased me later that he was having an 'off day'. Martin came through the ranks the hard way, like Julian Bailey, Mark Blundell and I did, so he is no stranger to a deal. In business, Marty is nothing short of relentless and he can be a ruthless negotiator. I can recall a few instances when we've played a battle of wills for several days, over sums as small as £50, and on each occasion he has eventually won. Yet when we're out socially, he is generous and when Karen and I have been totally cash-starved Yer Man has been good for a loan.

He has also saved me in other ways, such as the time a large crowd met up in a club near Zolder, Belgium. Everybody had been drinking and I pushed Thomas Danielsson into the indoor swimming pool, while Julian followed him soon after, complete with the palm tree he'd been hanging from. Several mechanics, who had been locked in a sauna, smashed its door down. The place then turned wild and the police were called.

In the meantime, I mistakenly thought it was funny to spit beer at Martin's team manager Colin Essex (a bloke who is probably stronger than Jaws in the Bond movies). He wasn't happy and said: 'You shouldn't have done that, Pel!'

He then picked me off the ground by my neck and pulled back his fist.

With enormous pressure around my throat, I sounded like Donald Duck as I croaked: 'Sorry Colin, sorry Colin!' but Martin put himself in the firing line and saved me from being well and truly 'plucked'. The Formula Three world then made a hasty exit as the sight of blue flashing lights told us the police had arrived.

The whole thing was definitely Martin's kind of night, but he also enjoys good gossip. His first words in any telephone conversation will be: 'So what's the dirt and filth?' If I can't provide any, he'll happily reel off stories of local action that makes *EastEnders* seem like a documentary. However, he'd had enough drama of his own and was now fighting to recover from a near fatal crash.

Damon was right. Martin was in such a bad way that, on visiting him for the first time, his Lotus team-mate Derek Warwick had felt physically ill. As I stood by his bedside with his fiancée Diane, I had a similar feeling but I was careful to control my reaction in front of her. Martin had broken his right leg and sustained multiple breaks to his left. His collar bone was snapped, he was heavily bruised above his left eye and he was in a coma, supported by dialysis and respirators.

Over the next five weeks I visited the hospital, hoping like everyone else for some good news. Finally it came. Diane told me Marty had regained consciousness and wanted to see me. His voice was almost like a whisper as he slowly beckoned me near, and I fully expected him to say something like 'Hi mate'. Instead, he smiled and said: 'You c. u. next Tuesday!'. As you'll appreciate, Yer Man had used the shorter version of this phrase and I roared with laughter and relief.

I continued visiting the hospital regularly and, to keep his spirits up, I often did something daft, such as the time I dressed as a surgeon. Buoyed by several drinks earlier with friends in the City, I borrowed a surgical gown, a facemask and a clipboard from a storage cupboard, and then entered the ward. Martin immediately knew it was me, but the other inmates didn't realise it was someone playing around. I made a bedside visit to each of these poor souls, then viewed their charts, had a quick chat about their damaged limb or whatever, and then looked over at Martin and made some highly visible sawing actions. Martin loved this but I don't think anybody else did...

Like Johnny Herbert, who replaced him at Lotus, Martin was very brave but sometimes his painful recovery was overwhelming. I remember one horrible occasion when it all became too much and, after the nurse asked me to leave, I could still hear Martin screaming as I walked out along the corridors. This upset me a great deal. Although his leg injuries were to spell the end of Marty-boy's career as a driver, he kept his promise of walking down the aisle with Diane by 13 April 1991 and I kept my promise of giving a speech.

I saw this as good practice, because I was now giving out speeches on a regular basis to the bank, the mortgage company, the phone company, gas, electricity and water. You name it, we owed it. I managed to convince them all to keep letting me have more time because I was 'a superstar waiting to happen' and the big money was 'just around the corner'.

It was proving to be a bloody long corner. The debts had now grown to £300,000, which was just about the total value of the house Karen and I had renovated. But the market by this time had plunged and nobody was buying. There were still some options though. My old sponsors Hawtal Whiting had offered me a highly-placed marketing position within their company, and one of the world's most successful racing car constructors confidentially approached me to become their managing director. I was flattered but declined. I realised that financially our life was in tatters but I had to say no because if I'd accepted a job then I would never make it to Formula One.

A guy called Richard Lloyd, who became a good friend, understood how I felt. My last race of 1990 had been in Mexico, driving a Porsche for Richard in the World Sports Prototype Championship. As an ex-driver himself, Richard knew that even saying the word 'job' was so painful to a racing driver that he referred to it only as 'J. O. B.'

So, once again, we stubbornly refused to accept defeat. Instead, we held our breath and risked everything on the slim hope of making it into Formula One.

A few months before Martin's wedding, Mark Blundell had become the fourth member of the Rat Pack to enter grand prix when he signed as team-mate to Martin Brundle at Brabham. This combination was a nightmare to Japanese TV commentators, as they struggled throughout the year to pronounce 'Brumdell and Blumble at Blab'am'. Julian Bailey, meanwhile, put a deal together to join Lotus and made his Formula One comeback as partner to Finnish debutant Mika Häkkinen. Julian was wondering how long it would last when, after signing his contract, he was presented with a set of race overalls that had the name 'Johnny Herbert' embroidered on them.

In Monaco Julian's car was to carry a sponsor's name along the engine cover that was far more unusual. Nobody had previously heard of a company called 'Ollocks', probably because there wasn't one. It had actually been City financier Ted Ball's tribute to a departed friend, and since it was his Landhurst Leasing company that was bailing out the troubled Lotus team, they were forced to accept it for that one race.

I had just finished three days of tyre testing for Goodyear in Atlanta when I decided to fly to Phoenix, Arizona, and meet up with the boys at the first grand prix of the 1991 season. I knew we'd have some fun, but I also wanted to meet this chap Ted Ball. Well, I didn't meet him, but I found out how to and I had our mutual friend, PR lady Jackie De Havas, arrange a meeting.

Once back in London, I arrived as scheduled and waited in the reception of Landhurst's offices for 45 minutes. Mr Ball still hadn't appeared, which I'd been told was pretty normal, but I was getting impatient. His secretary suddenly came in and said: 'Sorry, Perry, I'm getting fed up with this as well. Come with me.' So I followed her out of the building, down the street, and we turned into a pub where she pointed to Ted, who was standing at the bar with the boxing promoter Frank Warren. His face lit up from the other side of the room and he shouted: 'Perry McCarthy. It's *the* Perry McCarthy. My boy, come here!'

I thought this was quite funny and my mood lightened as I walked toward this thickset, charismatic 45-year-old. I was clearly there to get some backing because, quite simply, Ted was a very wealthy motorsport patron, but something about his look reinforced the stories I'd heard about his past. Now at close quarters, he smiled with opened arms, announced 'My boy!' and then threw a left punch. I saw it coming, so I turned, but it caught me hard on my upper right arm. 'Good boy. Good boy. You're fast... strong arms, boy.'

Fair enough, I thought. He obviously likes a 'big boy' greeting, but the greeting immediately went up a notch when he crouched like Joe Frazier and threw a combination of two left jabs, followed by a right hook. Surprised, I flicked into the same stance and blocked but I had no idea what was going on. Within 10 seconds of arriving, I'd found myself in a sparring match, in the middle of a pub, against the very guy I wanted to help me.

The blows were now coming in at head height and I was bobbing and weaving, desperately trying to defend against this maniac I'd never met before. I was hoping this would be over, fast. If I didn't try to hit my potential sponsor, then just maybe he'd settle for a points decision. The bout was something like 20 seconds old when he saw a gap and connected with a left to my jaw. It hurt. I drew back my fist to hit him and thought: 'Ollocks to the sponsorship!' Ted, however, knew the game was over and slammed forward to hold me in a bear-hug. He then kissed me on the cheek, told me we were gonna be great mates, put me down and then holding my arm up, he triumphantly re-announced to the bar 'This is *the* Perry McCarthy!'

He was right about that – I mean, who else could this happen to? For God's sake, all I wanted was some backing

so I could drive a poxy racing car! But Ted proved to be a great character. Our 'fight' was just his idea of messing around and we stayed all afternoon, chatting and drinking, while I kept an eye out for any sudden movements. There are a lot of Ted Ball stories, some good, some bad, but nearly all of them funny. He certainly wasn't everybody's cup of tea, but to his friends he was a generous, interesting and considerate chap. I liked him; he was different, and from that moment on, we did indeed become mates, up to and beyond the point where Landhurst Leasing crashed with debts of more than £40 million.

In the meantime, Ted had decided that owning two Formula One teams was enough of a commitment so, once again, I postponed my grand prix attack and returned to the States.

I took Karen out to see me race in Florida, but because of financial constraints, the team had also signed a second driver who brought money – and a pretty bad attitude. Within only eight laps, I blew this Miami circuit specialist into the weeds, but although I was second fastest to the Jaguar in the early session, a clogged filter prevented me from going for pole.

It didn't matter, though, because Albert Neon Jr. started the race and shortly afterwards he clogged the whole car into the wall. That was the last time Spice asked me to drive with a team-mate.

In Atlanta, I finished second with a new lap record and then scored seventh in Ohio. We then trekked down to Louisiana for the New Orleans 'Grand Prix Du Mardi Gras', where we arranged for some promotional girls from a bar/restaurant chain called *Hooters* to come along and create a bit of attention. They certainly did that because 'hooters' is American slang for 'titties', and there seemed to be a pert set of them everywhere I looked. Let's just say these girls will never drown.

I went out to qualify, fighting to keep my mind on the job, and when I returned, the team told me I'd set pole position. It was great news and the Hooters girls were jumping up and down with glee. I watched them closely and then I started jumping up and down with glee! In the race, I led from the start and I was determined to score a win around this twisting downtown street circuit. I pulled away and established a new track record, but the girls had inadvertently provided a clue to our fortunes when we retired with an engine problem and the dream went 'tits up'. I was so depressed that I just walked back to my hotel room, went to sleep, and tried to forget about the car, the engine and anything that looked like a melon.

It was all an uphill struggle against the factory teams, who were spending literally 20 times more than we were, but I reasoned that as long as I kept being a thorn in their side, it had to be worth the effort. David Tremayne at *Motoring News* was still making sure my adventures received a high profile, while my old mate John Wickham, who was now the Footwork Arrows Grand Prix team manager, was about to provide a major boost to my morale.

I was like a dog with two wotsits when I again returned to England and arrived at Silverstone in answer to John's invitation to help with some testing work. The Footwork trucks were all lined up behind the pit garage and the team mechanics were inside, busy preparing the beautiful Formula One car that was there, just waiting for *me*. Yes sir, I was about to be a Footwork Arrows driver.

Okay, it was just for the day but it was a fantastic opportunity. It had been 13 years since that fateful day when Les Ager had taken me from the music shop and over to Brands Hatch for my first drive on a circuit. Now, at last, I had a chance to put my foot down in a grand prix car. Part of me couldn't believe I was actually there: my manager Roger Cowman and I kept looking at the car and then at each other. We already had the biggest grins on our faces but I was positively beaming when the team's number one driver, ex-Ferrari star Michele Alboreto, came over and said: 'Hi, Perry. Welcome to Formula One.' He probably never realised how much that meant to me. Once I was strapped into the cockpit, we started the engine and I had the most incredible sense of fulfilment.

It was by far the fastest thing I'd ever driven. The performance was just phenomenal but I wasn't nervous and felt like I'd been driving the car for years. As I changed up through the gears, flat out with the Ford DFR engine screaming 'faster, Perry, faster', I knew more than ever that this was where I belonged. There would be no contract just yet, though, because this was only a systems check the team needed before their race in France. Nonetheless, it was great. I'd done what was asked and John Wickham was pleased. David Tremayne was also delighted and I knew he wanted to feature my test in the following week's Motoring News.

I couldn't wait to read about it, so I called him the day before the issue was on sale and asked him to fax me a copy of the story. I waited about 15 minutes for the fax to come through. Right below the large photo of me in action, my bold headline read: 'McCarthy tests Footwork'.

'That's great' I thought, but when I started reading the text, my mouth dropped in horror. I was quoted as saying: 'Yeah, well, the Footwork was all right, I suppose, but it's a shame I wasn't with a really good team like McLaren or something'. I stopped and read it again, but no, there it was, in black and white. This was like a nightmare and the public relations disaster continued with: 'I found it difficult to drive because the nerve damage in my leg from Formula Three has never got better and it's a big problem to me.'

Oh my God! I hadn't said any of these things. How could David, of all people, do this to me? I looked down in stunned disbelief at the report that would certainly end my career and I literally felt sick with worry. There just had to be some kind an explanation, so I called Motoring News immediately. It was 6pm on Monday, and the issue was close to press. 'Dave?' I said hesitantly. Suddenly, there was silence from him and the rest of the normally busy office. I hung on the line in frozen anticipation when suddenly they couldn't take it any more and I heard the whole newsroom explode into hysterical laughter. The fax had been a hastily-prepared spoof, I'd fallen for it big time, and now the rotten bunch of bastards were having a field day. Still, I was well overdue for a taste of my own medicine.

I tested several more times with the Footwork Arrows team and, apart from being valuable experience, it also provided other advantages. I could now go to an airport check-in and then request an upgrade because 'I'm a Formula One driver' and know, for a change, that I was only half lying.

When you travel a lot, upgrades become seriously important and I'll do anything to get one. I always wanted the same seat we've seen on the TV ads, where the guy reclines almost flat and shows us he can wiggle his toes. However, my flight tickets were always the cheapest available and put me with another 300 tormented souls way back in cattle class, where there's just about enough room to wiggle your ears. Other non-advertised pleasures in cattle class also include the 'mystery meat' food and the seven-hour psychological warfare over who gets the communal armrest.

Anyway, as I waited to fly back to the States for my next race, I felt lucky. I explained to the pretty girl at the desk how I was recovering from a leg injury I'd received in the Spanish Grand Prix and that I needed a good seat to rest because I'd been called out as a late replacement to save the British team's hopes in California. She went for this rubbish and I was upgraded all the way to first class! I was amused when I boarded with Sean Connery and we had a little chat. I asked him if he'd like to be my guest in Laguna Seca but he declined. I didn't press the point in case he strangled me with the wire in his wristwatch.

So, I landed in LA, home of the stars, and checked into a hotel. During my three-minute relationship with the vacant-looking receptionist, she noticed my 'Swedish' accent and of course went on to tell me that she wasn't actually a receptionist but that really she was an actress. Now there's a surprise. She then spotted my Footwork multi-sponsored sweatshirt and asked if I was in motor racing. She seemed impressed when I told her: 'I'm only a racing driver at the moment but really I'm an astronaut.'

I arrived for the first time at the Laguna Seca track and immediately set about learning the circuit. However, as I went to drive my rental car on to the pit straight, I was stopped by an official. 'Hey buddy, that's a no-can-do. We got course operatives on site preparation.' This basically meant a couple of blokes were putting up some banners.

'Okay, mate. What if I cycle round?' I enquired.

'Sorry, fella. It's a no-go situation.' What a wally. The way this guy talked, you'd think he was with NASA.

'All right mate,' I baited. 'What if I walk round and promise not to run anyone over?' He wasn't impressed with my sarcasm but as ever, I thought I was funny, which was handy given I was alone for so many journeys.

In fact, over the past 18 months, I'd spent about 330 hours in the air aboard 67 different flights, which I'd spent 115 hours waiting for. That's a lot for someone who isn't desperately keen on flying. The international leg of the journeys never used to worry me too much, but the palms of my hands would be covered in sweat on the internal flights. I just loved it when, screaming down the runway at 170mph, I'd read *USA Today* and find the airline I was on was actually bankrupt and they'd made 20 per cent worth of cutbacks in maintenance. And the landings... I'm sure some of our pilots were Vietnam veterans who kept having flashbacks. One time, going into Texas, I knew that if we'd hit the deck any harder, I would have been sitting next to the undercarriage.

Over at the beautiful Laguna Seca circuit in Monterey, I survived a crash in qualifying to finish back on the podium in third place, after a long fight with Geoff Brabham's Nissan. Then in the San Diego Grand Prix at Del Mar, I made a mistake while battling with Juan Fangio's Toyota, which cost us second place, and we finished fifth. That was the final race of the year and my time with Julian Randles and all the guys at Spice team had been great fun. But as I flew back to England, I knew the only thing definitely scheduled for 1992 was the repossession of our house. I was, as ever, praying that someone, somewhere, might give me a break.

Chapter 11

READY, STEADY, STOP

*Right on, baby! I was Andrea Moda Formula's new grand prix driver.
All I needed now was the correct competition licence and that
shouldn't be too difficult, should it?*

Although I longed for a chance in Formula One, there are times when the word 'desperate' has to be kept in proportion. Halfway through the year in which I had my last race for Spice USA, a terrible accident at Oulton Park resulted in tragic news. Paul Warwick, the 22-year-old younger brother of grand prix driver Derek, had been on the way to his fifth consecutive British Formula 3000 race win when he crashed at 140mph. A suspected front suspension failure caused him to leave the track and he was killed. The race was awarded to him posthumously and, later on, so was the championship. (By the end of the year none of the other drivers had succeeded in overhauling his incredible points tally.) But Paul will be remembered for more than his talent and achievements because he was a really nice guy. The funeral was, of course, a deeply sad affair. We were all very upset and I remember being choked at the sight of Derek, inside the church, in agony at the loss of his little brother. It's at times like this when I actually despise the sport of motor racing.

Back in the business side of motor racing, though, the Rat Pack were reaping mixed rewards. For Julian Bailey, seeing the name 'Johnny Herbert' on his own Lotus overalls the previous year had definitely been a sign of things to come because his sponsorship had run out after four races. And it was actually Little 'un who replaced him, to begin a four-year term with the team. Grumpy, who had finished sixth at Imola, then went to race sports cars in Japan, but later returned home to start a career in touring cars. Mega Mark Blundell, meanwhile, was also out of grand prix, but he stayed close and signed as McLaren's test driver. However, mid-way through the year, Mega drove for Peugeot in the famous Le Mans 24 hour sports car race and came away even more Mega than normal: along with Derek Warwick and Yannick Dalmas, he won.

So with Martin Donnelly on the sidelines, that left just Damon Hill and me still looking for a ride, and at the beginning of 1992 we were the only members of the Rat Pack who hadn't driven in a grand prix. Damon and I were friends from our time in Formula Ford and it was his future wife Georgie who taught me to pronounce his name as 'Day-mon' as opposed to my cockney-sounding 'Daymun'. Other people (including Martin Donnelly, who was his team-mate for one and a half seasons) frequently called him Damien.

If it was Damien (as in the kid with the mark of the devil in *The Omen* trilogy), that would probably explain a couple of evil moves he's pulled on me, such as the time I was over-taking him for second place in a Formula Three race at Silverstone. I'd gained a good slingshot from the previous corner, and as I went past at 140mph, I couldn't resist teasing him, by waving goodbye. Damon, however, didn't see the funny side and promptly barged me off the track. I was pretty pissed off about it at the time, although it was my fault for being stupid. It taught me a lesson, though: never confuse Damon Hill the racing driver with Damon Hill the mate. Damon is a fiercely determined guy who takes his job very seriously, but as a pal, I've always thought of him as a most considerate chap. When he beat me to the Footwork 3000 drive, for instance, he was at pains to keep me motivated.

He is quite a private man who often keeps his cards close to his chest, which is why we nicknamed him Secret Squirrel. However, he has asked my advice on many things in the past, but being an intelligent bloke, probably then did exactly the opposite – like the time I told him to stop waiting on a decision from Williams and sign instead for Ligier. That advice would have cost him 21 grand prix wins and a World Championship.

Whenever I think of Damon, though, I think of his humour. He has a very quick, dry wit, and when it's accompanied by some quizzical facial expressions he reminds me of John Cleese in *Monty Python's Flying Circus*. But when he has his sensible head on, he is still good company and in conversation he has a calm, clear and rational view of the business of motor racing.

Damon's past has been well documented but the death of his father Graham (and five members of Graham's racing team) in an aircraft accident left his mother Bette to raise both him and his two sisters alone and on a budget. No doubt, this tragedy so early on played a role in developing a man who really can absorb huge amounts of pressure in both his personal and professional life. His later upbringing, though, may have also taught him about the value of money and especially how not to spend it. In the junior formula, getting a round of drinks out of him could be like trying to pull your leg out of a bear trap. Difficult. Nowadays, Damon could probably buy the entire pub and maybe even the brewery, because he earned a fortune from winning grand prix races – even before he went on to make Britain proud by beating Michael Schumacher to the 1996 World Championship.

However, before his current tally of four children, and before he was team-mate to luminaries such as Alain Prost, Ayrton Senna, Nigel Mansell and Jacques Villeneuve, Damon Hill was hanging on, just waiting for a chance. This finally came in the middle of 1992, when he signed for Brabham: even though the team had definitely seen better days, he was now in Formula One.

A short time before Damon signed, my own options were looking non-existent. More and more teams were withdrawing from the IMSA series and the championship itself was falling apart. I couldn't get a ride in IndyCar or Formula 3000, because they needed money, and a court order had arrived at home asking for the house back. It really was all beginning to look completely hopeless and by mid-March, the season had once again started without me. We still had a TV at home so I was able to watch the races but later that month I received a phone call from Eddie Jordan's solicitor, Fred Rodgers.

I'd known Fred for a number of years: he was an absolute motor racing enthusiast who also had interests and connections outside EJ's team. The conversation went like this: 'Hi, Perry. It's Fred. How would you like to be a Formula One driver?'

I checked my diary. April: bank foreclosing. May: possible phone disconnection. June: house repossession. It took me about half a second to say: 'Yes, Fred. I'd love to.'

I was on red alert, the ball was rolling, 'engine room – full speed ahead'. Fred told me a new Italian team wanted to replace both its drivers and I should go and see their man in Banbury, a chap called Duffy Sheardown. By the time I got to Banbury, any pretence of calm assurance had disintegrated. I knew there was a chance – a real good chance – and I stared at poor Duffy like a dog looking at a bar of chocolate. Duffy got the point. He knew about my career and he knew I was determined, but although he wanted me, I would have to wait for a decision from the team owner, Andrea Sassetti.

As with nearly everything in my life, it had yet again been an unusual set of circumstances that led me to the door of a grand prix drive. Andrea Sassetti was a young, wealthy Italian who, with no previous experience, wanted to own a Formula One team. So over the winter of 1991, he employed Alex Caffi and Enrico Bertaggia as drivers, but a decision to buy the uncompetitive Coloni team was his first mistake.

After this purchase, they arrived in South Africa for the opening grand prix of 1992 but were disqualified because they hadn't paid the $100,000 deposit needed for a new team entering Formula One. Enzo Coloni, in a deal that Dick Turpin would have been proud of, had apparently sold him only the pile of junk known as the team's equipment and not, as imagined, the team's entry.

Soon after, Andrea decided he didn't want the Coloni car anyway. So Duffy took him to see Nick Wirth, whose Simtek design company owned the drawings for a Formula One project previously undertaken on behalf of BMW. A deal was struck immediately after Andrea literally emptied a plastic sack of lire on to Nick's desk. His band of mechanics stayed on at the Simtek factory to build the car in time for the second round of the World Championship.

During the evening, though, they received a bit of outside assistance. From six o'clock onward, the workshop was filled with about 30 guys from other teams who were moonlighting for £150 a shift. They all arrived directly from their day

jobs and since they were still dressed in McLaren, Williams, Lotus and Benetton shirts, the place looked like a grand

prix employment bureau. It was all too late though. Sassetti's cars were at the Mexican Grand Prix but were withdrawn and, in the end, he cited 'freight delays' as extenuating circumstances.

It was during this time that the drivers had been less than complimentary about the team's efforts. So Andrea fired them. The search for replacements was given to Fred and Nigel Mansell's ex-manager Mike Francis. Mike sought advice from his contacts in Formula One and apparently my name kept coming up. Fred, meanwhile, didn't suggest anyone except me. David Tremayne also called Sassetti and bullied him. So the vote was in and with fewer than 10 days to go before the Brazilian Grand Prix, Fred made the call I'd been dreaming of for years.

'Everybody agrees. Andrea wants you. Perry, you're a grand prix driver!'

I was just ecstatic. Those words were like a fanfare heralding my arrival to the big-time. I had an overwhelming feeling of achievement because I knew I had beaten the odds and I was in. After all this time, I was actually in! Me, Perry McCarthy, had now been chosen as one of the elite in the sport I had set out to conquer so long ago.

Okay, the team could have been *slightly* better, and I wasn't going to be paid, and I did have to find my own expenses, and... well, who cares? I had a chance and at least I didn't have to take several million dollars worth of sponsorship to pay for it. Karen and I called some friends, including Bob Tappin who came over with a few bottles of champagne,

then we cranked the hi-fi up loud and celebrated. We just couldn't stop smiling. Right on, baby! I was Andrea Moda Formula's new grand prix driver. All I needed now was the correct competition licence and that shouldn't be too difficult, should it?

For years, my competition licences had been issued by the UK's governing body, the RACMSA (Royal Automobile Club

Motorsports Association) and I'd held their top grade, the International A, for the past five seasons. However, the MSA had no direct control over a licence unique to grand prix and I needed one immediately – the Super-A, more commonly known as the super licence. Granting this licence is the sole decision of the Formula One Commission, but after I investigated the process I became worried – terrified, even – that my stop-start career wouldn't meet their requirements. Under the regulations I needed to be the current Formula Three champion of Britain, France, West Germany, Italy, Japan or South America (which I wasn't) or I should have competed in a whole season of International Formula 3000 (which I hadn't).

With qualifying in Brazil scheduled for 3 April, I needed help fast. But on the Saturday before the race weekend, the top man in Formula One, Bernie Ecclestone, told me he didn't rate my chances of securing a super licence too highly. Seeing the whole thing disappearing before my eyes, I kept talking and finally Bernie advised me to approach the RACMSA and tell them that I had his blessing to do so. I

was on the brink of disaster, but at least this was a straw to cling to.

On Monday, 30 March, the race and speed executive of the MSA, Peter Todd, went in hard and lobbied FISA, the world governing body of motor racing, on my behalf. Peter and other major players at the MSA felt I'd done enough to be a grand prix driver and were right behind me. There was a flurry of internal calls within the Paris offices of FISA, while back in Billericay the waiting was unbearable.

Karen was also getting edgy, mainly because I was being a bloody nuisance. I'd flit around and play the piano for two minutes; watch TV for five minutes, flicking the channels every eight seconds; turn the hi-fi on, then off; torment the kids; and then leave them wound-up as I went to play football in the garden. Then I'd return and ask her for the 50th time what she thought of our chances, after which I'd go through the whole routine again.

By midday on Tuesday, 31 March, Karen was close to shooting me when we heard that FISA representatives had faxed both the RACMSA and my team owner, Andrea Sassetti, with fantastic news. They decided that I was eligible for a super licence and I let out a major sigh of relief. Immediately after, Karen decided I could live. I decided to get busy.

The next 24 hours was mayhem. My fax streamed out messages of congratulations, the phone rang continuously and I was thrilled to give interviews to TV, radio and members of the press. Somewhere in the midst of my media glory, I called Karen's mother Val, to thank her for the latest batch of clothes she'd made for the children, and then I phoned my cousin Gary Denham, who lent me £800 for the airfare to Brazil!

The following day, Wednesday 1 April, my destination was South America and I proudly boarded the Varig flight to Sao Paulo as Britain's latest grand prix driver. Reality came back, however, when my economy ticket placed me at the back

of the plane and I was squashed like a lemon between two enormous women. Just before take off, they started attacking their personal supply of cakes and eyed me suspiciously in case I lunged for a chocolate éclair. At the rate they were munching, I thought they'd probably expand and crush me by mid Atlantic, so I called the flight attendant over. His English was almost non-existent but I held up a year-old photo of myself in a race suit and with the aid of sign language I told him: 'Me, Formula One driver. This for you!'

Brazilians love motor racing and his face lit up. 'Grand prix. You!' he beamed.

But as he reached for his present, I pulled it back and pointed to the head of the plane. 'Me go up there!'

He hesitated. 'You have... photos for my friends?'

'No problem, sunshine!'

We agreed on four and he then escorted me to the comfort of first class, which allowed me to sleep without the fear of being eaten alive.

On Thursday, 2 April, I arrived at the Interlargos circuit and was introduced to Andrea Sassetti for the first time. He was tall with dark hair and, in contrast to other Formula One team owners, was wearing wraparound sunglasses, a black motorcycle leather jacket, jeans and pointed cowboy boots. He could have been an extra from *Rebel without a cause*. Later, a representative from FISA came to our pit garage and I was delighted to be awarded the document I'd been fighting for – my very own super licence. Andrea paid the appropriate fee and I slipped into my race suit.

Everything was so exciting. I had my licence, and in accordance with the regulations, I went for the 'driver weigh-in' and performed a timed cockpit escape test. The further I went through this routine, the more I felt like a proper, real life, honest to God, grand prix driver, and most of the people I knew in F1 came along to congratulate me. Ken Tyrrell came to the front of our pit and stood there smiling with his arms open wide in a 'So you've finally done it' kind of way, and that just made my day. It was a lovely gesture. Yes Ken, yes *everybody*, I was an F1 driver and I was ready to race on the same track as Ayrton Senna, Nigel Mansell and Michael Schumacher.

It was just all too good to be true. And so it proved. My bubbly mood suddenly turned to massive anxiety when race director Roland Bruynseraede came over to ask me what time was I leaving the circuit. Then he added: 'Please don't leave the circuit until I return.'

'Why does he want me to stay at the circuit?' I asked myself. It had to spell trouble because he couldn't be that desperate for a dinner date. Sure enough, Roland returned at six o'clock and asked to see my licence. I felt sick. 'Why?' I asked.

But he repeated: 'Just give me your licence please, Perry.'

I had it in my pocket but said: 'No!' I had a horrible feeling that I wouldn't see it again.

'Give it to me now, please!' I really had no choice and, hardly daring to breathe, I cautiously handed it over and waited for some kind of bombshell. It didn't take long, and when it came, it was more like a nuclear warhead. Roland looked embarrassed as he said that there had been a mistake, that my licence should not have been issued, and that it was now rescinded. I stared at him open mouthed. The ramifications of this hit me like a blow to the stomach. I couldn't enter the grand prix and Andrea Moda would have to replace me for future races.

After a career in Formula One spanning about seven hours, I was out. I felt furious. Distraught with disappointment I was shouting my head off at Roland – who is a really nice guy and one of the key people within FISA who had helped me get the licence. I didn't understand how this could happen to me. Everything I wanted was wrapped up in that licence and it had just been taken away. All those years had gone down the drain. We'd lost everything in trying to get to Formula One and now *this*, just when I thought I'd made it. My finest hour turned into my worst nightmare. It was cruel.

Over the next couple of hours, I desperately tried to hold myself together but it was no good. This little episode had torn my heart out and I walked to the back of the garages, out of sight, and cried uncontrollably. It was a complete emotional collapse. I hated myself for it but, standing there alone, thousands of miles from home, I was in despair.

After a while, I started thinking clearly again. Then Johnny Herbert, who'd heard the news, came and put his arm around me. When I saw *his* eyes fill with water, I smiled and said with a lump in my throat: 'Don't *you* start John, otherwise I'll crack again!'

The following morning I was back to being Mad Dog. I was ready to fight. I knew it wasn't over because I wouldn't let it be over. I called the RACMSA, told them what had happened and they started faxing FISA. I called Karen, Roger Cowman, Fred Rodgers, I called everyone, and if I'd had their number, I would have called the RSPCA as well and reported FISA for cruelty to dumb animals! I then arrived back at the circuit to find that the team hadn't finished building my car, so I wouldn't have been driving anyway. However, the car that was ready, driven by Roberto Moreno, managed only two laps before something broke, and it failed to qualify. I put all that to one side, though, because my immediate job was to get that licence back.

I went to see Bernie Ecclestone again. DT had been with me in the Moda garage that morning when Bernie walked in. David demanded to know why I hadn't got a licence. Bernie was kind enough to listen and it was clear when he replied that it was 'all a mess-up', or words to that effect, that he was on my side. We all talked for a bit and DT was pushing my case very hard.

Now I positioned myself outside the circuit office Bernie was using. It was like waiting outside the headmaster's study, as I had done on numerous occasions as a schoolboy. After a while, the door opened. Bernie looked at me thoughtfully and then invited me in. I was about to find out if I was going to be expelled and my heart was beating hard. I was face to face with Mr Ecclestone: if I had one chance, then it would come from him – right now.

He knew all about my situation, but when I asked him directly if I could have a new licence, the knot in my stomach tightened as he said: 'No'. He told me the licence should not have been issued by FISA and that only the Formula One Commission could decide on these matters and he believed they would say that I should have had a year in F3000.

There was a small silence. My chin and bottom lip started quivering and I was struggling not to crack. I had to go on the attack fast, firstly to save my career, and secondly so that I didn't start bloody crying again. I wasn't shouting but I did tell Bernie that it wasn't fair, that I hadn't raced a full year in F3000 because of money, and that I'd raced and beaten 11 of the drivers currently in grand prix. I told him about the house and how Karen and I had struggled, but above all, I told him I was good enough to be in Formula One. I think Bernie liked the fact that I wouldn't give up and he said: 'Okay, Perry. They tell me you're a fighter, here's what you do... '

Mr Ecclestone, boss of the Formula One Constructors Association (FOCA) and FIA vice president of promotional affairs, then told me that there was a provision for 'exceptional circumstances', where my results and maybe my reputation could be judged by the 13-member F1 Commission. Five of these seats were held by team principals, and Bernie said that if I convinced them to vote for me, then he would have a chat with the others. Well, Bernie is a formidable character and when he has a 'chat' with someone, they normally see his point of view. I felt as though I'd just grabbed a breath after being trapped underwater: I had another chance. I wasn't finished yet and now I knew *exactly* what I had to do.

The meeting finished and Bernie showed me to the door but, as he opened it, there stood a Brazilian gentleman who was waiting for his own moment with the most powerful man in grand prix. As luck would have it, he was one of the *others*; he was a voting member of the F1 Commission, and on seeing this chap (who I'll call 'Guido' because I can't remember his name) Bernie signalled me to wait a moment. I was then fascinated by the following conversation.

'Guido, this is Mr McCarthy and Mr McCarthy has a problem.'

'Yes, Mr Ecclestone. I know.'

'Well, Guido, Mr McCarthy needs votes for his licence. How would you vote for him?'

I could see the look of fear on Guido's face. He wanted to please Bernie but what should he say? Maybe it was some procedural test Bernie was setting him so he threw the dice, but his answer sounded more like a question: 'Er... well, I would talk to my colleagues... here at the circuit and... discuss the situation... and make a joint decision?'

He smiled weakly, almost willing Bernie to say 'correct' but instead, I could almost hear him squeal as Bernie patiently said: 'No, Guido. How would *you* vote for him?'

Guido had got it wrong and his eyes were pleading: 'Give me a clue – a wink, a nod, anything!' He changed tact and nervously went in for a second attempt: 'Er... I would speak to other members of the commission... and others in the pit lane... to hear their thoughts on Mr McCarthy?'

A short silence followed, and Guido remained static with the growing realisation that he had crashed once again. Even though my own problems were far from over, I was darkly amused to see someone else suffering, but then Mr Ecclestone gave up trying to navigate him toward the answer and said directly: 'Look, Guido. *I want you* to vote for him!'

The Brazilian instantly smiled in relief. His torment was over. He now knew the answer and he almost laughed when he put out his arms and said: 'No problem!'

As I left the office, I was convinced Bernie Ecclestone was now trying to help me and I walked toward the pit lane determined to keep my side of the bargain. This newcomer to grand prix, now with one-thirteenth of a super licence, was about to pay a personal visit to Frank Williams at Williams, Ron Dennis at McLaren, Flavio Briatore at Benetton, Giancarlo Minardi at Minardi, and the Italian lawyer Marco Piccinnini at Ferrari. I had a lot of talking to do.

Meanwhile, the British press had gone ballistic about the whole affair and were pushing FISA for answers. FISA, however, issued a statement that must have been inspired by Hans Christian Andersen, because they said I never had a super licence. This was a fairy tale, and someone, somewhere, was covering up for the procedural mistake in issuing it.

As the motor racing journals were to point out relentlessly, though, it wasn't a mistake to give me the licence: it was the regulations that were at fault because under the current rules, the likes of Ferrari's Gilles Villeneuve might not have been granted an application. Conversely, we'd recently seen a couple of moneyed but real no-hopers get in just because they'd had that crucial year in F3000. My plight had brought this matter to light and Mr Ecclestone pledged that the procedure would be significantly revised for 1993.

Back in England, though, I had to sit and wait for the decision of the F1 Commission. It was a tense time but in the best traditions of a courtroom drama, I was supported by a great defence team. David Tremayne at *Motoring News*, Joe Saward at *Autosport*, Peter Todd at the MSA and many others were all working hard on my case. I'd done my bit with the team principals and Bernie was no doubt true to his word in talking with the other commission members.

I just couldn't be sure of the verdict, though, and for the moment, I had to be content with my one vote from 'Guido', who was probably still in Brazil trying to work out who I was...

I didn't think I could have been under any more pressure but it transpired that there was another little story going on in the background over in Italy. Apparently, one of Andrea Sassetti's original drivers, Enrico Bertaggia, had found serious sponsorship and he wanted his drive back. So with multiple zeros pulsing before his eyes, Andrea had kindly faxed Max Mosley, the president of FISA, and told him not to bother with my renewed application.

Jesus! What next? I mean, give me some more aggravation please. Just shoot me. No hang on a moment – the electric chair. Yeah, give me the electric chair; I can handle it.

As promised, Max called me at home. I was on edge: a negative message from Max would spell the end and there would be no second chances. I asked him if the Sassetti story was true and when he confirmed it was, my grip on the receiver tightened. But then he gave me the news I'd been waiting for. He and Bernie had voted for me, the teams had given a thumbs-up, and the other members had followed suit. I had the licence and it would be reissued to me at the Spanish Grand Prix.

'Thank God for that,' I gasped. 'But what about Sassetti?' Well, dear old Andrea had already upset quite a few people and Max sounded amused when he told me that Andrea Moda Formula had already had its quota of driver changes, so as I now had a super licence, that was it. Sassetti couldn't change.

This time it was done. This time I was an accredited grand prix driver but even though it had been a test of nerves, I had in fact been very lucky. If FISA hadn't made their original mistake, then my application through the correct channels would have been turned down flat. It was only the emotion generated by my predicament that had forced the licence decision in my favour, and then having endured all the fuss, FISA made sure I kept my place in the Andrea Moda Formula team.

For the second time in my career the driver change regulations had helped me, but if Roger Cowman had previously winced when he was forced to use me as his reserve driver back in Formula 3000 (instead of another driver who had £100,000 in sponsorship), then my new team manager must have been spitting blood. By having to reject Bertaggia, he had a driver who was proving to be *one million dollars* more expensive. Unlike Roger though, Andrea didn't see the funny side!

Chapter 12

WHATEVER IT TAKES

*I tried to calm myself down from the morning's adventures
that had included my own version of Home Alone, multiple
near-misses on the road, and near cremation – and it wasn't even
quarter past eight yet.*

A week later, I flew to Italy for the team's first test at Imola. I
hadn't been invited but I went anyway. Andrea's face creased
to a frown when he saw me, but he quickly regrouped and
activated a big smile. I wasn't sure which expression I preferred;
the frown was disappointing but the smile worried me.

The car completed several laps, but they still had only
one running and it was again occupied by my team-mate.
Nonetheless, I was excited to see our all-black beast pass the
pits at speed. For Roberto Moreno the experience was nothing
new. Although he was fresh from a year at Benetton, he'd
previously worked with several of the small teams and he
warned me: 'Perry, don't to expect too much.' Point taken, but
one of the small things I did expect as a Formula One racing
driver was to actually drive.

It became clear that it wasn't going to happen that day,
though, especially when the old girl broke down. With nothing to
do, I went to have a cup of coffee with Mark Blundell, who was
testing for McLaren. We sat alone in the Marlboro hospitality
suite but the atmosphere had been badly contaminated by
Marky-boy's stomach. Mark had obviously eaten something that
was out for revenge and he was now able to pass wind at will.

He loved demonstrating this and I knew when a new deposit of gas was coming because he'd give an evil little grin and then whoosh! It was really bad – just one stage short of germ warfare – and I was beginning to feel sick when who should walk in but none other than the current World Champion, Ayrton Senna.

Ayrton began his approach to our table smiling but almost immediately his progress slowed, his nose twitched and his mouth started to turn down. He must have risked one last gulp of air as he quickly shook hands and darted off to a glass-partitioned room. He looked out a couple of times to check we were still alive, while we were trying to stop laughing.

I was also watching him, though. Ayrton was checking a new delivery of overalls, but somebody had forgotten to include balaclavas and this sent him off the Richter scale. Item by item, the stuff was launched across the room at high speed and Ayrton, who was totally fluent in the darker side of the English language, called the miscreant every name under the sun and then stomped out to find him. Mark, who was building up to another whoosh, just looked at me and said: 'He gets like that sometimes!' He then let out a little grin and I quickly went in the same direction as Senna.

Senna's balaclava strop reminded me of an incident in 1986, when I had my balaclava stolen from my road car the night before a race. All of my racing equipment disappeared in the break-in, so it looked like I was not going to be able to compete in the Croix en Ternois round of the French Formula Three championship. However, I was saved by two drivers from another team who, between them, lent me a set of gloves, boots, overalls and a crash helmet.

It was pouring with rain for the race and there was a mad dash into the first corner with a group of drivers I didn't know. I dived for a gap but made contact with someone who then went off. Within the same lap, I'd rubbed wheels with someone else and he went into the wall as well. Shortly afterwards I was also out of the race due to an engine misfire. So I got changed and once the race had finished, I walked over to return the race clothing that had been so kindly lent to me. But as I approached, both the drivers and all their mechanics were standing together and looked at me in stony silence. Then, just behind them, I noticed two rather damaged cars. It dawned on me that these were the very guys I'd hit on the first lap. It was bloody embarrassing. They'd helped me, and in exchange I'd taken out their entire team. As I delicately placed the kit next to their pile of wreckage, I grinned sheepishly, said 'merci, monsieurs' and retreated.

Later I joined Eddie Jordan and Wham! pop star Andrew Ridgeley at a golf club in Le Touquet where, after a few beers, we decided to pool our combined musical talent. I played the piano, Eddie played the spoons and, to the envy of several million fans, Eddie and I listened closely as Andrew sang. We had a great time, but considering Andrew had made millions from singing, he remains to this day the luckiest person I have ever met in my whole life. I stayed around him a while, hoping some of it might rub off on me.

I was hoping for some luck when I arrived in Barcelona to drive in the Spanish Grand Prix. I received a similarly warm welcome from the Formula One pitlane as I had in Brazil and everyone seemed genuinely pleased that my problems were at last over. My racecar still wasn't ready but they were working hard to complete it, so at least I had a chance of making my much-awaited debut in the following morning's pre-qualifying session.

Pre-qualifying was different from official qualifying. Back then the regulations for official qualifying allowed up to 30 cars to be on the track at the same time and during the two days leading up to a grand prix, these cars tried to set a fast time and claim a good slot among only 26 starting positions. So, usually, there would be four non-qualifiers.

However, the addition of Andrea Moda on the grid had raised the total number of car entries to 32, and this activated the embarrassing spectacle of pre-qualifying. Six cars now had to compete in a 'knock-out' session held at 8am on the Friday before the race. As newcomers, two of these were from our team and the other four were from the two worst performing teams of the previous year. The fastest four of our group of misfits would then be allowed back to compete in the official qualifying sessions, thus whittling the entry back down to 30 cars. The two slowest cars, however, would be finished there and then. It was the end of their grand prix weekend.

I was well aware of this system, but as our immediate competition would only be two cars from the Fondmetal team and two from the cash-starved Brabham team, it might just be possible to clear the first hurdle. To do this, though, my car had to be reliable and I needed to be fresh and on-form. At 11pm on Thursday night I was still with the team in our garage and my car wasn't finished. I was tired and I'd been begging for someone to take me to the hotel for the past four hours, but now, finally and reluctantly, Andrea arranged for a mechanic to drive me to my executive penthouse suite on the other side of Barcelona.

When I arrived, I realised my dream of luxury was a trifle premature. The place looked more exhausted than I did. The lobby could be described as early Dracula and when I entered my room, I noticed there were five beds more than I expected. But who cares? It was midnight, I needed sleep, and I was thinking about my big day. As I seemed to be sharing with most of the team, I didn't bother booking a wake-up call because I'd already been assured that someone would wake me at six.

The following morning I woke unaided to find the room fairly well lit from the daylight that had pierced through the paper-thin curtains and I looked around uneasily. I was alone. None of the beds had been slept in. My pulse started to race as

I called reception to ask the time. 'The time, sir, is 7.25am.'

Seven twenty-five? *Seven twenty-five*! No way. Please God, no! I was supposed to be out on the bloody track at eight, and here I was in bed, on the other side of Barcelona, with no rental car. Why hadn't somebody called me? I knew why, I knew bloody why! Those stupid bloody maniacs never came back to the room, that's why! Andrea had obviously had them working on the cars all night and it had slipped their mind that they might need a silly, inconsequential thing like a driver.

Oh my God, I've made it to Formula One, I've had a licence problem, but because everyone thinks I'm so serious, Bernie has backed me, Max has backed me... the other teams... all the press... And to say thank you to them, I'm not even going to turn up!

The next few minutes were a blur. The only person who could have got washed and dressed faster was Superman. I ran downstairs to the foyer in a blind panic. The guy on reception informed me he couldn't get me a cab for at least half an hour and I began a desperate search for someone from my team, from any team, from Battersea Dogs Home, anyone. I needed a ride to the circuit and I needed it immediately! Oh God, help me, please!

Well, it seems like He did. The thing with old God, though, is that when it comes to me, He's got a pretty wacky sense of humour. Just as I thought I was finished, I got seriously lucky when Andrea's brother walked through the main door. He'd just got back from some nightclub and looked like death but it was a total miracle. It was my only chance and we had 25 minutes to complete a journey that on a grand prix weekend could take over an hour.

Halfway across town I needed another miracle, because I thought I was going to die. Andrea's brother was now on a total mission to get me there on time. He was flat out at 90mph to 100mph through the city streets and going straight over red traffic lights at the same speed. I was numb with fear. It was insane, this situation was insane, my bloody life was insane. I gripped the seat and prayed while trying to avoid eye contact with my driver, who I thought was the devil incarnate. Unbelievably, though, the crazy bastard did it and, with smoke seeping from the brakes and radiator and a knocking sound coming from the engine, he dropped me off outside the Formula One paddock with about two minutes to spare.

I glanced back to the poor little rental car which had given up its life for my career, and then ran like hell toward the truck. Once inside, I scrambled into my race kit and, with eyes darting wildly like a savage who'd just discovered fire, I burst into the garage. It was 8.05 and there was no time to talk to the mass of press who had been waiting for me to arrive, or indeed, to strangle that bastard Andrea for leaving me abandoned in the hotel. I jumped into the car then signalled my wonderful team that I was ready to go on to the circuit and become a grand prix driver. That, of course, would have been too easy.

The engine wouldn't start, so they immediately sprayed a highly combustible solution called Quick-start into the air intake directly behind my head. But they used too much and the whole lot ignited which sent a jet of flame around my new crash helmet that had been painted in the colours of Gilles Villeneuve. I screamed in surprise, released my belts, and pushed myself forward to avoid being fried. Someone threw a blanket over me and thankfully the fire was out quickly.

I wasn't sure how much more I could take but I refastened my harness and this time my British-made Judd V10 engine coughed and spluttered into life. I selected first gear and tried to calm myself down from the morning's adventures that had included my own version of *Home Alone*, multiple near-misses on the road, and near cremation – and it wasn't even quarter past eight yet.

I pulled out from the garage and drove on to the pit lane. I could see the track ahead of me and with a thrill of expectation I accelerated towards it. But as I crossed the white line marking the start of the circuit, the engine once again coughed, spluttered, stalled, and I slowly rolled to a halt. And that was it. My debut was finished. I couldn't restart the car because there was no onboard ignition system and even though I was still close enough to talk to the team, they weren't allowed to pull me back because I was *officially* on the circuit. All I could do was get out and stare back down the pit lane in disbelief. At a distance of 20 metres I, Perry McCarthy, had set a new Formula One record – the shortest ever attempt at qualifying for a grand prix!

Roberto Moreno made it a clean sweep for Andrea Moda Formula when his car broke down after about three laps. I left the circuit in the company of Julian Bailey and moved out of my multi-guest room. Over the next two days, Julian and I based ourselves at a five-star executive suite that had been booked and paid for by a non-arriving Ted Ball. We then hit about every bar we could in the beautiful city of Barcelona. We had a good time but it was of little consolation because, from my first two grands prix, I had now completed a grand total of zero laps. A lot of people say motor racing's dangerous, but it isn't the way I do it. I did, however, want a little more danger because for the San Marino Grand Prix in Italy I was hoping that I'd actually get to drive out on the circuit – just like the other Formula One drivers do.

At last I got my wish. I did eight laps but then I pulled in with a differential fault. Roberto and I again failed to pre-qualify, but at least this time I had attempted to put the car through its paces. However, if I thought the fast and flowing corners of Imola had been an experience, then the next venue, to a newcomer in a tricky car, was nothing short of frightening. The Monaco Grand Prix is the jewel in the World Championship crown, but maybe it should be called the eye of the needle because although the circuit is beautiful, it's difficult and hard to get around; just like Karen.

Now, I don't want to become a bore on this subject, but leading up to the race, our money dramas were as bad as ever. While the other drivers were busy skiing or testing, or doing all the things F1 drivers should be doing, I had to find a way of financing my trip to Monte Carlo. And to make matters worse, I had promised to take Karen with me. It was, in fact, the promise I'd made to her after Fred had called to tell me Andrea Moda had accepted me. To be precise, it was the promise I'd made after I'd drunk two bottles of wine following Fred's call. KJ's power of recall in such situations is dazzling and so is her ability to remember and randomly mention just about anything I'd ever done wrong. So the deal was done and she was coming.

The deal proved easier than expected when I called a friend of mine, Gary Howell, who was involved with the motor racing tour operator Chequers Travel. He suggested that if I acted as a courier on their behalf at Gatwick Airport and gave a speech to their group during the race weekend, then he'd provide our flights and accommodation. I'd already done a similar thing to pay for Imola (with an American company called Grand Prix Tours), so I agreed.

A week later, I was standing around the check-in area at Gatwick, wearing my Chequers Travel badge and handing out tickets. I was busy greeting about 50 different people who needed a little direction and my patter went something like this: 'Mr and Mrs Brown? Yes! Good morning. Here are your tickets. Please check in here and then go through to the departure lounge and make your way to Gate 15 where the flight will be leaving in one hour.' Not one of them had the faintest clue why I was really there. However, during my little performance, one middle-aged lady politely asked if I was going with them.

'Oh yes, madam. I have to be there,' I smiled.

'Why's that, then?' she enquired.

'Well, I'm one of the grand prix drivers.'

Her eyes lit up: 'Oooh! Do you all do this?'

'Absolutely, madam. Nigel Mansell's just over there with Page & Moy!'

Karen and I looked at each other and grinned. Sure, this whole situation wasn't ideal and, yes, our home problems were a nightmare, but we had to remember what it was all about. We'd held on and come through, and even though Andrea Moda was turning out to be a nightmare, we still had a chance. But more to the point, our journey so far had been an adventure and it was important to try to live it, to enjoy the moment, and grab a laugh whenever or wherever it presented itself. No matter what my Italians had in store for me, I was determined that Karen would have a great weekend and forget about home, debt and reality for at least the next few days.

We landed in Nice and joined our group of enthusiasts on a coach for the 40-minute journey to Monaco. I love a captive audience and, en route, told our party a string of jokes and motor racing stories. By the time we arrived, nobody was left in any doubt that I did more than hand out tickets. In fact, just about one hour later in the hotel, I talked one of them into sponsoring me for a few pounds in exchange for a small sticker on my crash helmet, and this provided our spending money.

Karen joined me as I walked around the circuit, mingled among the super-rich, breezed past the yachts in the harbour and then... tried to work out just what the hell we were doing there.

Unfortunately, I had the same feeling after qualifying. My efforts lasted a total of three laps, during which I had scared the hell out of myself. The team still hadn't made a proper seat for me, so I had taken a beating inside the cockpit, but I kept my foot down and desperately tried to remember where the next corner was.

I knew the tunnel was taken flat because I'd seen it on TV, so I did just that. I took it flat out on my first lap but as I came back into daylight at 170mph, I was being bounced around so badly, I had double vision and I vividly remember speeding downhill toward the tyre barrier wondering if I should turn left or right. Anyway, I was called back to the pits and that was my run for the day. Three bloody laps! I was beginning to feel like I was on some new kind of Chequers Travel deal, a kind of Gold Class option for clients: '*Fly* with us to Monaco. *Stay* with us in a top hotel. *Eat* with us in nice restaurants. Then, following breakfast, *drive* three laps of the circuit in an out-of-date Formula One car. And then *watch* the race from your room... Yours for £900.'

However, a miracle was about to happen because Roberto had an uninterrupted session and he brilliantly qualified for the race. I was delighted. I hoped this would mean that in future the team would run two cars correctly and give me a proper opportunity. Well, I could hope...

I shrugged off my latest non-qualification and joined Ayrton Senna, Nigel Mansell, Michael Schumacher and the rest of the drivers for a group photo shoot. It felt good standing as part of this elite gang and it was like a school photograph: 'The class of '92'. Okay, maybe I was the class mascot.

Then I took Karen over to a local café where I gave a speech to the Chequers Travel crowd. They were a great bunch of people and afterwards, we joined a couple of guys who looked like fun. They were. Graeme Sutton and Mark Callahan turned out to be terrific characters and we became instant friends. In fact, we got on so well that Graeme offered to sponsor me to the tune of £10,000. So another chance deal was done. All I had to do was wear his company badge on my overalls and join him every other week for lunch in London's Langham's Brasserie where I'd talk to his clients. Over time, these sessions in the company of a personality like Graeme became increasingly boisterous and would include drinking, arm wrestling with Graeme, drinking some more, arm wrestling with anyone, and, of course, tormenting the staff. Actually, we were extremely good at tormenting the staff, but most of them gave as good as they got. What a sponsor! This kind of deal was right up my alley.

The trip had definitely shown signs of progress and, in the small principality of Monaco, Karen and I continued to have a good time. During the day, Eric Silberman and his colleagues at Honda made a fuss of KJ with their superb paddock hospitality, which we both greatly appreciated, and in the evenings we met with friends who included my fellow non-qualifier Damon Hill and Georgie.

For race day, however, we were invited to Ted Ball's suite in the Hotel de Paris. From a balcony overlooking the famous Casino Square, we watched Ayrton Senna lead. We drank champagne and then travelled back home, where we success-fully delayed the repossession of our house until September.

Several days after our return I received a call from a chap who'd read about me in one of the newspapers. He said he owned a small aviation company and wanted to help out by flying me, in one of his many light aircraft, to the remaining races in Europe. It was a great offer and I said I'd take him up on it but, in the short term, I had to devise a new travel plan for my trip to the Canadian Grand Prix.

The plan worked and, as I reclined in the business class section of my Canadian Airlines flight, I held on to the little Canadian badge I'd promised to wear on my race suit. Upon landing in Montreal, the second part of my 'travel the world free' scheme progressed nicely when, as planned, I met Chuck Hoggard, who owned a company called F1 Promotions.

Chuck became the third tour operator that year to provide my accommodation in exchange for a speech to his clients.

So, half a world away from home, I wondered what my team had ready for me this time? I mean, it couldn't be any worse than the previous races could it? Unfortunately, it could. I arrived in the pit lane and, sure enough, there was the team, there was Andrea and there were the cars. Two things were missing, however – the engines. It transpired that they had been withheld by the freight forwarding agent against alleged debts owed by Andrea Moda Formula, and keeping the units back was the agent's way of adjusting Andrea's thought process. Anyway, with nothing to power our black beasts I started looking for a circuit that ran downhill. The team eventually borrowed an engine from Brabham for Roberto's car but even by my standards, this latest episode was difficult to believe.

As Julian wasn't around, I linked up with Gary Howell and, at about the same time Gerhard Berger was busy winning, we hit every bar in the beautiful city of Montreal. I wasn't the only one with problems, though, because one of the barmen was complaining about how Canadians feel threatened by America. He said they were dominated by American culture, its TV, advertising and products. Then he told me that a national newspaper recently held a competition to create a phrase that could establish an independent identity for Canada, something that would fill his nation with pride, a phrase similar to 'As American as Mom's Apple Pie'. So the paper ran the line

'As Canadian as... ' and asked for the slogan to be completed. He paused and gave a melancholy smile before telling me that the winning entry read: 'As Canadian as... possible under the circumstances'. At that moment, I found this one of the funniest things I'd ever heard. If his story was true, I'd suddenly met a whole nation who was as insecure as I was. Maybe I could live there.

I was probably still smiling about it, sitting in my study back in England, when my pal with all the aeroplanes called. He was making arrangements to get me to France for the forthcoming French Grand Prix but it was even better news than before. Now he said I could also take Karen with me. A few days before we were all supposed to leave, he called again and apologised because there'd been a change of plan. The change was that he couldn't do it; but he'd definitely be okay for several of the other races. So having promised Karen she was coming with me to France, I did another 'speech for accommodation' deal, borrowed a car from Mark Callahan and we drove out to the Magny Cours circuit, south of Paris.

We arrived at the circuit via a curious route because it was the time of the French lorry drivers' strike and they had used their trucks to block many of the roads around Paris. I can't actually remember why they did it. Maybe it was something about British lamb or maybe it was a bet they made with some of their equally temperamental mates in air traffic control. Maybe it was a desperate act to show French waiters that truck drivers could also be obnoxious.

Anyway, we were slightly delayed, but we made it there and as we walked into the Formula One paddock I was comforted by the fact that things just couldn't possibly be any worse than my experience in Canada. They could. My paranoia quickly returned after we had twice walked past all the team trans-porters in the Paddock without seeing the black one belonging to Andrea Moda Formula. I started making enquiries and it became clear why I couldn't find them: they weren't there.

Out of all the teams in the pit lane and the scores of ancillary and support vehicles, guess who had found themselves trapped in the blockade? I looked up to the sky, right up to 'them up there' who kept tormenting me, and I was impressed with the ingenuity of their latest trick. Nice going, boys – in Canada the engines hadn't arrived, and now the whole bloody team hadn't arrived! Karen reached breaking point and burst out crying. I did my best to comfort her and assure her that, one day, I'd be a star.

Andrea turned up and apologised about that thing with the trucks and then promised me faithfully that I'd get a proper chance the following week in the British Grand Prix. For some strange reason I was beginning to have my doubts.

The build-up to Silverstone was exciting and, like the other four British drivers, I was getting a lot of press attention. Nigel Mansell was big news, especially as he was on course for winning the championship, and Martin Brundle was having a pretty good season with Benetton. Johnny Herbert, driving for Lotus, was as popular as ever, and Damon Hill's inclusion evoked memories of his father Graham. My own story, though, was also beginning to fascinate a lot of people.

I told my various tales in colourful detail to any journalist who wanted to listen and they would laugh at the black humour of my punch lines. But I have found one can only laugh so much at someone else's misfortune and these journalists and personnel from rival teams began to get angry at the hand my team were dealing me.

Only the previous year, press reports on my American races read: 'McCarthy set a brilliant pole position' or 'Perry was in irresistible form'. Now they could only talk about my predicament rather than my driving. It was a difficult situation because although I was frustrated and angry, I just couldn't help finding a lot of this funny. It was all so bizarre: I was becoming infamous rather than famous. *The Times* called me 'the world's unluckiest racing driver', *The Daily Telegraph* headlined me as 'a new cult hero', and America's *Sunday Express* said I was 'a comedian locked inside a racing driver's body'. But they were united when they implied that Andrea Moda Formula was useless. Still, this was *the* British Grand Prix and, with renewed optimism flowing through my veins, I was intent on doing something special in front of my home crowd.

As ever, pre-qualifying began at 8am and the circuit was still wet from overnight rain. I took my position inside the cockpit and then sat in the pit lane, waiting for the crew to do something sensible like put the wheels on the car. Well, I waited and waited, and over the next 30 minutes my previously jovial mood turned as black as the clouds overhead. During this time, the pit lane commentator Bob Constanduros was putting pressure on the team when he repeatedly told the crowd that he could not understand why on earth I was being kept stationary. It worked and, finally, Andrea cracked. They turned their attention away from the number one car, put wheels on my car and I screeched away.

I didn't stand a chance, though. They had sent me out onto what was now an almost dry circuit with the worn rain tyres that my team-mate Moreno had previously used on his car. This was stupid and dangerous, but I was way beyond caring. On my first lap, I drove my balls off. I had been sideways through the sixth gear right-hand Bridge corner and then my tyres gave me such little grip that I slid off the track as I came through the Woodcote curve leading on to the pit straight. I held the drift and with all four wheels on the grass, I changed up and continued accelerating. I wasn't backing off for anything: I was either going to qualify or crash. I crossed the start/finish line and was later told that I'd set joint-fastest time. By now, I had totally lost my temper so I gripped the steering wheel hard and took an equally kamikaze approach to my second lap.

Blessings do come in disguise however because, halfway around, the clutch exploded and I was forced to cancel a lunatic plan, in a crazy situation, that could very easily have got me killed. I was furious when I returned to the pits and I packed my things and left without saying a word.

I returned on Sunday to watch the race but, more importantly, to raise money by selling some T-shirts I'd designed. However by 10am, I was still three miles away from the circuit, stuck in a traffic jam. I was pretty bored, but then I noticed a motorcycle cop by the side of the road, so I took a gamble and called him over. 'Officer, my name is Perry McCarthy. I'm a Formula One driver and I need to be at the track right now.'

He looked at me and then picked up his radio. He was soon joined by one of his colleagues, and after about another minute there was a squawk from his handset that must have confirmed I was telling the truth. Luckily enough, nobody mentioned the fact that I hadn't actually qualified, so they revved up and gave me a high-speed escort all the way there. Well, it beats waiting around, doesn't it?

The T-shirts, incidentally, sold like hot cakes. Considering how the team constantly kept me in the pit lane, I'd designed these with a pseudo-political message and drawn a cartoon of me standing in front of a wall, spraying the graffiti message: 'Let Pel Out!' On the reverse side I wrote: 'Car 35... where are you?' Luckily enough, more than 1,000 people either felt sorry for me, or thought it was pretty funny. Either way, I made some money.

Nigel again won for the Williams team but the following day I decided to do something about the mob I was supposed to be driving for. Julian Bailey was with me when I phoned the team and I found their receptionist was as bright as the rest of them.

'Pronto, Andrea Moda Formula,' she said.

'Hello,' I said. 'It's Perry.'

'Perry... Perry who?' came the reply.

'Perry McCarthy', I answered, patiently.

'What company are you from?'

'I'm not from a company. I'm your bloody racing driver!'

'Oh yeah,' she said, with a total lack of enthusiasm. 'Andrea not here'. Well there's a shock!

Julian was in hysterics and so was I, but I knew I wouldn't be able to sort this out over the phone. I needed to make a personal appearance. My man with the planes once again offered to take me, and then once again cancelled. By now, though, my sponsorship from Graeme Sutton had started coming through, so I spent some of it on a flight to Italy and set off determined to have a heart to heart chat with Mr Andrea Sassetti.

I landed in Bologna and one of our mechanics collected me from the airport. We drove for a long time, way out to a remote spot called Ancona on the east coast. I didn't know where the hell I was and the scruffy building we pulled up to looked more like a criminal's hideout than a Formula One base. There was definitely something not right about Andrea and I don't just mean mentally. His money was supposed to have come from shoe manufacturing but nobody knew for sure, and after trying a pair of his boots on, it seemed highly unlikely it could be a successful business. What we did know, however, was that he had enemies. One month before, somebody had burnt his night club to the ground. Then, just a few days before my visit, one of the mechanics had been sent out for some spare parts. A few blokes who recognised the team mini-van had started shooting at him.

Anyway, Andrea kept me waiting for several hours and, during this time, I watched some of our rag-tag army struggle to load a large tool chest onto a truck. As the truck didn't have a tail lift, they'd propped two scaffolding boards against the rear-end and their efforts reminded me of a Charlie Chaplin movie. One of these boards was sagging badly, due to a massive split, and while three mechanics pushed the chest gamely uphill, another one rammed his back against the side to stop it falling over. By the mid-point, the board was bent in half, the tool chest was tilting at 45 degrees and the boys were covered in sweat. I was in silent hysterics at this performance:

it was very different from the high-tech operations of Williams and Benetton.

I walked over to the poor bastards and said slowly: 'Guys, I have good news!' Each of them was at their physical limit but they listened eagerly as I continued. 'I know Andrea is talking with a big sponsor... many many millions.' I waved my arms around for effect. 'When he gets the money,' I continued, 'he told me to tell you... he is going to buy you... *a new piece of wood*!' They started laughing, lost their concentration, and the whole thing slid back down to ground level.

Life became distinctly more serious when I eventually got to see Andrea. Within seconds we were yapping at each other like wild dogs and all hell broke loose. He was obviously still mad at the world for not being allowed to dump me after Enrico Bertaggia had offered him $1million to rejoin his team. In fact, Enrico still had access to the money and Andrea told me that without it, he could still only attempt to run Roberto's car and use my one just to comply with the rules of entering two cars. I told him I didn't care who was offering what: I'd been signed to do a job and I expected to be allowed to do it. In other words, I wasn't going to stand down.

Our meeting had accomplished nothing except bringing our mutual hostility out into the open, but part of me knew I had to be a little careful. There was a million dollars at stake, and I wasn't on home ground.

By eleven o'clock at night, I'd been waiting for somebody to take me to my hotel when, suddenly, the sliding door at the end of the workshop was pulled back. In walked about five blokes, a couple of whom were heavyset, and my alarm bells started ringing. I wondered if this was going to be Andrea's way of persuading me to leave the team and, if so, guessed it might involve a few bruises. Well, I wasn't going down without a fight, so I grabbed a handful of iron bolts from a workbench and clenched my fist ready to get the daylights kicked out of me.

The biggest fella came over to me and, standing about five foot away, he looked at me without smiling and said: 'Are you McCarthy?'

I gripped the bolts tightly, judged the distance to his thorax and prepared for action as I said: 'Yes'.

Now, it was quite lucky I didn't hit him with a pre-emptive strike because his expression then changed to a big grin, and as he offered his hand, he said: 'Oh, this is good. Perry McCarthy... you are a great driver. I watch you race in America.'

Ooops! Only two seconds before, I'd been so damn scared that I'd planned to punch his windpipe and then pile into his mates, but now I could see everything was all right. I breathed a sigh of relief and said: 'You really don't know how much that means to me!' And just before we shook hands, he looked puzzled as I opened my fist and put all the bolts on the table.

When you're averaging two laps per grand prix, and when you think your team owner is plotting to have you beaten up, you have to start wondering if it's all worth it. But I did think it was worth it. All I needed from the remaining races was just one chance to show what I could do.

A few days later, though, my one lap at Hockenheim in the German Grand Prix showed that nothing had changed. And that included my mystery man with the plane, who had again offered a flight and again cancelled.

For the Hungarian Grand Prix, though, both he and my team excelled themselves. First of all, matey-boy called me and swore that the deal was done, that there'd be a plane ready and waiting to take me out there. The day before I was due to leave, though, he cancelled. I was hugely annoyed and told him that, far from helping, he'd actually been messing me around and that I had no back-up plan to get out there. A short time later he called back and said he felt bad about letting me down, so he'd purchased a regular ticket for me to pick up at the airport. I thanked him and the following day I turned up at the appropriate airline desk, gave the reference number I'd been issued with, and they checked me in.

I was relieved that this chap, who I'd never even met, had kept to his word. Then I looked at the ticket closely. Then I looked at it again to make sure I wasn't dreaming. And then, alone, in the middle of Heathrow Airport, I started laughing. The ticket was one-way. The more I thought about it, the funnier it got. Maybe if I learnt how to crouch down with my arms folded and kick my legs out, I could make a new life as a Hungarian street dancer. It was like something from *Candid Camera* but at least I was going. I'd worry about getting back later.

However, the *team* didn't seem too worried about anything. During Friday morning pre-qualifying, they kept me in the pits for very nearly the entire session and finally gave me the signal to go, with only 45 seconds remaining. Well, I couldn't even get around the circuit to begin a flying lap before the chequered flag came out, and I was once again livid.

I pulled into the pits, jumped out of the car and ran inside the garage, where my patience snapped. I screamed obscenities at Andrea and his team. It was the first time I'd behaved like that and they thoroughly deserved it. But in typical McCarthy fashion, my timing proved disastrous.

As I went to get changed, John Wickham from the Footwork Arrows team told me that his boss, Jackie Oliver, wanted me to test for them. 'Sure thing,' I said. But John then told me that Jackie had insisted I have Andrea's written permission.

Andrea Sassetti almost started laughing when I made the request, and as he walked away without a word, I had a rough idea that he wasn't mentally composing anything beginning with 'Dear Jackie'. Roberto Moreno turned to me and said: 'I think you've just screwed yourself.' Maybe I had, but I was also getting a lot of help in that department.

Not everyone was out to get me, though. Lynden Swainston, who worked for Bob Warren Travel, helped me when she provided a return ticket to England for just £20 and then my mate Gary Howell, who had again provided my hotel room in return for a speech, took me out on the town where we hit every bar in the beautiful city of Budapest. We did the same again on Saturday night and it was in one of these bars that an over-friendly American enthusiast recognised me, put his hand on my shoulder and asked how I was getting on.

'We had some problems,' I replied deadpan. 'And we failed to qualify.'

'Oh well,' he smiled. 'Good luck for tomorrow!'

He didn't really get the failing to qualify bit, did he? Considering it was nearly midnight and I was half-drunk in a Budapest pub while my mega team had loaded the cars and were heading for their hideout in Italy, I'd need a bit of luck for the race tomorrow wouldn't I!

Given my earlier predicament I knew I could have left Andrea Moda and then tested with Footwork Arrows, but the next race was at Spa in Belgium. It was a circuit I knew well and, as the Brabham team had just collapsed, there would only be 30 cars entered for the race. That meant the dreaded pre-qualifying would be scrapped and I'd be straight into the official sessions. The governing body FISA had also given me new hope because, after the shambles in Hungary, they'd told Andrea that if he didn't start making a legitimate effort to run my car, there would be dire consequences. So, all in all, it was an opportunity I couldn't afford to lose and I stayed put. But if I'd known what was about to happen in the Belgian Grand

Prix, I would have chosen differently.

Once again, I strapped myself as tightly as possible into the small confines of my Formula One racing car, but this time I had a morbid feeling that I was never going to get back out.

I was near completing my warming-up lap when out of the blue came World Championship leader, Nigel Mansell, driving his Williams. God, it looked so fast as he dived down my inside and braked hard for the second-gear Bus Stop chicane, but suddenly I found myself closing up on him at high speed.

I'd been so busy watching him and the way his car was working that I'd braked too late and was now heading straight for him.

It all happened so fast. There was no time to think and as I desperately pressed the brake pedal to the floor, the wheels locked up and I silently screamed: 'Oh no, not Nigel. Of all people, please, not Nigel!' I missed him by a few inches and tried not to think about imaginary headlines such as 'Complete idiot wrecks Mansell's championship-winning car'. Nigel pulled away but I decided that, as I'd now had one whole lap's worth of experience in a grand prix car around Spa, I should launch a qualifying attempt before it broke down.

I crossed the start/finish line, braked late into La Source hairpin and then accelerated hard through the gears on the way downhill toward the extremely fast Eau Rouge corner. The approach begins with a gentle left-hand sweep and the entire series of curves demands absolute precision. However, as I lined the car up at 170mph, I'd felt the steering slightly tighten. Something was wrong and I immediately hit the brakes.

I managed to take some speed out of the car but I was already deep into the first section, heading toward the barriers, and committed to turning sharp right for the tricky uphill stage. The steering had now virtually jammed and, with unthinkable consequences only half a second away, I strained with every ounce of my strength to turn the wheel. It was a desperate fight and I pulled a muscle in my shoulder as I forced the car to change direction. At the last possible moment she responded, but I wasn't out of trouble yet. What should have been an instant turn-in had taken a fraction longer and I was way off line. I went off the track, on to the grass and, still scrambling for control, I *juuust* missed the wall.

It had been a very close shave. I knew I was lucky to be alive and, back in the pit lane, I told Andrea that I believed the steering rack was flexing. 'Yes, Perry, we know,' he said.

I looked at him dumbfounded. 'You know?' I said.

'Yes, we tried it on Roberto's car last week, and we see this problem then.'

'So then, of course, you put it on my car!'

'That's right,' he replied, without the slightest sign of understanding or remorse.

Well, this wasn't Formula One: this was bloody stupid. If I hadn't trusted my instinct and backed off after the initial increase in steering load, then I would have gone into the wall, head first, at 170mph.

I knew it was over, or at least, I was finished with them. But just when it couldn't possibly get any crazier, it did. Several officers from the Belgian police force turned up at our pit and Andrea Sassetti was arrested on allegations of fraud. FISA later banned the team from the rest of the World Championship for bringing the sport into disrepute, and the last thing I ever saw of Andrea was when he was bundled into the back of a squad car. As they drove him away, he glared at me through the back window and I imagined his wild brown eyes were saying: 'I hate you McCarthy. I'll hate you till the day I die!'

Chapter 13

DOWN AND MAYBE OUT

The Angel was saying: 'Trust your judgement, Perry.
You know it can't be done.' And the devil was yelling: 'Schumacher
can do it, but you? You're a poof, a nancy-boy.
Go on, prove me wrong – take it flat!'

The Spa circuit may have been the last I saw of Andrea but it wasn't the last I saw of the Belgian police. On the way back to Calais, Karen and I were stopped for speeding. The cop was particularly bad tempered and, apart from recording 120mph on his radar, I was sure something else had already upset him. I told him I was a Formula One driver returning home from the race but he didn't like that and, looking like he was about to explode, he said: 'Oh, really? Well, let me tell you, zee first man we stop zis afternoon is your friend Olivier Grouillard.'

Well, he was five years too early on the friend bit but, having known Ollie for a while, this bloke's mood began to make sense. Anyone who's tried telling Grouillard to behave, especially after he's crashed in a race, has probably come in for a hard time. I smiled helplessly and paid the £80 fine, which added to our misery and left us with £20 for fuel.

We reached Calais just in time for a 10-hour ferry delay. As we sat by the dock, looking across the port, there wasn't really a lot to talk about. The season had crashed and burned, we'd lost everything, my reputation was worth about as much as a bag of crisps and the future looked fairly bad. I was desperately upset, and deeply hurt at how I'd been made to look like such a fool, but I wasn't going to let Karen – or anyone else – see that. I gave KJ one of my lectures on life and said: 'It's simple. We can roll over and forget it, we can drive into the bay and end it, or we can fight back and make a new start.' She didn't go for the 'bay' option because she'd just had her hair done, so she dried her tears and nodded solemnly with the toughest choice. We agreed to fight back. Now all I needed was a plan!

A couple of weeks later the repossession came due and we said bye-bye to the house. Everybody was exceptionally nice about it and as we stepped out the door for the last time, the elderly chap who was changing the locks put his hand on Karen's shoulder and said softly: 'Don't worry love. It'll be all right.' Back in 1992, he probably had a lot of experience of seeing people lose their homes, but I doubt if he'd ever met anyone like KJ because, turning to him without a trace of sadness, she smiled and said: 'I know'.

We were relieved that it was all finally over but, unbeknown to our locksmith, my new plan was well underway. I had already put a deal together to pay a very low rent for a better house, only five miles away in Shenfield, Essex. The place was in disrepair but a lot of people were keen to help so, a few days before our move, some mates and I used the free materials provided by a local merchant to work 30 hours straight and paint every room, door and ceiling. Then as soon as that was done, Hamilton's Carpets sent a couple of their people round, again without charge, to re-cut and fit the carpets from our place in Billericay. The house now looked great, Karen was happy and I flew out to show my face at both the Italian and Portuguese Grands Prix in an effort to keep my career alive. Expenses were courtesy of Chequers Travel and Grand Prix Tours, while speeches were courtesy of P McCarthy esq.

Without a team I no longer held a pass, but as I approached the Formula One paddock in Monza, I was holding a race programme. I lent against the fence and smiled to the security guard as I opened the cover, pointed to my own photo, and then held it up next to my face for comparison. I could see he was slightly confused by my performance, since this didn't exactly happen every weekend. With the driver page still next to my head, I continued: 'Look, me driver, me in programme, me here, me want to be in there!' I guess he finally decided that only an Andrea Moda boy would actually need go through this, so he let me past the gate and wished me good luck.

Now, you might think that I'd feel a bit stupid doing this but I didn't. I was so used to having to improvise, even to get the simple things I wanted, that it all just came as second nature. The main thing I wanted, though, was to drive and, with my sights set on the following season, I needed to start talking with some team owners. I succeeded in meeting two of them but I knew it would be an uphill struggle: with 10 non-qualifications in a row, I must have looked like second choice to Donald Duck.

However, it seemed that far from thinking me an idiot, they had actually admired my determination and I was offered a drive if I could bring a million dollars worth of sponsorship. I was delighted they'd taken me seriously and, moreover, a million bucks was cheap. In reality, though, they might just as well have said: 'Get lost. We're not interested.' The recession was in full swing back at home and there was no way I could attract that kind of money.

I was beginning to attract *some* money, though, with my work as an after-dinner speaker. I was averaging an appearance a month and I was keen to develop new work when I agreed to meet a lady from a booking agency in London. We met in a bar just off Oxford Street, talked about my life as a grand prix star and, by 10.30 that evening, we were both three-quarters drunk. Still feeling thirsty, I called Karen to tell her that I was going to be pretty late getting home but she didn't allow me to speak because she had some urgent news: 'Perry, Gordon Message from Benetton has called and they want you to do several days of testing for them at Silverstone.'

I was delighted. 'Oh, that's fantastic, darling. When is it?' I slurred.

'They want you at the circuit at 8.30 tomorrow morning.'

I looked around. The room was spinning like a roulette wheel. I could imagine someone with the voice of a fairground announcer saying: 'Place your bets, place your bets. Will McCarthy make it home? Will he get to Silverstone? How long before he crashes Schumacher's Benetton?' I put my head against the wall to slow the room down, but then the wall speeded up. 'Oh God... Call Gordon back and tell him I'll be there.' I put the phone down, garbled something about 'a big chance' to my drinking partner, told her to make a 30 quid bet on me lasting about four laps and then willed the train to go faster on my journey back to Essex.

The following day I found myself at the circuit and walked into the pit garage trying to disguise my hangover. I knew most of the crew and my last-minute chance had come about because their regular test driver Alessandro Zanardi, or Alex as we call him, was ill with pneumonia. Well, I didn't feel too great myself, so I took a painkiller and sat in the car. I was very excited and felt totally at home, but when I went onto the circuit, I thought I was going to throw up. The noise and vibration from changing gear at 14,800 revs made me feel like my head was in a blender and every time I hit a bump I could taste Carlsberg.

The car was dynamite, the precision and response were fantastic, and with its incredible grip in the corners, I was pulling an amazing 5g. Yes sir, *this* was a Formula One car;

this was what grand prix is all about and I started to relish every moment. During one of the test days, the team's number one driver, Michael Schumacher, showed up to see how we were progressing with the development of the new active ride suspension system. We had a chat about the car and the circuit. He described a typical lap and told me that he took the Bridge corner flat out. I was amazed to hear that. Okay, I knew he was brilliant but I'd been lifting off the throttle at that point because the car was already sliding right across the track. However, I was now inspired, and a McCarthy decision was born: 'If Michael can do it, then so can I.'

I went out on another run, with a war between good and evil raging in my mind. The angel was saying: 'Trust your judgement, Perry. You know it can't be done.' And the devil was yelling: 'Don't listen to him. Maybe you're a coward. Yeah, you heard me. Schumacher can do it, but you? You're a poof, a nancy-boy. Go on, prove me wrong – take it flat, take it flat, take it flat!'

The devil won. On my second lap, with the engine screaming and the scenery flashing by, I braced myself, summoned up every bit of courage I had, kept my foot nailed to the floor and turned in at about 170mph. It was a bad decision. The car was already sideways before I reached the apex and my hands moved around the steering wheel faster than Bruce Lee against 15 baddies. I knew I shouldn't have listened to the devil. But then the Benetton finally forgave me and I got it straight again just after I'd paid non-scheduled visits to both sides of the track.

I returned to the pits because I thought the tyre pressures, or at least *something*, must be wrong: surely Michael couldn't drive like that every lap. Once parked, I chose not to mention my little brush with disaster and waited while the team invest-igated my concerns by downloading data from the onboard computer. Several minutes later the team's chief engineer, Pat

Symonds, knelt next to the cockpit and grinned at me: 'Have a little moment, did we?'

'What do you mean?' I replied, innocently.

'The steering readout shows you on full opposite lock while flat out!'

Ooops! I'd been rumbled. 'Ah well, Pat, I asked Michael how he drove the circuit and he told me he could take Bridge flat, so I took it flat.'

Pat shook his head in amusement: 'That's right, he does – when he's on new qualifying tyres and a very light fuel load. You, on the other hand, have worn race tyres and half a tank of petrol!' This meant that I had nothing like the same grip. He teased me with one of those looks that suggested I was insane and I grinned back, like the stupid rock-ape that I was. It just seemed like such a good idea at the time...

We continued with checking and running the new systems, which meant the car wasn't trimmed for ultimate speed. But with those used tyres and the extra fuel weight, I set a time that was only 1.2 seconds slower than the British Grand Prix qualifying time set by Benetton's other driver, Martin Brundle. Everybody was very happy – and I was delighted to have driven for a proper team. Finally, I'd had some success. I'd shown I could do it and it felt like a reward for staying around and not giving in. Perhaps my luck was changing.

In fact, I was sure it was changing when, immediately after the test, Nissan called and offered me $25,000 to drive for them in the Daytona 24 Hours. I flew to Florida and joined my old mates Arie Luyendyk, James Weaver and the man who'd pushed Nissan to sign me, lead driver Geoff Brabham. It was a big programme and a lot was riding on it. The Japanese giant had turned away from its successful turbo engine and had spent millions designing, developing and building an all-new, multi-cylinder, normally aspirated motor. Over the next five days, we had to evaluate its potential.

Pooling our combined talent and experience, we eventually proved beyond all shadow of a doubt that the motor was... useless. What a pity! Still, on the up side, the local entertainment was great.

Unfortunately, though, Nissan decided that they couldn't justify the programme based solely on us having a good time at Molly Brown's lap dancing club, and they pulled out of the race, which in turn slashed my pay by $20,000. I wish they'd told me before, because during the week I'd spent about 500 bucks ramming dollar bills down the dancers' knickers!

Maybe my bad luck wasn't over yet, but back in England fresh hope came from the 1992 British Touring Car Championship winning team owned by Vic Lee. Vic, an old mate of mine, had said he wanted me to drive for him in 1993. The BTCC series was starting to get big. It was featured regularly on BBC TV, it drew crowds of about 30,000 every race, and the drivers were well paid. So, a bit of fame, good money, close racing and a top team: yup, I liked the sound of it.

I arranged to test one of his BMW racecars but it didn't happen because, two weeks later, something came up that would occupy a lot of Vic's time. Actually, it would occupy all of his time for the next six years because, in a major shock, he was arrested on an allegation of drugs trafficking and sent to a high security prison.

So Vic was locked up, Nissan had pulled the plug, Zanardi resumed his testing role with Benetton and I'd spent a fortune on American go-go dancers. Okay, a few minor setbacks, but I still had one big hope. Over the past few months, journalist David Tremayne and ex F1 team owner John MacDonald had been lobbying the top team in Formula One to give me a chance. Finally, I received a call from Frank Williams.

Frank's driver, Nigel Mansell, had won the championship but after a dispute over the team's new signing, Alain Prost,

Mansell took up an offer to drive in the American IndyCar series. Damon Hill, who had been testing for Williams while racing for Brabham, then got the biggest break of his life and was drafted into the team full time. That in turn meant Williams now needed a new test and reserve driver.

This little fact had not escaped my attention – I was fully aware that Frank's call at the beginning of April 1993 could lead to something big. I subsequently completed two days of ABS brake development running at Silverstone, with the feeling that this really was my final chance. I needed everything to go well from the start but I had a problem because I didn't get along very well with their test team manager, Brian Lambert. I didn't like him at all and it was obvious he'd already made up his mind about me. However, I beat the odds and managed to keep my mouth shut because I knew their driver choice was between me and a Scottish F3000 driver called David Coulthard.

I knew David and I knew he was a serious threat because, apart from his speed, he had a lot going for him behind the scenes. I didn't want to think about it, though: this was going to be all or nothing. If I got this I'd be on the way to the top so I just had to get it. They just had to choose me. But after a long wait, they made their decision and unfortunately they chose David. That's when I chose to stop. DT still has a fax from Frank after that test, promising that I would get back in the car, but it never happened.

I was devastated not to be picked. I sat down and decided that enough was enough. I just couldn't take any more disappointments. I'd tried everything and I'd fought the world but now, at 32, I'd lost faith. I just didn't believe there was a way through any more and I couldn't keep expecting Karen and the kids to live in an unstable environment, with what many presumed to be an unstable bloke...

I just had to come to terms with the fact that I'd given it a bloody good go, but ultimately, my mission had failed. I wasn't going to be World Champion, so it was time to forget the past and do something else. I would have to start a new life. The bell had tolled and it was the end of Mad Dog.

Well, that was the plan, anyway...

The following year was like some form of rehabilitation but, like most addicts, I found it tough to kick the habit. I definitely had withdrawal symptoms. I never got to the stage where I found myself boxed into a corner by a pack of flesh-eating gear levers or looking at someone as their face gradually turned into a steering wheel, but I did spend a lot of time daydreaming. All I had to do was close my eyes for a while and suddenly, there I was again, going for a quick lap, driving flat out toward a corner and pushing the limits. I would easily lose 20 minutes like this, as I raced wheel to wheel with Nigel Mansell or Ayrton Senna and somehow beat them to the finish line. The spell was always broken, though, when the phone rang or my children jumped on me shouting: 'Wake up, daddy – look at my new drawing!'

Well, daddy certainly needed to wake up because daddy was currently going nowhere fast. I was earning just enough to get by, from trading some cars, office furniture and even welding rods, but scampering around like this wasn't exactly building for the future – and I still owed about a hundred grand. My thoughts would sometimes return to the time I brilliantly turned down senior positions with two major companies in favour of motor racing, but what the hell: I'd thrown the dice and they'd come up snake eyes. I wasn't the only one in trouble, though, because my dad, Dennis, had been ejected from the millionaire club several years ago.

Back in 1979, Dennis had originally pressed the button marked 'big risk' and won. However, he wasn't content so he kept on pressing, but with his purchase of the jet and various subsidiary businesses, he never noticed that the button was now labelled 'financial suicide'.

By 1986, his costs had the same trajectory as an Apollo space rocket but his income could no longer fuel the mission. A decision by OPEC (Overseas Petroleum Exporting Countries) also did little to help because they cut the price of oil from $32 per barrel to just $8, which forced Western producers to make sweeping cost cuts on all aspects of their business. Unfortunately for Dennis, this surgery included their rig maintenance budget, but that wasn't the end of it. DJM Construction had also been facing increased competition from other contractors. Putting aside his own mistakes, circumstances were definitely contriving against him, but I'll never forget that, against the odds and in a unique display of skill, he took the time to show me how to make matters even worse. Like an anthropologist finding a vital clue to man's development, I was about to understand how the mutant genes dad had passed down were responsible for some of my own problems.

The episode took place in 1986 and dad, seeing the work dry up from his one remaining client, decided he wanted a meeting. It was early July and I was staying close to dad's offices in Holland in preparation for the Formula Three race at Zandvoort – the one where we squashed all those ducks. Dennis invited me to attend so, along with his general manager Mike Welch, we descended on the corporate offices of the client, an American oil company. I knew it was going to be an important meeting because Dennis was being handed an ever-smaller slice of a shrinking cake and it was now vital for him to reverse this process. We were shown into a large boardroom, where we said hello to seven or eight executives, and the meeting began.

They were a serious bunch, and to begin with, so were we, but we'd all noticed that the senior contracts manager, who was Dutch, couldn't pronounce his Rs, and like anyone with this impediment he sounded them as Ws. Now this was okay until he started using the word 'ranking'.

Given that the future of DJM Construction was in the balance, it was a good idea not to laugh. However, the problem gathered momentum and the guy was now using this as his favourite word and, when he gave a little speech, I thought I was going to have an internal injury: 'Dennis, as you know, we have a wanking list and we wank our contractors relative to their performance. For many years, you have been in our top wanking group but, recently, you have now gone into the lower wanking group.'

We sat there with pursed lips and straight faces, but the water was welling up in our eyes. We didn't dare look at each other. Then dad stood up and addressed the only people who could save his company. The reply had been handed to him on a plate and he just couldn't resist it. In a decision that made Hitler's attack on Russia look like a smart move, he said: 'Thank you for discussing your wanking list with us. We know that you wank us and that you have actually been wanking us for quite a long time. Now, if I understand you correctly, if we can again cut our costs, work longer hours, and then do everything you say, with a bit of luck, we will once again become your number one wankers.'

The guy was nodding solemnly, but seeing him actually agree just made matters worse. Mike and I collapsed into hysterical laughter. It was like opening the floodgates of a full dam and we couldn't stop. The old man joined in but the contracts manager didn't. He realised Dennis had been taking the mickey out of him and Dennis knew he knew, but that was how dad was. He was fed up with their attempts to run his ship and, rather than be boarded, he went out with a laugh and finally pressed the button he had been saving for just such an occasion: the one marked 'self-destruct'.

Soon after that, he lost everything. After a brief spell in Spain, he and mum moved back to England and bought a small bungalow just a couple of miles down the road from our house in Shenfield.

There was a lot to be learned from dad's rise and fall, and I did take some of it in, but it was tough to apply the lessons because, in many respects, my own character was so similar. I was no stranger to the 'self-destruct' button and by the beginning 1994 I was in trouble. I'd been in trouble before but this time the trouble was with me and my character. I was living with failure. I had little respect for the guy staring back at me from the shaving mirror, because he had no direction, he was shell-shocked and he was definitely unhappy.

Although my motor racing career had been tough, it had been bearable because trying to get to Formula One had, in a way, been a noble cause. It had been romantic, and we had been living an adventure. But now, having no rainbow to chase, I was up to my neck in reality and I guess that was the main thing I couldn't bear.

We trudged on with life. Remembering the plan of giving the family the best I could, I did a new low-cost deal to rent a beautiful house in the village of Great Warley, just outside Brentwood in Essex. It provided a bit of excitement in our lives and Bob Tappin helped us move in, but during the two days we spent unpacking, my mood turned from optimism to stunned disbelief.

It was the weekend of the San Marino Grand Prix, held on the Imola circuit in Italy and an old mate, the Austrian driver Roland Ratzenberger, was killed in final qualifying. Roland had been on a quick lap when he went wide and took to the grass while exiting the Acque Minerali chicane, but he recovered and brought the car back on to the circuit. However, his on-board telemetry, which records data, later showed that he must have suspected damage before or after this 'off' because the steering trace revealed that he then started to weave the car from side to side. This is something we do at low speed if we have a nagging feeling that something's not right and it's a relatively safe check procedure.

Qualifying time was running out and Roly must have either ignored his doubts or at least satisfied himself that everything was okay, because instead of returning to the pits for a check, he made the decision to begin a new, flat-out lap. Two corners later, his front wing collapsed from its mounting and this took away the aerodynamic downforce needed to turn in. Roland went off the track and hit the barriers head-on at about 180mph.

I sat by my stack of unpacked furniture deep in thought about Roland and all the years he had spent fighting to reach the top. I remembered being so happy for him when, only a few months earlier, he had finally got his chance by signing for the Simtek team. Now, in the blink of an eye, he was gone. Poor Roland, he was a lovely guy.

Roland's death seemed unbelievable, but the following day the absolutely unthinkable happened. The great, triple World Champion Ayrton Senna, possibly the fastest, most charismatic racing driver of all time, was also killed.

Having moved from McLaren to the Williams team at the beginning of the year, Senna had been leading the field and was determined to stay ahead of Michael Schumacher's Benetton. Suddenly, in a manner similar to Ratzenberger's crash, Senna speared off the circuit at the fast left-hand Tamburello corner. Like millions of others, I watched the TV broadcast in horror. With the force of that impact, I knew he had to be badly hurt. But when the medical team arrived to remove him from the car and then lay him on the track, I had the awful feeling he was dead. I didn't watch the rest of the race and the news that Ayrton had indeed passed away was confirmed a few hours later. The arguments still rage over what caused him to crash, but I find it very difficult to consider driver error.

For the second time in two days I found myself thinking about the death of a racing driver. With no disrespect to Roland, though, Ayrton Senna was more than just a driver.

I'd known him for about 12 years. We weren't great friends but I had met him on numerous occasions and found him to be charming, polite and interesting. I admired the guy so much that sometimes I found it difficult to avoid just standing there and gawping at him.

As a racing driver, he had been a big part of my life and an inspiration to many others. His talent and stature had earned him global fame, but Senna was beyond even that. He was an icon, he was a standard to aspire to, he was the indisputable best, he was the racing driver of our generation. Perhaps as a man, though, he was even more special. He was highly intelligent, he believed in God, and tales of his generosity to the underprivileged in his home country of Brazil were widespread. His esteem was such that he was granted the honour of a state funeral, during which his adoring nation, his fans and the world of motor racing grieved. His close friend, the grand prix medic Professor Sid Watkins, who cared for Ayrton at the crash site, caught my emotions when he wrote: 'Senna's gifts had he survived would have won a place in the history of mankind, not just motor racing.'

In times like this, Julian Bailey uses the old expression: 'There for the grace of God go I'. It's worth thinking about. How many times had Julian, myself and the rest of the Rat Pack crashed when, if we'd been an inch to the left, two inches to the right or hit at a slightly different angle, we could have met our maker? I told myself that maybe it was just as well I was out of the game. I didn't believe it though. I had lived with risk for a long time and my new life wasn't giving the required rush of adrenaline. By the middle of 1995, the cracks were beginning to show in my self-imposed rehabilitation and when the German manufacturer Audi called, I was definitely in need of a fix.

When this came, it was a short call with a big message. Richard Lloyd, boss of Audi Sport, phoned toward the end of August and told me they were planning to enter the 1996 British Touring Car

Championship. His question was simple: would I come out of retirement to drive for him? The answer was easy: 'Yes!'

I had been working in sales for a new telecommunications company in London and I hated it. After I put the phone down, I was hoping the way I said 'yes' hadn't betrayed my desperation. I was hoping it hadn't sounded like a 'please help me, get me out of here, I can't stand it any more' kind of yes.

The advantages of talking people into moving their custom to our particular network had provided me with a regular income, but it had also run the risk of losing me friends. The system kept crashing and companies I'd personally signed, such as Reynard and Lola, were beginning to get fairly pissed off about not being able to make phone calls. The worst example of this happened a few days after I'd signed the Benetton Formula One team to the exchange, and their top man, Flavio Briatore, had flown in from Milan to find that the lines had gone down.

This nonsense was reflecting badly on me and I wasn't very happy about it. After several rows with my employers, I decided I'd go back to taking my chances for a few months before driving for Audi, so I walked out and left the company. On the way home, I stopped to have a beer with some friends in the city and it was late by the time I boarded the train for Brentwood. Surprisingly, I was in a really good mood, and I was still in a good mood even when the train broke down short of my destination. I wasn't in a good mood, though, when I tried to get a taxi.

The shaven-headed rank controller was a bit of a hard nut and, for some reason, he chose to show off in front of his mates. I could understand his rudeness if I'd signed him to my former telecom employer but I hadn't, so I handed some abuse back. The whole thing then started to escalate. It was obvious this was only going to end one way and, unbeknown to me, someone had already called the police when matey-boy pushed me in the chest. Half a second later, I connected my fist to his nose and he dropped to the floor. It was a good punch and it seemed his friends thought so too because thankfully they all stepped back.

The person to step forward was a police officer, who suggested I accompany him to Romford police station. This seemed like a great idea because my bloodied opponent was now standing and his pack, realising that odds of 6 to 1 were pretty good, had begun to find their bravery.

I was allowed to call Karen from the station, although I didn't know if I wanted to. Basically, we had been going through a bad patch during the past year and I suppose, like anyone who's unhappy, I was tough to live with. Anyway, standing next to the desk sergeant, at one o'clock in the morning, the conversation with Karen went like this: 'Hi, darling. Guess where I am? I'm at Romford police station. I've been arrested for fighting, but don't worry about anything because I've quit my job and I'm going back to motor racing.' The line went dead.

I was asked to have a seat and waited for someone to come along and take a statement, or charge me, or do whatever it is they do, when in walked a tall guy wearing a police uniform that was unusually elaborate. He approached me smiling, with his hand outstretched, and said: 'Hello, you're Perry McCarthy, aren't you? I was told you were in here. I'm just on the way back from... ' Well, I can't remember where he'd been or what his name was but he introduced himself as Commissioner so and so, and continued: 'I was at the British Grand Prix when you tried to qualify that Andrea Moda. Bloody good effort, son!'

I smiled back and said thank you, then he turned to the desk sergeant, had a hushed chat, wished me all the best and was gone. The remaining cop looked at me with a crooked grin and just said: 'Lucky boy.' Then he arranged for my arresting officer to take me home. En route he privately congratulated me on flattening the bloke, who was apparently well known to them. Wowee – what a day!

The following months weren't so action packed, but with my mind now refocused on racing, I tried to stay cool as I waited for Audi to stamp my return ticket. It's important to have a hard head in this game: the constant pressure of waiting for someone's decision is enormous and it can wear you down. If you're lucky, you might have a couple of people around whose judgement you trust, whose input can recharge your batteries, to ward off the destructive nature of doubt. Well, I had and still have such a mate, and as I continued the agonising wait for Audi, I spent a lot of time with my close friend Alex Hawkridge.

I admire and respect Alex. He is highly intelligent with an enquiring mind and I am fascinated by his depth of knowledge and range of experiences. He has a great sense of humour and we talk about many things, including life, relationships and motor racing. Hell! I think so much of the guy that I even follow his advice, which is something I'm not used to doing with anyone.

Although he was now chief executive officer for Reynard, Alex was also the guy who signed Ayrton Senna when he ran the Toleman Grand Prix team. I realise Ayrton was a one-off but I've always been proud of Alex's faith and confidence in me. So when Audi finally called with a negative decision in December 1995, I needed all the moral support I could get.

However, Karen was in far more need of a shoulder to cry on. We still loved each other, but she felt motor racing was a lost cause and was tired of struggling. She'd been seriously unhappy about my decision to return and, after three months of tension, she was now totally pissed off with this new disappointment. She wanted me to pursue a job introduction in the City that had been put together by Johnny Dumfries, and I assured her I would. If she'd known that I had instead opened negotiations with another manufacturer, she might very well have stabbed me.

By late January, though, I'd bought myself some protection because a drive with the works Lotus Team in the GT World Championship was looking good. However, they needed £100,000 worth of sponsorship so I brought a few friends in on a plan. I was absolutely determined not to miss this opportunity and, after a bit of lateral thinking, I called in some guys I'd worked with in telecommunications. Now employed by different companies, both Tony Ford and Steve Burgess looked at the phone bills of the Norfolk-based car constructor and calculated they could make them a saving of £60,000. Lotus agreed to put this against my budget and, in a similar contra-deal, my old sponsor Mike Theobald agreed to supply the team's fireproof clothing requirements through his Advanced Wear and Safety company. I then talked to some guys at Hewlett Packard, who agreed to further discounts on a computer order to Lotus Cars.

All this took my expected contributions to a total of £80,000. I needed one more deal, and with time running out and other drivers chasing the seat, I needed it fast. Karen was now fully aware of my scheme and I considered the personal health risk of any news short of total success. There was nothing left to do except go down to the pub.

Normally, I'd agree with those, including Karen, who say that you won't find answers at the bottom of a glass, but The Thatcher's Arms was only 200 metres away from our house in Great Warley and engaging in lively banter with the other regulars was a good way to relax. It was nearly always good fun there and the place had its fair share of characters, whose names had somehow evolved over the years to include something relevant about them. This made it easier to remember everyone after drinking four pints of Heineken. There was security Phil, Jim the roofer, Gary the window, Steve the painter, Mike the builder and... *Paul the multi-millionaire.*

Chapter 14

MAD DOG BITES BACK

*Having made the decision to return to motor racing as a
career, I really needed a top-class programme in a top-class
championship*

Paul Whight, chairman of the highly successful property
group Grantchester, and I had become very good friends
over the past year and we shared many interests, which
included motor racing. He knew I needed the last part of my
sponsorship and decided he wanted to help. Like a knight in
shining armour, he sat me down in The Thatcher's, bought
a couple of pints, smiled and announced that he'd like
Grantchester signage on the front of the Lotus, a badge on my
overalls, and a few promotional days from me – and if that was
possible, he'd provide the £20,000.

'Yes,' I said. 'That's certainly possible.'

My return ticket had been stamped. I called the team, drove
to their Norfolk base, signed the deal – Mad Dog was back.
I was beginning to make Frank Sinatra look like an amateur
when it came to comebacks.

I was teamed with ex-Formula One driver Jan Lammers and
we would share the Lotus Esprit Turbo V8. It sounded good,
but it wasn't. Jan, 'the flying Dutchman', is a great guy with a
terrific sense of humour and we got on very well, but I couldn't
say the same about the team principals. I really didn't like
these guys and, in my opinion, they were out of their depth in
running a team. I don't think they were too keen on me either,

but after the third race I vowed never to speak to them again.

The whole thing kicked off badly. We withdrew from our first event in Monza, Italy, because of brake trouble in testing. We had a car failure in our second race at Jarama, Spain. In our third outing we scored a great result and came second on home ground at Silverstone, which maybe could have been a win if I hadn't made a stupid mistake in the pits. (Forgetting to start the engine again after a driver changeover always costs a bit of time.)

Tempers were frayed after that race and this was their chance to pay me back for some of the lip I'd been giving them – such as the time I went ballistic during a test at Snetterton circuit. The test ended the very moment we started the engine because a hose clip, which had been left on the manifold by someone, fell into the timing belt which resulted in one mangled and very dead V8. Anyway, after Silverstone, we had yet another argument and they fired me – but they never got close to repeating our Silverstone result.

I was furious that I could be fired by people for whom I had zero respect. I was even more furious that I'd had no time to leave the team before they fired me. However, I was pleased that at least my mate Paul had the choice to cancel his sponsorship instalments to the team.

It had also crossed my mind that I was going to have to tell Karen about our latest bit of good news, and that was going to need more careful handling than neuro-surgery. It had taken a massive effort to return to racing, with what was supposed to be one of the top names in the business, and once again it had ended in massive disappointment. For once, though, I had a back-up plan.

A few days before the Silverstone race, I had been contacted by the Oreca team, who would be running the works Chrysler Le Mans team in the 24 hour race. So, now with no Lotus contract, the call proved to be a major stroke of luck and, a few days after my Lotus divorce, I signed to drive one of Chrysler's all-new V10 8.0-litre Dodge Vipers. This time I was teamed with fellow Englishman Justin Bell (son of five-time Le Mans winner Derek) and Dominique Dupuy. It was an exciting opportunity. However, a couple of days before the race even started, we had a little mishap.

Justin had arrived at the circuit and offered to take me and team regular Olivier Beretta to the chateau we were all sharing with the team. JB was in a good mood because the call-up to the Chrysler squad was probably the biggest break of his career to date. To celebrate, Chrysler UK had lent him a beautiful, brand spanking new Cherokee Jeep. Although we were riding in comfort, our local map provided little help in locating the chateau and we were soon totally lost on some country lane in the middle of farming country. 'I reckon it's back the way we've come,' said Justin. So forget a nice, gentle three-point turn: in true racing driver fashion, JB put his foot down and reversed as fast as possible while the gearbox whined like a kamikaze fighter plane in a final dive.

We must have hit 30mph as Justin attempted something that those Japanese pilots would have been proud of. Reverse spin turns in a confined area are tricky to perform at the best of times. In a four-wheel-drive with a high centre of gravity, it was suicide. As Justin threw the left side of the steering wheel down, not one of us had a chance to say 'Tora! Tora! Tora!' before the right-hand wheels dug in, the beautiful, brand spanking new Cherokee leapt into the air and then aged considerably as we barrel rolled along the road.

Both Justin and Olivier were still in their seats when we came to rest. We were upside down, but they were still there hanging by their seat belts. The cascade of noise that included the shattering of every piece of glass and the re-shaping of every body panel was now over and, lying in my new seating position across what used to be the vehicle's roof, I decided to break the silence. 'Justin, me ol' son,' I piped up. 'I think that Chrysler contract of yours might be in trouble!'

We all crawled out on our bellies through a small gap that used to be Justin's door window. Olivier had cut his head slightly, but now three of Chrysler's works drivers stood by the side of the road just staring at what used to be a 30-grand motor. We could all see the funny side, although the thought of how our team boss Hugues de Chaunac would react didn't invoke violent laughter.

A local farmer helped out by ramming the scoop of his bulldozer under the car's roof and then flicked it back on to its wheels. It didn't look any better the right way up and mild horror was beginning to register on Justin's face. Our new mate then called his neighbour who owned a flat-back truck and, not only did he winch the thing on board, but he also knew where the chateau was. So we prepared a little cover story, then prized a door open, got back in and sat there with the CD player pumping out chart hits as we were carried aloft through a small town, waving to astonished on-lookers from the remnants of the Jeep.

We arrived at the chateau to find the entire team waiting, most of whom were trying not to burst out laughing, although some of them did, as the three of us explained in detail how we'd nearly been killed by a reckless driver coming toward us – and it was only Justin's skill and cat-like reactions that had saved us.

I had escaped from the crash without injury but pain was about to follow. The following day, Olivier, Dominique and I joined two other French members of our driving squad, Eric Hélary and Philippe Gache, for a swim in a local lake. Philippe, my old mate from Formula Three and F3000, was already standing up to his neck in the murky water 10 feet away when he shouted: 'Perry, come in! The water is very nice!' So I ran through the shallow part before launching into a full-on dive towards him. However, I stopped dead within one second when I head-butted the lake bed. It really hurt. I rolled over, first stunned and then surprised, to find myself in only two foot of water. Philippe, who was now standing up and looking down over me, couldn't stop laughing. The bastard had actually been lying down when he called out!

Our Le Mans week was really enjoyable. Hugues de Chaunac and his Oreca team, who were contracted to run the Chrysler programme, were top-class professionals. In the race, though, our car lost a cylinder and we finally withdrew from the Le Mans 24 Hours at one o'clock in the morning. So it was back to finding a drive with another team.

My friend and ex-manager Roger Cowman introduced me to a real character called Kevin Sherwood, and before long I was back in single-seaters with his newly formed DKS Team. To be precise, I competed in one BOSS Formula event and three British Formula Two races, recording a second place, a third place and two mechanical retirements. I enjoyed it and we'd earned some money through personal sponsorship from a lovely chap called Pas Ruggerio. But having made the decision to return to motor racing as a career, I really needed a top-class programme in a top-class championship, and I was very interested in the racing plans of a new manufacturer owned by American billionaire Don Panoz. In the meantime, though, the rest of the Rat Pack had been experiencing different fortunes.

Damon Hill had finally done it. He drove his Williams to beat both his team-mate Jacques Villeneuve and his arch adversary Michael Schumacher in the Benetton to become the 1996 Formula One World Champion. It was a brilliant achievement and one for which he would be awarded our 'King Rat' trophy, but unbelievably, like me, he was looking for a drive for

1997 because Frank Williams had signed Heinz-Harald Frentzen earlier in the year to replace him. However, Secret Squirrel could be sure of a few offers, and eventually chose Arrows.

Mark Blundell was lucky to have any offers, though – not because he wasn't good enough but because he was lucky to be alive. Mega, who at the beginning of 1995 had stepped into a McLaren race drive after Nigel Mansell's brief spell, was in turn replaced at the end of the year by David Coulthard. So early in 1996, he took up an offer to drive for the Pac West team in IndyCar racing and, in a mixed season, he surprised the world by walking away from a 200mph crash full on into a concrete wall after brake failure in Brazil. Lucky he's got a neck the size of a tree trunk, otherwise his head would have come off. After surviving that, Mega thought he was totally invincible and the team were impressed enough to re-sign him for 1997.

Martin Donnelly was poacher-turned-gamekeeper. Yer Man, after surviving that terrible crash in Formula One in 1990, had started his own team running aspiring racing drivers in the Vauxhall Junior Championship. Since his accent mysteriously became broader Northern Irish every year, it's a wonder they could understand anything he told them.

Grumpy was experiencing the highs and lows of 'tin tops'. Julian Bailey was driving for the works Toyota team in the British Touring Car Championship. He was a front-runner in the series but the team was a trifle upset with him directly after the prestigious British Grand Prix support race. Toyota had been dominating the event, with Will Hoy leading and Julian second all the way through the race, when in the closing stages Jules tried to reverse the order and go for a win. Unfortunately, he slammed into the side of Hoy so hard he turned his team-mate upside down and put both Toyotas out on the spot, which handed the race to Nissan.

Johnny Herbert, after being teamed with Michael Schumacher at Benetton and winning both the 1995 British and Italian grands prix, had now moved over to Sauber, but although he would receive a little more attention, he wouldn't win again until he transferred to the Stewart-Ford team a couple of years later.

By the beginning of 1997 Andy Wallace, James Weaver and David Brabham had all signed for the new Panoz team, which would be run by the highly-respected David Price Racing operation. 'Pricey' was a good choice and had massive experience in top-level motor racing, but he was going to need a little convincing to sign someone who'd actually had fewer than 10 races in the past five years. However, they had a good budget, the car had been designed by top constructor Reynard (to contest the GT World Championship and the Le Mans 24 Hours), they needed one more driver, and I wanted in. Alex Hawkridge was centrally involved in the operation and was pushing Pricey hard to sign me, as was my old mate Andy Wallace.

Late in January, Alex arranged for me to test a Panoz that would be run by the French team DAMS. We flew to the Paul Ricard circuit in the south of France and I completed a handful of laps. The test went well but over in the UK there was still no decision.

I had re-laid the groundwork for my career in 1996 and it was now very important to consolidate my return by securing this drive. The money I had from last year was gone – as ever, I had no reserves – negotiations had been going on for nearly three months, and I was unemployed. Funnily enough Karen had noticed all this, and as the pressure built to bursting point, KJ and I had what Mark Blundell calls one of our 'quarterly reviews'. It was actually 3 March, my birthday, when Karen went sub-orbital and pointed out, in detail, the error of my ways.

She reminded me that we now had three children to support – Poppy was nine, Frederica was seven and our new addition Finella was only eight months. 'Who are these people you keep talking about?' I quipped, but she'd now gone beyond speech and was just making loud screeching noises. Mid-way through the attack, however, the phone rang. I picked it up, careful to keep an eye on the red-faced madwoman who was glaring at me from across the room.

'Hi Pel, it's Pricey', said the south London voice. 'Listen, son. We'd better get this done. Why don't you come over tomorrow and we'll sign.'

I took a moment to grin widely at Karen in a 'nar nar ne nar nar' kind of way and said: 'Great. See you in the morning.'

Wow, happy 36th birthday, Pel. I put the phone down, KJ put the knife down, we had a big cuddle, and I let out a sigh of relief that the gamble had paid off. Dave was generous with the pay. When added to several personal sponsors and a separate drive DP had introduced me to with the URD team (racing in America), it all meant we were about to earn serious money. Pricey had given me a big chance and teamed me

with David Brabham, but I wouldn't have got it without

Andy, Alex, and a bit of Australian sweet-talking from 'Brabs' himself.

I now had the financial security to go into full-time training and my pal, fifth dan karate expert Simon Kidd, gave up a lot of time to put me through my paces every day of the week I was in England across the season. It was sheer torture but worth it, because even though we share the driving with our team-mates and might get three to four hours rest in between shifts, I was more than aware that a 24 hour race in a tough car can be exhausting.

A few years earlier, Eddie Irvine had been driving for Toyota, who had produced a car that was quick but looked like hard work. I remember bumping into him in the Le Mans paddock and he was in a real state. He was covered in sweat, his overalls were unzipped, his head was hung down and he was limping badly.

'Wow, Eddie!' I said. 'Just finished a tough stint?'

He looked up: 'Piss off. I'm just about to get in the bloody thing!'

By the time I got to Le Mans I was very fit, which was handy in dissuading my team-mates from beating me up. Well, they did have a valid reason. TV personality Noel Edmonds was involved with our Le Mans programme and he had introduced Nescafé 21 as a sponsor to the team. It made good promotional sense to the coffee brand because Noel had also arranged for the BBC to film a documentary on our campaign.

Nescafé told me they would be interested in putting a badge on all our crash helmets and suggested we'd get £2,000 each. I relayed the story to the boys, who looked very pleased. Then I told them I'd rejected it on all our behalves and insisted we get four grand each instead. It was probably about two days later that I had to tell them that Nescafé had changed its mind: they'd now even cancelled the first offer and spent the money on something else. Er, sorry. Good job my team-mates had a sense of humour.

During the race there was a far more significant dis-appointment. The engine blew to pieces on the last part of the Mulsanne straight at about 2am on Sunday – the same bit of track where, only a few hours earlier, Julian Bailey and I had been racing side by side (Panoz versus Lister) waving to each other at 210mph. The disintegration of our 6.0-litre Roushe V8 put an end to our attack, but it also provided a dramatic ending to the BBC TV's *Noel's Le Mans Dream*. This wasn't totally bad news, though, because the Panoz wasn't exactly driver-friendly. The thing constantly gave off the most mind-numbing roar from its twin exhausts and regular cockpit temperatures were higher than 120 degrees. I laughed when James once said, in his best public school accent: 'Do you know what, old boy? With the heat in that car and the noise from that bloody engine, it just makes you lose the will to live!'

After the engine blow-up, I attempted to walk back toward the pits, which were about two miles away. However, I got lost in a pitch-black forest before the headlights of a car transporting a few spectators around spotted me wandering about like the ghost from Hamlet, but in fireproof overalls. They were scared at first, then kindly offered to give me a lift.

Le Mans had been enjoyable, but in the World Championship Mercedes and McLaren-BMW were giving us a severe beating. We had reliability problems, and when we did keep going we were not quick enough even to finish in the top six. However, Brabs and I got a major result in the rain over in the United States on the Sebring circuit. David had driven a great first stint, but when we changed over, the rain came down hard and in the final laps of the race ex-Formula One Finn JJ Lehto was closing fast on me in his Michelin-tyred McLaren-BMW.

I was doing everything possible to keep our car on the track and ahead of him and just to give you an idea how hard I was trying, I was around two seconds a lap quicker than Olivier Grouillard (who was standing in for James) in the team's sister car. We desperately needed a good result but I was sure I'd never be able to hold JJ off. Suddenly, though, something caught fire in the McLaren's engine bay and JJ pulled to the side. It was a welcome sight and we were delighted to score third place and our only podium result of the year. Brabs, Pricey, Karen and I then spent the evening celebrating.

Back in England I had cause to celebrate again, this time

in the company of the Rat Pack. With three wins in IndyCar, Mark Mega Blundell became the new holder of our trophy and title King Rat.

For me, Sebring was a high point, but my competitive instinct wanted more. To win in a top-level sports car series one needed to be with a German manufacturer – Mercedes, BMW, Audi or Porsche – but available drives in these works teams were rarer than Johnny Herbert buying a round of drinks. So the following year I went back to the States.

Driving for the Dyson team in the company of Butch Leitzinger and John Paul Jr., I led the Daytona 24 Hour race by three laps when, with only four hours to go, the engine took the rest of the day off. We just looked up to the sky and said thanks a lot.

A few hours later, we were looking up at something else when we all went along to Molly Brown's lap dancing bar. We drowned our sorrows surrounded by some very well-proportioned young lasses and while sitting at our table one of them decided to inform us in a southern drawl that: 'Huh, ya knowe, I thank sex is a beautafull thang.'

James looked up from his 14th bottle of Corolla and in clipped tone announced: 'Not the way I do it!' I literally fell off my chair laughing.

The following race for Dyson had the same net result but without the laugh, and they decided they didn't want me back again after I shouted at a mechanic for failing to bring me something I needed in the closing moments of qualifying. Maybe I should have just punched him when no one was looking. Actually, it was a shame really because I liked that team.

It was back to Panoz for Le Mans. After some interesting negotiations with Panoz Motorsport chief Tony Dowe, James and I were chosen to drive the new multi-million dollar technological marvel known as the Hybrid, which used both a petrol engine and an electric engine that cleverly worked together to give more power and lower fuel consumption. In fact, it was so good that we actually didn't use any fuel at all in the race, mainly because with the battery system taking up half our available cockpit area, the car was so overweight that we failed to qualify.

Three races was hardly a gruelling season but I was very busy giving a lot of after-dinner speeches and working as a TV presenter for Sky and a TV commentator for Eurosport. In the background, though, I was pushing to make my dream of driving for a top German manufacturer come true – and I was getting closer. As a driver, I really wanted a big prestigious contract, but I also needed it to cover our spiralling cost of living, because having had money around us for a while, we found several ways to spend it as fast as possible. At the end of 1998, we sent the kids to private school and then on 4 January 1999, we moved into a big ol' Georgian farmhouse that needed more paint than the Forth bridge.

Up to my eyes in gloss and emulsion, I knew that my German target Audi was committed to entering Le Mans. I also knew that their driver line-up hadn't been finalised. I did have a few advantages, though – especially if they wanted the car rubbed down and painted in vinyl white. There was to be both a German and a British team, and the British team would be run by two of my biggest supporters: Richard Lloyd and John Wickham.

Competition for this drive was fierce. Audi Germany already had touring car champions Frank Biela, Emanuele Pirro, and Rinaldo Capello within their squad. They were then joined by another touring car champ Yvan Muller, ex-Le Mans winner Laurent Aiello and ex-Formula One superstar and ex-Le Mans winner Michele Alboreto. Meanwhile, the UK team had a shortlist of 40 international drivers from which they had to select six.

By early February, I was once again on tenterhooks until the chosen few were announced. They were: ex-Le Mans winners Stefan Johansson, Andy Wallace, and Stefan Ortelli, then James Weaver, Didier Theys and – wait for it – ex-Formula Ford Champion (only 16 years earlier) and ex-Formula One non-qualifier Perry McCarthy. I was now determined to repay the faith shown in me by Richard, John, and another good friend, David Ingram of Audi UK.

So you'd think I couldn't be happier. But within a couple of weeks, the German team decided they wanted me to drive for them as well and I joined Frank and Emanuele in their car for the Sebring 12 Hours, where we finished fifth.

I found the Germans to be the complete reverse of the national stereotype. From Dr Ulrich (head of motorsport) down, the whole team were great fun, massive enthusiasts, incredibly hard working and they didn't once threaten to shoot me. Oh boy, I really was so happy. I was testing regularly for both the UK and the German squad, I was being looked after, I was earning a lot of money and I was fit, confident, and very fast.

Unfortunately, I didn't manage to finish Le Mans. We had been plagued with transmission problems and finally the gearbox seized on me at the end of the Mulsanne straight. I used the in-car radio to inform the team and try to get some advice on how (if possible) to get the car back to the pits for repairs, but the reception was bad.

Standing next to the car by the side of the track with the others flying past me at 220mph, I used the mobile phone they'd provided as a back-up to call my team manager. I then allowed myself a small grin. 'Hi, this is John Wickham,' came the familiar voice. 'I'm sorry I can't take your call right now but please leave a message.' We connected pretty soon after and the team came out to me and confirmed that we were, in fact, finished.

It was a shame, but what a year! Even though we didn't win, the whole season had many of the elements I'd always been looking for. However, I knew it'd only be a matter of time before Audi would dominate.

Well, unfortunately Audi cut their race budget for the year 2000, which meant that the British team and I wouldn't be competing with them. So I made a new corporate decision: I decided to retire. I didn't want, and actually couldn't face, anything less than I'd recently had. It was as simple as that.

Leaving motor racing was different this time though. I wasn't confused, I wasn't distraught. I was very much in control. I had moved on and it was out of my system. I had been there, seen it, done it and didn't need it now. The chapter was closed and I opened a new one mid-2000 when I started putting together an internet sports betting operation.

The Rat Pack nights out in London were still part of my life of course. As always, we reeled off our old stories but there were also a few new ones to tell. Damon Hill retired from Jordan Formula One and racing full stop at the end of 1999. Julian Bailey won the British GT Championship the same year and then went on to win the FIA Championship in 2000 for the Lister team. Johnny Herbert and Mark Blundell were replaced in Jaguar F1 and Pac West IndyCar (then both switched to racing sports cars) and Martin Donnelly was continuing to run his race team using a language that occasionally resembled English.

My Dad though was in the wars a bit. After a triple by-pass heart operation he was then diagnosed with prostate cancer and emphysema plus a few other things, none of which you'd want for Christmas. Dennis sometimes asked how Julian, Mark, Damon, Johnny, and Martin were getting on and, before he passed away in his sleep he could entertain with a few stories of his own – but I'm still not keen on the one where he threw a builder's knife at me!

And Audi? Well, my earlier prediction that they would dominate was proven right when, 12 months after my gearbox had seized, the German team scored a 1-2-3 finish at Le Mans. I was absolutely delighted with their result because my relationship with the Audi group was still so strong that I continued to feel a part of it. There again, I did start thinking how I would just love to have actually been with them, making the move, taking the risk, sliding the car, living on the edge, dreaming of glory, going flat out... but preferably not flat broke!

Chapter 15

RESISTANCE IS FUTILE!

*I was finally going to do what I
dreamed of as a kid... I sat next to the Captain
of the Starship Enterprise*

Following Audi's progress was something of a hobby for
me, not that I had much choice because drivers and team
members would often keep me up to date with news of what
was happening on and off the track. But it was interesting,
especially as the final part of the internet sports betting business
I was pursuing was proving very tough to arrange.

The general feeling was that Audi would win Le Mans again
in 2001 but I knew they would be facing increased opposition
from a determined squad who were bringing back to the track
a very famous name. Bentley.

I knew more about this than a *retired* racing driver should
know, but I wasn't returning to motor racing so it didn't hurt
to keep in touch with my friends Richard Lloyd and John
Wickham (who were running this new project) did it? There
was no opportunity anyway. I had left motorsport, I was busy
creating a business, plus the fact that Bentley had announced
their drivers: six of them for a two-car team. So, it wasn't a
route back and I wasn't looking for one.

Because the famous Le Mans 24 Hours attracted so many
entries there was a separate 'pre-qualifying' event held at the
circuit in May, just over a month before the race itself. This
was an important test session for the teams and drivers but
its main role was to exclude cars recording a slow lap time

from each of the different categories, thus providing a final entry list.

At 9am on the Friday morning before pre-qualifying I was just waking when my mobile phone rang: 'What are you doing?' It was Richard's voice. I laughed. I always laugh when Richard begins a call like that. 'I'm in the Berkeley Hotel, Knightsbridge… I was out with Mark last night but he left about 5 o'clock this morning to fly straight to the circuit.' 'What are you doing this weekend?' he asked. I stopped laughing. The question had my complete attention. I was now fully awake because I knew he was in France, organising the Bentley race team, and I had a rough idea he hadn't phoned to ask if I could videotape *Stars in their Eyes* for him.

The call lasted less than two minutes and the small fact that I no longer held a race licence didn't stop me ending the chat with: 'I'm on my way!'

Twenty minutes later I had showered, dressed and checked out of my room. Richard had let me off the leash and I was running headlong back to motor racing. During my cab ride to Liverpool Street Station I cancelled my day's meetings, I then called my doctor's surgery, used the word 'emergency' about seven times and succeeded in arranging a medical for 10.30. I then called the Motor Sports Association, used the word 'emergency' *eight* times and had them fax a medical form (needed for a race licence) over to the surgery. I held my breath and then called Karen to tell her Bentley had a 'driver problem'. I added that Richard hadn't said who or what the trouble was but he needed me as a replacement fast and I had agreed. Sensing that this decision might create a whole new driver problem I winced as I waited on the other end of the line for a sentence that might have included 'AARRRGHHH… BUT YOU SAID YOU WEREN'T RACING AGAIN!' However, I was off the hook when she said enthusiastically:

'that's great news!' Phew. One day I might actually know what she's thinking, but that would spoil the surprise I guess.

I arrived at the surgery in Shenfield, Essex, just in time and the results from my blood pressure, heart rate, eyesight and waterworks tests were entered onto the faxed medical form, then signed. Afterwards, I met Karen outside as arranged, had a quick kiss, and then took the car she'd arrived in while KJ got a cab home. My target destination, 70 miles away, was Colnbrook, Surrey, home of the Motor Sports Association. I arrived at 12.30, just in time to catch the licensing department before they went to lunch. I filled out my application, ticked the 'express handling' box (a slight understatement in this case) and handed over the required fee along with my medical form. They were really helpful and by mid afternoon I was back home in Billericay with my 2001 international race licence. By 8.30pm that same piece of paper and I were in my car travelling underneath the English Channel on what was the first available train heading for France.

During the missile-like trip from Calais, my 160mph Audi S8 was returning an average of 12 miles per gallon as I headed south through Boulogne, Abbeville, Rouen and Alençon en route to Le Mans where I started to find out just a little more about the 'driver trouble' that had launched me into action.

My friend and ex-team-mate James Weaver had some concerns as to certain aspects of the programme and made the difficult decision to stand down. I'm afraid I can't be more specific than that. I was disappointed, for him and for me, to hear that it was James I was replacing. He wouldn't be racing with a top team and I wouldn't be working with someone who's always great fun to be around.

So, having made the journey to Le Mans very quickly indeed, I checked into a hotel near the track. Well, that's if you can call it a hotel: most of the places we end up in out there have about as much character as a coma victim.

The following morning in the race paddock it struck me that only 24 hours earlier I was an ex-driver, with no licence, asleep in a London hotel room. Now I was in France and, more importantly, Le Mans, about to join Bentley. Richard and John introduced me as their new racing driver to various personnel from the Bentley factory and I received my branded race kit, signed on with the organisers, then had a race seat made to the shape of my own back in preparation for driving duties on Sunday. But, that would be too easy wouldn't it. Just 24 hours later I was an ex-driver again!

Tony Gott, chief executive of Rolls-Royce and Bentley Motor Cars, had apparently arrived at the circuit and not been too pleased that the race team directors – yes, the ones who run the race team, who know what they're talking about – had chosen me without consulting with him. He then seemingly decided that, as I hadn't raced in the previous year, I didn't have enough experience. Therefore, he insisted that I shouldn't drive in pre-qualifying and that I be replaced with his choice of driver the following week. Richard, John and I weren't particularly happy about this, especially me. But that was it. I went home. I wasn't at all upset with the team managers for bringing me out to the circuit – they wanted me in the team and paid me well just for turning up – but I wasn't too impressed with Mr Gott, who incidentally never had the courtesy of speaking to me at the circuit. I did, however, allow myself a little smile when, at a later date, he left the company 'to pursue new challenges'.

In June, Audi scored a 1–2 victory and I was getting frustrated with my internet venture. I was starting to dream once more of motor racing. Unfortunately though, a basic fault in my DNA didn't allow it to just stay as a daydream. The Bentley deal had acted as a catalyst and my genetic need for speed had totally resurfaced. Within one month of being a Bentley driver who didn't drive the Bentley I zipped my overalls back up, laced my race boots, pulled my crash helmet on, closed the visor, strapped in tight and tested for Audi.

Even worse was to follow: I was quick and I loved it! There was only one thing to do and that was to make sure I would be racing a car, in a big event, for a major team, as soon as possible.

It proved easier than expected and early in 2002 I signed a contract with the respected French team DAMS which included the phrase *Le Mans 24 Hours*. And just to add to the fun, our efforts were to be a major part in the production of a new motor racing movie based on the adventures of European cartoon strip character, Michel Vaillant. Personally, I'd never heard of Vaillant but the French think he's great. There again, they think eating frogs' legs is great.

The race – driving an out-of-date 6-litre Panoz with a giant movie camera strapped next to me and making pit stops for reloading film – proved a trifle frustrating, but it served a purpose in providing some much-needed race laps, because there was a McCarthy mega plan brewing.

Kevin Rose and David Ingram of Audi UK were talking of entering their own team and car in the 2003 Le Mans... and they were talking about it to *me*. Furthermore, it had not escaped my attention that while the DAMS team and I were still discussing focal points and lens sizes, Audi scored another 1–2–3 result in their brilliant R8R. I was very excited. I knew they wanted me for the next season but I just had to be patient and wait for the whole project to receive a final decision.

Throughout the year, my German friends had proved they were now to sports cars what Ferrari was to Formula One and I was frequently telling TV viewers about both manufacturers after Mr Bernie Ecclestone had invited me to be a studio analyst on his interactive *F1 Digital+* show, working alongside presenter Matthew Lorenzo and Damon Hill. We invariably had a lot of laughs and our style was to talk, comment, joke and argue about events in each Grand Prix just as mates would who were watching the race in a pub. It was no problem to get into the role pre-broadcast because fortunately there actually was a pub only 100 metres from the studio. Watching top level motor racing so closely though was just making me more and more hungry to be back with a top team again.

However, my 'off track' adventures were still accelerating.

My book – yes, this one! The first edition was officially launched in hardback mid season, on 1 July 2002, and wow what a party we had (starting in the Audi Forum Piccadilly and finishing in Langan's Brasserie in the early hours). With the exception of Johnny, who was in the States, the whole Rat Pack was there, and loads of mates from outside racing, the national press, racing press, television, radio and just about all the main motoring and motor racing TV show presenters, came to back me up. Karen was there of course, having fun, and our daughters Poppy, Frederica and Finella were playing 'spot the celebrity' but were most impressed when Daddy and Ulrika Jonsson were posing for photographers. There again, I was impressed that Ulrika was posing with me! Maybe in a certain kind of light I look a bit like Sven-Goren Eriksson?

We all had a wonderful time and the following day I started a promotional book tour – but, shortly afterwards, two of my party guests began talking to me about a secret project. The legendary car expert and TV presenter Jeremy Clarkson, along with producer Andy Wilman, had an idea to include me in their all-new BBC *Top Gear* programme. It was an idea with a difference. They needed a racing driver to test the various cars they would be featuring throughout the series but... they wanted the driver's identity to remain a mystery to the viewing public. The driver would be totally flat out in everything, and he would wear black overalls, black boots, black gloves and a black safety helmet with a black visor. All the driver would do is drive. He would set lap times. He would never speak. He would be called the 'Gimp'.

Hmmmmm! Not be seen or heard? Not exactly my style, is it? Well, I was still waiting on the crucial Audi decision so, with the potential of a good television project waiting in the future, I agreed, but with one main condition: there was no way I was going to be called the Gimp.

It was a potential deal-breaker because Andy was insistent. But my problem with the name was that I recalled it as a character from the film *Pulp Fiction*. The Gimp was a total nutcase who wore a black leather mask, was chained up in the basement of a shop, and did some pretty nasty things to other chaps! Even though no one was ever supposed to find out it was me underneath the black disguise, motor racing had taught me that nothing remains a secret for ever and, for obvious reasons, if my identity was exposed I didn't want the tag to stick. I wouldn't back down and eventually we settled on a name change. After a few suggestions were explored I agreed to being called the 'Stig'. I then chose to use a *Star Wars*/Darth Vader-type helmet manufactured by Simpson (which produced a slightly menacing look) and I drove everything on offer from exotica to hatchbacks, saloons and people-carriers, all as fast as I could while being filmed on our *Top Gear* test track in Dunsfold, Surrey. In dry or wet weather I was always full-on and several times went way past it as I spun cars, costing three times more than our first home, into the surrounding fields. I never actually hit any of our makeshift barriers, but several times I was bloody close!

Each week I'd also tutor a celebrity guest to drive around the track in our little Suzuki and this section of the programme was called 'Star in a reasonably-priced car'. Once I'd shown them (off camera) the racing line, braking points and how to balance the car, I would step out and it would be their turn to put in a timed lap that was recorded while the cameras rolled.

Some of them had a real natural talent, especially my old mate Jay Kay (the singer from Jamiroquai) who I've been on track with before. Also, the super model Jodie Kidd who, in between laughing, kept making 'giddy-up' sounds, pretending to hold the reins of a horse. Another mate, the actor Ross Kemp, looked as if he wanted to kill someone as he pushed to bring his lap times down. I didn't tease him too much because, like most of the characters he plays, he can pack a punch. Film star Sir Michael Gambon was really up for it when he turned in to the final corner too early, hit a bump on the grass, went way up on two wheels and very nearly flipped the car over. We subsequently renamed the bend Gambon Corner. American actor David Soul ('Hutch' from the hit TV show *Starsky and Hutch*) was really good fun but both our main and reserve Suzukis broke when he was driving them. Given the amount David smokes I was impressed he found time to break *two* cars! Anne Robinson really let herself down though because, instead of being the tough cold-hearted nightmare she pretends to be on *The Weakest Link*, she was actually a really lovely person with a terrific sense of humour.

The TV chef Jamie Oliver had a great time: we filmed a segment where, dressed in my black Stig outfit, I drove his Volkswagen camper van (equipped with a Porsche engine) around the circuit at speed while he attempted to prepare a salad in the rear living space. Predictably, Jamie ended up on the floor, looking like he was in a Marx Brothers movie, with lettuce and vegetables all over him. Off camera, I then took him out in his private Maserati and, as requested, drove it at full power sideways nearly all the way around the track... except for the last corner where I went wide and damaged his right rear wheel on some loose stones. Ooops. He looked at me and came out with his familiar phrase 'Pukka' or at least it sounded like that. He was OK about it, but a couple of weeks later Karen and I went to his London restaurant '15' and I gave him one of my old crash helmets and a set of Audi overalls to say 'Sorry mate!'

Then of course we had perhaps our most famous guest. My past caught up with me and I was finally going to do what I dreamed of as a kid. 'Engage!' 'Make it so!' Yup... I sat next to the captain of the Starship *Enterprise*. Apart from flying 20 feet up into the air in my old Formula Ford it was the closest I'd got to becoming an astronaut. We stayed on impulse power in the Suzuki and Patrick Stewart, alias Jean-Luc Picard, repeated many of the manoeuvres he used to escape from the evil Borg, even though they always say things like 'resistance is futile!'

Just about all our celebs were friendly and approachable people who were thrilled to take part on the programme. With the exception of Harry Enfield and Richard Whiteley I could see what competitive characters they all were. Going faster on each attempt was obviously addictive and they really tried as hard as they could. They sampled a small part of the world I've inhabited for most of my life and they loved it. The only one I wasn't too happy with was a certain female guest, especially after I had to grab the steering wheel from her to avoid crashing and, while I was attempting to control the car from the passenger seat with one hand, she started hitting me! I then gave her a very stern lecture on her lack of ability to listen to instruction and she started crying.

The mystery idea was working well. However, one of Britain's biggest weekend newspapers, the *Sunday Mirror*, had only one theory and after the first series they published a three-quarter page article naming me as the Stig. The good thing, of course, is that I wasn't called the Gimp!

'Stiggie', though, was already smiling about something else. Audi UK confirmed they were indeed entering an R8R for both the 2003 Sebring 12 Hours race in America and for Le Mans. They also confirmed me as their driver, alongside German Frank Biela (who'd won the 24 Hour race for the past three years) and recent Formula One driver Mika Salo from Finland. The highly-experienced Mike Earle, through his Arena motorsport squad, would run the team while engines, gearboxes and a range of technical support would come directly from Audi Sport mission control in Germany. The dream of winning Le Mans was real and I was training every single day of the week to make sure I was physically and mentally prepared for this brilliant opportunity. From a choice of nearly everyone who owned a crash helmet, Audi had picked me. My return to the top was complete and I was intent on proving they'd made the right decision.

Our first race date arrived in March and we came sixth in Sebring, with the two Bentleys and our sister cars from Audi America and Audi Japan finishing ahead of us. Although the result was a little disappointing we'd learnt a lot about the car and accepted the event was predominantly a test session for the build-up to our big race in three months time. Yup, being fast for 14 and 15 June was the real target and everyone was working hard towards it. This was easily the best shot I'd ever had at winning one of the world's biggest races and the thought kept repeating around my mind like a broken record.

In pre-race mid-week testing at Le Mans, Bentley underlined what we already knew: they were faster than us by roughly two seconds per lap. That's not so bad over an eight-mile course, especially as we were sure we wouldn't have to make as many pit stops as them for fuel and that we could count on the car's reliability (which over the past three years had been fantastic).

On the Thursday night, 12 June, Frank produced a terrific lap time and kept us in play by qualifying third fastest, behind the Bentleys but ahead of the other two Audis. On Friday afternoon, 13 June, I was smiling to the huge crowd that greeted us in the centre of Le Mans town as Frank, Mika and I took part in the traditional drivers' parade. The support was wonderful. Every turn we took there were shouts of 'win Perry win!' and 'go Pel go!' There were also an awful lot of people shouting something else. Frank looked bewildered and asked 'What does *Stig* mean?'

Mika and I returned to the track where I met up with Karen, who had just arrived from England with our friends Bob and Dawn Tappin. We spent a relaxed evening laughing with other friends, David Ingram and of course my Bentley rivals Mark, Johnny and David Brabham. The Bentley boys and I were pretty confident we'd all be on the podium come the end of the race: it was really just a question of which order this would be in.

The following day a combined mix of excitement and pressure grew inside all of us. Jay Kay arrived at the circuit as a guest of Audi UK, and although it was good to see him my slight disappointment was that I wouldn't be able to hear him perform in the evening concert they'd arranged, because I would of course be on track and hopefully leading the race. At just before 4 o'clock in the afternoon our combined total of nine Audi drivers (from the three cars) and six Bentley drivers (from their two entries) had a chance for one more back-slap, wisecrack, and hand-shake together on the grid before the race started. I leaned into the cockpit of our car and wished luck to Frank, who was strapped in tight and ready for the off.

From the start it was Bentley 1–2. I watched it with Karen from the Audi hospitality suite above the pit lane. We fell to fifth but then Frank made up ground and retook third place. Frankie would be in the car for at least another two hours before Mika jumped in and then it would be my turn. As I wouldn't be driving for about another four and a half hours I decided to get some sleep in our small team room at the back of the garages.

An hour and a half later I heard Mika's clipped Scandinavian accent. 'Perry wake up!' I looked at him. 'We're out of the race!' I knew it was a wind-up, a joke, a tease. We'd been doing stuff like this to each other across the past four months. 'Yeah right-oh mate' I smiled at him. 'Perry!' he repeated, 'we're out of the race, we've run out of fuel!' He wasn't smiling and even though he's got a good poker face I can normally tell when he's up to something because his lip slightly tightens in one corner. The trouble was, his lip hadn't tightened. I just stared. 'Frank has missed the pits.' I couldn't speak. I couldn't think. I was numb. I pulled up my overalls and walked over to the pit garage where the thought that was too horrible to consider was confirmed on the TV monitor. Frank and our car were stationary. Several of our team members had tears welling up in their eyes. I looked over to David Ingram, the guy who had been so instrumental in making this project happen, and then to Kevin Rose, who had enthusiastically bought into the whole thing. I felt for them, maybe even more so than for myself. I looked over to Mike Earle and we just stared at each other in disbelief. But I was also feeling for my mate Frank. I knew he'd be distraught at his mistake. A totally unusual mistake that we would expect nobody to make, especially Frank, had just cost us the race and the chance for me and Mika to actually *drive* in the race.

I caught up with Frank a few hours later and the poor guy just couldn't stop saying sorry as he explained how he overtook another car on the left-hand side just before the pit lane entry but misjudged the manoeuvre and hadn't cleared him in time, thus blocking his own entry on the right. It was a real career low for Frank. Think of it from his point of view: he had to face everyone in the race team, everyone from Audi UK and

Audi Germany, all the press and, to a degree, other race teams and drivers. You have to be very strong at a time like that.

So, in a terrible situation like this, we formed a new plan. Me, Mika, Frank and the rest of our Audi UK team turned up to Jay's concert, had a few beers, enjoyed the music and tried to somehow raise a smile. The following afternoon the Bentley number 7 car won with Tom Kristensen, Rinaldo Capello and Guy Smith, while the Bentley number 8 car of Mark, Johnny and David came in second. Afterwards they all commiserated with us and then me, KJ and a few friends celebrated with them.

The following day I did what I'd set out to do. Well, part of what I'd set out to do. I brought home two trophies to the UK. OK, they belonged to Mark and David but they asked me to put these in the car because they were off to an awards ceremony in Paris.

I was keen as ever, though, on a return to Le Mans and maybe a chance to collect my own silverware at some point in the future, so I carried on with my training and stayed fit. Sadly, I would have stood more chance if I had instead decided to attend every beer festival in Europe.

Part of my programme was sprint training in my garden. I would run as fast as I could between two cones I had set out 20 metres apart, squatting to touch one before accelerating back to the other, continuing the process over and over until exhausted. Thankfully, I have no neighbours because anybody catching sight of this would have thought I'd completely lost my mind or had rabies. The postman actually did see me once, then got vaccinated in case I ever chased him up the driveway. If he'd seen my one-off sprint training 'upgrade' he probably wouldn't have delivered mail ever again.

On the approach to one of the cones, I lost my footing. This resulted in a less-than-graceful backward somersault and I landed with my full weight on my left elbow. This pushed the rest of my arm upwards and deep into my shoulder socket. It hurt badly and I knew I had a serious injury. I called Professor Sid Watkins, who kindly arranged for me to visit a specialist he knew in London. It was the first step in what was, hopefully, going to be a long road to recovery and one where I would repeatedly hear the catchy phrase 'subacromial impingement and superior labral tear'. After two operations, a lot of physiotherapy and no track time, I was able to say with complete self-assurance: 'I'm finished'. The pain and movement restrictions persisted and there was no way I could race with confidence.

It's ironic that across my career I had survived some huge high-speed crashes and managed to recuperate on separate occasions from a broken back, fractured neck and nerve damage to my leg. But now, this was it, the garden had succeeded in doing what many tracks across the world had failed to do: end my career.

For quite a while I had a difficult time dealing with this fact. I had always been used to finding some way out of a problem, some solution, some kind of answer, some way to fight back. 'It's over' was a phrase that hadn't even been in my vocabulary before but one I was now completely forced to accept. I was 43 years old and had imagined at least another seven or eight years of racing ahead of me. Why not? It was only the previous year that a top manufacturer like Audi had chosen to sign me above so many highly respected names. But this injury would now, at best, cost dearly on lap times and, at worst, hurl me into a wall at 200mph because my shoulder sometimes collapsed under load. I wouldn't be rejoining my old team or any other because the market isn't that great for slow and possibly dangerous racing drivers.

Everything comes to an end and it doesn't take too much imagination to work out the various career-ending options available for a racing driver. This was *my* time.

Chapter 16

TO STIG OR NOT TO STIG?
THAT IS THE QUESTION

Richard Hammond was proud of the fact
'they had taken the mouthiest driver in motor racing and
found a way to shut him up'

As a kid, I'd never even heard the name 'Stig'... well, except late one night when I walked in on Mum and Dad watching a movie about a half-naked plumber who'd popped around to help a housewife. I was asked to leave and never found out how it ended. Indeed I had no idea that this name would change my future life a lot more than the housewife's, although she did look happy at the time.

I'm OK with Stig stuff now. I have been for a long while. But at the time, I slowly became disenchanted because there were some things happening behind the scenes and a couple of them have been consistently misreported. Here's the deal.

As I've mentioned, the whole concept of the Stig was secrecy and I took it seriously. I would drive to work in normal clothing but pull on my black helmet just before going through the security gates at Dunsfold aerodrome. As they didn't have a superman phone booth for me to change into my overalls, I would fully metamophose in a room behind the gatehouse. It was always a private moment of switching identities coupled with a routine I am more familiar with, one where I began to exclude the outside world and everyday life, allowing my concentration to naturally build and prepare to do nothing except drive fast and on the limit.

Then over at the studio and test track areas, as requested, I kept conversation with anyone, including the film crew, to a minimum. However, when I *did* speak, I put on a very heavy French accent, desperately suppressing fits of giggles while smiling wide and unseen behind my mask. Jeremy, who obviously knew it was me, sometimes struggled to keep a straight face when I talked to senior producers and it was nothing short of hysterical to hear these guys in return, change their own speech pattern as one does to help a *foreigner*: 'You very fast, yes I think you have good English, Paris is lovely this time of year, I have two of Charles Aznavour's albums.' One of our star guests, Sir Michael Gambon, was slightly more suspicious when he stood in front of me and said 'that accent of yours is a bit dodgy'. It took everything I had not to burst out laughing and say 'OK, you got me'. Actually, I *should* have said just that, but in a *German* accent just to really convince him Stiggie desperately needed psychiatric help. However, I did later laugh out loud when alone after I read on the internet that someone, who had heard me speak French at the track, knew that Stig is a Frog and, therefore, the mystery boy *must* be my old mate and ex-Ferrari F1 driver Jean Alesi. But I guarantee that Jean, being French Sicilian, would not have enjoyed lunchtime. Along with the cast and crew, I would line up in my Stig suit to get fed from the catering truck, but trying to eat and drink with my crash helmet on caused most of my planned intake to land on the floor. By mid-afternoon, Stig's tummy often rumbled... in French of course. Occasionally in German.

In episode one, Jeremy showed the viewers the Dunsfold test track and then continued, 'Right, that's the track. Now we needed someone who could tame it, so we got ourselves a professional racing driver who could post consistently fast lap times. Now this thing is called the Stig. OK, we don't know its name, we really don't know its name and we don't want to know its name because it's a racing driver and racing drivers have tiny little brains and therefore worthless opinions and they're very dull. Doctors actually call it Mansell syndrome.' I probably found all that a lot funnier than Nigel did.

More poignantly, though, Jeremy's co-presenter Richard Hammond was proud of the fact that they had taken 'the mouthiest driver in motor racing and found a way to shut him up'. Again, I thought that was a good gag. However, contrary to the rest of the planet, I was beginning to think that being the Stig was not a great *job*.

Sure, it was the most amazing experience to hear so many people talking about the Stig. It had captured everyone's attention. People talked about Stig like a comic book super hero and I was thrilled to bits that I was the one, that they loved my driving and that the character seemed to bring a share of fun and excitement. Even though I wasn't saving runaway trains or falling airliners, I was just bursting to say 'It's me!!! Really, it's me! Honestly!' I was proud and chuffed that this new adventure had happened to me – a new and unexpected addition to a crazy career and story.

Wow, running flat-out in the world's best supercars is always so much fun, especially if you're not paying for tyres, trying to avoid any car slower than 150mph or scanning for tiny dots on the horizon that could be Police. Obviously, the race cars I had driven were so much faster but I was always determined to drag every last nanosecond possible from the screaming Ferraris, Lamborghinis and other cubically expensive works of art I had the luxury of powering and sliding around a test track there just for my use. From the moment of strapping myself into their stitched leather seats, I felt totally at home and happy inside. Mentally, I would have a quick pre-launch conversation with the car to say what we were about to do and that she's 'my good girl', just to settle her nerves. Don't read too much into that, OK? Then, we would begin and together we would find out exactly how fast we could go while actually testing each other during our time together. OK, that's probably beginning to sound weird.

But, these thrills apart, there was a downside. For all the passion I had, I also had to produce income and the Stig's pay was as small as his speaking parts. My wage was pretty close to having three stars at McDonald's. But yes, I accepted the job because I really wanted to be part of the new *Top Gear* and nobody needed to stuff a quarter-pounder in my mouth to force me into it. In my original meetings, though, there had been the lure of becoming one of the main presenters and that was an exciting prospect for a long-term career. By the end of the first series, *Top Gear* was a big hit and Stiggie, unexpectedly, was huge.

Andy Wilman, the series editor and (along with Jeremy Clarkson) the brains and creative force behind the show, wanted me to continue as the Stig. At the same time, there had been a reshuffle of presenters; Jason Dawe was let go and James May was brought in to join Richard and Jeremy. Result: I was to stay hidden.

So, what was the problem with that? What was the problem with continuing as this soon-to-be iconic character? Well, there are a whole bunch of TV presenters who don't earn a fortune for their role. That's not necessarily a disaster because the compensation is that their face becomes recognisable unless they're fronting something produced for 30 quid airing at 3.20am every other Wednesday. With a familiar face come opportunities: TV adverts, other TV shows, endorsements, appearances – in fact all the things one needs to earn a living from that industry. Being the Stig, though, life was slightly different.

I couldn't show my face, of course, and no matter that Stig was rapidly becoming a massive brand, I couldn't talk about it. With international TV sales of *Top Gear* getting set to become almost global, I was surprised to hear that they couldn't pay their star driver a decent salary. In fact, I was surprised to hear it several times because, not having an agent to represent me, I had started pushing to improve my position. So that approach failed and I was a little frustrated. I had naively thought I was part of the *Top Gear* team but it was now disappointingly clear that I was only a hired hand and one that could be replaced.

OK, I thought, let's give it another try. I'll carry on but introduce an idea that might suit everybody, especially me. Merchandise! The public have a soft spot for Stiggie, so why not? Andy Wilman once wrote: 'The whole point of the Stig is the mystique – the bizarre characteristics he has, the wonderment created about what he might think, feel, do or look like. Kids adore the conceit, and I believe adults, although they know it's a man in a suit (or is it?), gladly buy into the whole conceit because they find it entertaining.' I agree, so why don't we put the Stig's name on a few things? Why don't we make Stig dolls? Why don't we put Stiggie books together? Stig triple-fast moisturising cream! I can see the tag line: 'Look craggy? Try Stiggie!'. The more I thought about it, the more sense it made – but all this was being overlooked by the BBC. If they didn't have the budget to pay me properly for the services of a 'top racing driver', I could work with them to actually create that budget and more. The idea of this secret racing driver had indeed come from the production team but at least I had been involved with not letting them name it the 'Gimp'. In fact, in my mind, I had been involved with a bit more than that. Apart from doing the job I was paid for, the 'Stig' had 'Perry' in it and still has to this day, because my natural on-track demeanour is to stand with my arms folded and I had fun bringing in the grumpy, off-hand, dismissive act to the character.

I checked out who had the trademark on the term 'Stig' and found it was available. So, I met with my lawyer mate Philip

Lamb and after a while, including a three-month period during which third parties (such as the BBC, just for example) may seek to oppose the application, I owned the trademark to 'The Stig' and 'Stig'.

I had already set up a company called 'The Stig Limited' and now it was time to put my idea forward. I talked to Andy and others at the BBC and said, 'Hey, I have this company and these trademarks. Let's do a deal that gives me an interest and a future. You guys take 51% and now let's go out and market the hell out of the Stig together.' Quite soon it was averagely clear in a letter from their legal department that they weren't too keen on the 'together' bit. In fact, they were, shall we say, not in a great mood altogether that I'd even pulled this stunt. Basically, they said... Hey, we have an idea too! Stig was our creation, we own the intellectual property rights to it, so, Monkeybrain, transfer the trademarks (oh, and the website domain names you also registered) over to us soon or we will send trained assassins to kill you. OK... they didn't actually say the last bit, but it was similar – BBC lawyers.

I knew I didn't have a leg to stand on. It was their property plus I reckoned they had a legal budget large enough to sue everybody living in Northern Europe. So, I'd taken a punt to get their attention and it was my only shot at trying to be in business with *Top Gear* and the BBC. It was unsuccessful but subsequent communications from them stated that I could now refer to myself as 'The Original Stig' and that was a win that maybe I wouldn't have achieved if I hadn't constructed something to negotiate with. It was a win worth having – unlike some of the press attention I had been receiving.

In series two we featured a 'priceless' 1953 Le Mans-winning Lightweight C-type Jaguar as driven by Duncan Hamilton. Old '053' has been owned and preserved for years by Duncan's motor trader son Adrian. I drove it with James May as passenger.

After the show was broadcast, I took a caning in the press. The criticism was first aired in the *Daily Telegraph* by eminent motoring historian and author Doug Nye, and subsequently reported (with additional, damning quotes from Hamilton Junior) by London's *Evening Standard*, the *Daily Mail*, the *Daily Star* and *The Times*. Doug stated that I 'burned out the rear tyres, twisted the drive-shafts and destroyed the clutch in televised sequences of over-revving, doughnut spins and getaways'. Really? I don't remember it quite like that! I also don't remember Doug even being there when we filmed. I was so upset that he had written this without even checking with me. My reputation means a lot to me and my reputation wasn't about needlessly vaporising classic racing cars. I called him to explain I was angry and that maybe he'd been used. He was gracious enough to apologise, which I was grateful for, at least on a personal level. At the same time, it was reported that Adrian was asking the BBC to cover a repair bill.

Jeremy Clarkson responded to the article with a typical one of his own in *The Sun* and wrote that 'a crusty old historian' was the only man to object to the car's treatment and warned: 'I know the man in question and I know where he lives. And if he'd like to see some real hooliganism he should try objecting again.'

Ha! That's Jeremy all right. I'm a big fan of his. I like him a lot. He's highly intelligent, funny, mischievous, a brilliant writer and a superb TV presenter. But no one from *Top Gear* or the BBC had actively gone on record to defend *my* name and it really did hurt reading that I was a 'Hooligan', a 'Philistine' and, of course, my favourite – 'Bleedin' idiot'.

With this kind of rubbish coupled with my merchandising non-starter, it was clear that *Top Gear* and I were sadly running out of fuel. I wasn't even able to supplement my earnings with additional work from *Top Gear* magazine because a Formula 3 driver called Ben Collins was happy to wear my Stig kit and stand around with his arms folded in shopping centres or test cars for next to nothing, thus destroying the market.

I hope you're getting the point. The simple fact of life was that they didn't care too much who was in the Stig 'uniform' and there was no importance for them in *me* being the Stig. I was left to ponder that no matter how enjoyable this episode of my life had been, I was now probably the wrong bloke in the wrong job and after 20 shows we all knew it was time to part company.

I don't believe I've been apportioning blame here but only stating how things were and how they happened. However, time for my opinion: I think they wanted it all their own way and never really considered they should be paying not just for the services of a racing driver but also, and perhaps uniquely, for the services of anonymity. My close friend Richard Farleigh, from TV's *Dragon's Den*, always says 'a really good deal has to work for *everybody* involved with it'. I agree. On the other side: some people will think I expected too much.

In my final conversation with Andy Wilman (at that time), he told me they'd arranged a big send-off for me. We were all about to find out what that was in the first episode of series three!

A lot of people still ask me if it hurt when the car hit the water. Well, yes... if I'd actually been in the car, it would have seriously hurt – as in end-of-story hurt, as in dead. However, although I was unscathed, a high-speed accident *did* kill the Black Stig!

The scene: HMS *Invincible*, 22,000 tonnes of aircraft carrier and home to a fleet of Harrier jump jets. These aircraft do 0–60mph in 2.8 seconds and hit 100mph by the time they reach the end of the 200-metre take-off runway. And, as Jeremy was to tell viewers, 'that has given the Stig his biggest challenge yet [to match or beat it] and obviously he needed a very special car [*enter the Jag*], the old *Top Gear* Jag XJS bought for just a couple of hundred quid... it was stripped of everything and fitted with nitrous injection... that meant 500bhp. In a drag race in the last series it beat just about every other supercar on the planet. But is it enough here? *Top Gun* versus *Top Gear*. So, 100mph in 200 metres but, unlike the Harrier pilot, the Stig must leave himself enough space to pull up again.'

The deck crew gave the thumbs-up, the deck light turned green and the Jaguar began its run while Jeremy commentated as the old girl accelerated hard. But approaching the end of the ship, Jeremy dramatically shouted '109 miles per hour! That's too fast!'. The car didn't stop and flew off the ramp at the end of the runway to begin its nose-dive into the sea. 'Er... that was not supposed to happen,' explained a convincingly shocked Jeremy, 'and that is unquestionably the end of our Jaguar... but what about the Stig?' The camera focused on one black race glove floating and then cut back to Jem: 'That is all that was there... the Navy divers went down but they couldn't find anything... so tune in next week and we'll bring you up to speed with whatever developments have happened.' The divers, if they had indeed gone for a swim, would have been wasting their time: there was, of course, no-one in the car when it was launched off the flight deck and the 'dead Stig', having never been on board HMS *Invincible*, was sitting safely at home in Essex with a glass of wine, smiling. It really was a brilliant piece of TV and a great send-off.

The send-off actually did prove to be convincing. My alter ego was common knowledge by then and the following day my daughters were surrounded with concerned school friends asking, 'Is your Dad OK?' Poppy, Frederica and Finella all found it amusing but were never too keen on their new nickname – the 'Stiglets'.

Like many others, I did tune in the following week to see what indeed had 'happened', but I had a pretty good idea I wouldn't be returning from the deep to greet the cameras with a fish hanging from my visor. JC sorrowfully told the world I couldn't be found. A nice montage of my driving was played as a tribute before announcing I was dead. 'But don't worry,' Jeremy exclaimed, 'we've got ourselves a new Stig!' The uniform had now changed to white and the guy within it stood and crossed his arms, the same way he'd practised in shopping centres and would continue to practise for the next seven years. Well, that was before going on to release a book where he tried to convince everyone he was faster than everything, including electricity. I could go on about how I and a few other racing drivers viewed that, but I won't. However, in a bizarre twist of fate, Stig number 2 had more than he realises to do with this book and the fact that I became the Stig in the first place.

Back in 2001, as a day job, Ben worked for Scalextric. Haynes Publishing held a promotional evening in London to publicise a new book about the famous miniature racing cars and Scalextric in turn supplied a display layout for guests to enjoy racing each other via the delicate use of a hand control. I was invited and chose to accept because in the past I'd been told I needed to work on delicate hand control issues. OK, maybe not, but I had known Ben from my time presenting the *F3 ON 4* racing show, I knew they had beer there, I was bored and so I went. After only three laps of racing, it was obvious I still had all the delicacy of The Terminator with PMT. I decided to leave them with a few working models intact and sloped off to chat with senior members of Haynes while I imagine Ben was desperately trying to beat my lap time. I told them I'd written a book. They asked to see it, I sent it through and within two days they wanted it. So, my book was to be published! Then, at the book launch the following year, as you know, Jeremy was at the party, we talked about *Top Gear* coming back on screen and before you could utter 'Some say... he is illegal in 17 US states' I became the Stig.

I will always be grateful that the Stig, and my part in it, has indeed become a part of motoring history. It was a totally new concept and in my opinion it reached out to millions of people in an important way: it made them smile. Life is often about creating or spotting opportunities and *Top Gear* had certainly provided a few. The first opportunity was to be part of the show. Box ticked. Second opportunity was to be part of the main presenter team. That failed. Third opportunity was to be part of a merchandising programme. That failed. The final opportunity was to do the only thing available to me: take this gift with both hands and make the most of being The Original Stig. That has worked big-time and changed my life.

Across my year as the Stig there had been massive interest in Stiggie and even more interest in 'Who is the Stig'? Unbelievably, that question was to become one of the most frequently asked on the internet. Number one was 'Am I pregnant'? Now, for most people, you would have thought there might be some clues to both queries. The pregnant one may be easier: 'Check to see if you have quite a large stomach bulge and, secondly, has your boyfriend recently applied for a job abroad'? Back to Stig and, personally, I would have thought the publicity I received from the *Sunday Mirror* exposé might have given a small hint. You might have also thought that, as my name had been splashed everywhere for melting down the 'priceless' 1953 Jaguar into a soap dish, the answer was at hand. But no, the internet forums, the chat rooms, discussion threads and several on-line mental asylums were swamped with people who knew the truth. They totally knew it was Michael Schumacher or Kimi Räikkönen. It made complete sense that two current F1 stars, earning millions while fighting for a World Championship, would somehow manage to get to Surrey every Wednesday for two Big Macs and medium fries. Maybe they took turns. Many thought it was Damon who, getting bored with the question, told me he was planning to get a T-shirt made saying 'I am not the effing Stig'.

During series one, it had become an open secret inside motor racing that it was me. In fact, my very first memory after episode one is receiving a text from my pal, TV presenter Mike Brewer, saying 'Morning Stig'! Personally, I had kept my big mouth shut to the outside world but I did confirm it in the second edition of this book, which was actually published a couple of months *after* my split with the show. Many of the internet fraternity, who had survived murdering each other over the Schumacher/Räikkönen debate, now decided they totally knew I had been fired from the show for *revealing my own identity*. I just couldn't be bothered to go and try to make them believe they were wrong. There were too many of them. It was like a virus. It was like one of those Zombie films where their numbers keep growing while they froth at the mouth chanting 'Stig got fired, Stig got fired'. Who populates these sites? Why do they believe they know about everything? Why do they get so mad and vicious when anyone disagrees with them? I was half expecting to read detailed plans, even covering refuelling sites, for the attack helicopters they were deploying to destroy me.

Chapter 17

GOOD EVENING, LADIES AND GENTLEMEN...

If they sense any weakness, they'll devour you
faster than Mark Blundell eating... well...
pretty much anything really!

As so many self-employed people know, once a contract ends there's *normally* no severance pay or pension. It was the same for me. I had recently finished with Audi, finished as a racing driver and finished with *Top Gear*. However, I did have something I could use; I could now talk about being the Stig. But, as the undead of the internet had shown, I couldn't count on everyone knowing that, so it was important that the various agencies who book me for after-dinner and motivational speeches did know, and that they in turn let their clients know. Since my wonderful year in Formula One, many companies had booked 'Perry McCarthy' as part of their conferences or seminars. However, now, they could book a bigger name, a character the whole nation knew, an iconic, need-to-meet name: the Stig. Believe me, I'm not being sarcastic. So many people love the show, love their car, love driving and, here it was, opportunity knocks; I wrote a lot of new material and my corporate appearances and charges accelerated.

I like performing and, as a trait from my early childhood, I enjoy making people smile. As with motor racing, though, the pressure is on to deliver and you *will* be judged. My audience sizes have ranged from 50 to 1,000 and one needs to get their attention fast. If they sense any weakness, they'll devour you faster than Mark Blundell eating... well... pretty much *anything* really! I really hope to make everyone laugh every 45 seconds or less, so I get through a lot of material. It's fun but again, as with racing, I want to be good, I want to be recognised as being good and I want to get the job done. I never use standard jokes: I like to write my own stuff but here's an old gag that works perfectly to illustrate my approach to anything I do. A guy gets into a cab in New York City and asks the cab driver 'How do I get to Carnegie Hall?' and the cab driver replies, 'practice, practice, practice'. Very droll, but spot-on. I shake my head in disbelief when some 19-year-old contestants on TV's *X Factor* look to the camera, crying and shaking and pleading, 'This is my last chance... without this I'm finished'. The girl contestants often get upset too. I don't mean to be pitiless because I guess I also thought, at 19 or 20, that it would all happen at the speed of light – experience, though, has taught many of us otherwise.

As a professional speaker you can win, or, if you're not ahead of the game, you can crash, even though crashing doesn't cause physical injury... however there was that one night in Birmingham. I'm experienced in this role now and ready for it. Just as I always was before qualifying or a race, I again mentally remove myself from my surroundings. Then, about ten minutes before start time, I focus on my stories and gags, leaving just enough mental capacity to hear my cue before *Bammmm!* The decision is made, there's no turning back, walk up on stage, full power and here we go!

'Good evening, Ladies and Gentlemen...

'Thank you, Bob, for the introduction. Yes, I was the *ORIGINAL* Stig, the one in black, so please don't confuse me with this new poof in white.'

I've also opened with 'Bon soir', 'Guten abend', 'Buona sera', 'Buenas tardes', 'Ni hao', 'Howdee' and something unpronounceable in Russian ending with 'Comrade' because, to date, I've given about a thousand speeches all over the world at top hotels, race tracks, conference centres, cruise liners and even large tents for my friends at Camping F1.

There's normally no end to questions from an audience asking 'What's Jeremy Clarkson really like?', 'What's your favourite car?', 'Who's the Stig now?' and 'Am I pregnant?'. However, people at – or even away from – an event, seem almost spellbound to meet the original Stig; not Perry I hasten to add! Honestly. I'm often introduced to people in all sorts of places who don't know me or my background. If the conversation comes around to 'What do you do for a living?', I'll say 'I was a racing driver who made it to Formula One.' Reaction ranges from mildly impressed to pretty interested, depending on whether they follow the sport. However, when it's revealed that I was the Stig... oh boy! Even if the company I find myself in hate F1, their eyes widen and, as I've previously mentioned, they smile a big smile! The mobile phones come out: 'Talk to my boy!', 'Talk to my girl!', 'I don't have any kids but leave a message for my cat'! The Stig effect is amazing. It's great to see people happy and I'm always willing, of course, to join in the fun. Andy Wilman got it just right when creating this character and it serves to show the power of television. It has also left me in a unique position with a story to tell...

Chapter 18

STAYIN' ALIVE

From oil rig worker to racing driver, from selling
welding rods to selling sponsorship, from presenting
TV shows to becoming The Stig

It has been 31 years since I had my first proper race and 21 years since I forced my way into Formula One. So, as Cilla Black once sang: 'What's it all about, Alfie? Is it just for the moment we live?' Good point, but I really don't know. Who does? I've rolled the dice and taken a chance. Have I lost? Well, I've seen others win both races and championships and I've seen others lose the most treasured possession, their life. Both inside and outside motor racing I've seen people succeed but I've also seen many people living life in a way they don't want to. All I know is that I wanted to race and I wanted to do it my way and cram life with as much fun and adventure as possible. The funny thing is that it's taken a hell of a commitment to do that.

Trying to succeed in anything, especially motor racing, is tough. So why put yourself through it? Well, I believe President Kennedy offered a few clues in a speech he gave concerning the American space programme when he said: '*We choose to go to the moon in this decade and to do the other things, not because they are easy but because they are hard, because that goal will serve to organise and measure the best of our energies and skills, because that challenge is one that we're willing to accept, one we are unwilling to postpone, and one we intend to win... and the others too.*'

What d'ya think? Yeah, I'll have one of them! I think if it'd all been too easy I probably would have got bored. I believe in effort and I believe in challenge but, there again, failing to win time and time again eats at my soul, so I guess a sense of humour can be handy.

I failed to win in Formula One – hell, I even failed to qualify – but I don't know if anyone could have tried harder to forge a career at the top level and I'll always believe I was good enough. But is that what life's all about? Is a World Championship the measure of a man?

After reading this book you may think (like my Dad used to) that I'm a 'bleedin' idiot'! But I do regard myself as a very lucky chap. In Karen I have a soul mate who I adore. I have three healthy daughters who I love so much. I have a wide variety of close friends who are interesting, talented, loyal and funny. And… I can't help it, I am still optimistic and full of enthusiasm, which really you would have thought might have been kicked out of me by now!

So, my life on track has been replaced with a life on stage and the message hanging just inside the gags is 'go for it'. Got an idea? Try it! Have a dream? Do whatever it takes. My dear friend and Audi team manager Richard Lloyd, who was tragically killed in an air crash in March 2008, would have been proud of me because my work, although still fun and exciting, doesn't qualify for what, as you may remember, he could only bring himself to describe as a 'J.O.B.', pronounced as 'jay-oh-bee'.

In between appearances, I'm also keen to produce a follow-up book to this one called *Flat Out, Incredibly Wealthy*. I just need to work on the 'wealthy' bit now! But I'm getting there because we now owe no money to the banks, credit card companies or anyone else, and it only took 30 years. Mind you, the fun I've had has been worth millions.

So here we are in the closing moments of the third edition of *Flat Out, Flat Broke*. My publisher, Haynes, recently told me they believe it's the longest-running autobiography by a racing driver. They also told me its sales so far put it among the top 20 motor racing books of all time. I am sincerely proud. I'm proud and honestly now feel I have achieved something within my career and made some success out of quite a lot of failure. My book has done better than my Formula One career! Well, it certainly takes longer to read.

I hope you've had a lot of laughs and just maybe a couple of cries with me. The memories I've described, good and bad, are priceless but I'm determined that here, now and tomorrow will prove every bit as valuable. Although I can't end by saying 'Mad Dog is back', I can tell you that 'Mad Dog' is on tour and still Flat Out!

INDEX

Figures in italics refer to illustrations in plate sections, unfolioed pages *P1–P16*